Preparing for TAAS
Teacher's Edition

D1371471

McDougal Littell

THE LANGUAGE OF
LITERATURE

GRADES 6–8

McDougal Littell
A HOUGHTON MIFFLIN COMPANY
Evanston, Illinois • Boston • Dallas

TEACHER'S EDITION CONTENTS

ACKNOWLEDGMENTS

Ana Mercedes Palés: From "The Hurricane" by Luis Palés Matos, translated by Alida Malkus. Reprinted by permission of Ana Mercedes Palés.

Abiodun Oyewole: "Another Mountain" by Abiodun Oyewole, from *Rooted in the Soil*, First Edition. Copyright © 1980 by Abiodun Oyewole. Reprinted by permission of the author.

continued on page 206

ISBN 0-618-03207-X

TAAS Skills Practice Workbook: Teacher's Edition

Forward: About This Workbook

Preparation for the Texas Assessment of Academic Skills (TAAS) is a gradual process. The TAAS is designed to assess how well students have mastered the skills taught by the Texas curriculum, which includes skills that are developed and refined over several years. Through regular participation in classroom activities, students develop essential knowledge and skills and become comfortable with their own abilities. This *Preparing for TAAS* workbook builds upon this preparation by helping students to review skills they have developed in class. Moreover, it encourages them to think critically about the processes involved in reading and writing. By strategically approaching test questions, students will perform better on the TAAS.

Preparing for TAAS is composed of three sections. The first two sections, Preparing for TAAS: Reading and Preparing for TAAS: Writing, correspond to the two language arts portions of the TAAS. Each section includes the following:

- a chart or charts that identify the TAAS objectives and correlate them to the TEKS for each grade level
- test-taking strategies for answering test questions that target each objective on the corresponding section of the TAAS
- lessons designed to improve students' understanding of basic skills targeted by the TAAS
- leveled practice for each skill—when appropriate, a separate practice page is provided for each grade

In addition, the Writing section includes Guided Writing Practice for two modes of writing—persuasive and informative: classification—plus additional prompts and evaluation materials.

The third section, Anticipating TAAS 2003, includes instruction and practice in skills that address important TEKs and which may be tested in future versions of TAAS. The state assessment program in Texas is changing as a result of Senate Bill 103, which was passed during the 1999 legislative session. The new TAAS test will have new objectives that are expected to encompass a greater portion of the TEKS. The final TAAS objectives have not been approved as of this printing. As decisions are made in the upcoming months and years, visit our Web site at mcdougallittell.com for updated TAAS preparation materials.

The different sections of this workbook may be used jointly or discretely to prepare students for the TAAS. You may wish to incorporate individual lessons into your own lesson plans throughout the school year. You may also wish to use them as the basis of review sessions in the weeks leading up to the TAAS.

Answers for all exercises are found at the end of this Teacher's Edition. As well, the answer key includes answers to the practice tests provided in the *TAAS Practice Test Copymasters* books for Grade 6, Grade 7, and Grade 8, and help with error analysis and remediation.

Instructional Materials: TAAS 2000–2001/2001–2002

For students in middle-school in spring of 2001 and 2002, the language arts portions of TAAS will include a Reading test at each grade and a Writing test at grade 8. Even though not all students will be tested on writing in the current school year, because writing skills do take years to develop, you may wish to assign the writing lessons in this *Preparing for TAAS* workbook to all students.

The following pages describe the instructional materials in *Preparing for TAAS*. The first two sections of the book provide instruction and practice targeted to the six Reading Objectives and seven Writing Objectives to be addressed by the TAAS in 2001 and 2002. They consist of nineteen brief instructional lessons—fourteen in the Reading Skills section and five in the Writing Skills section—plus practice and support materials for two types of written composition.

Reading Skills

This section of the workbook includes lessons that address the following skills.

- **Using Context Clues**
- **Using Word Parts**
- **Recognizing Supporting Details**
- **Understanding Sequential Order**
- **Identifying the Main Idea**
- **Summarizing**
- **Perceiving Cause-and-Effect Relationships**
- **Predicting Probable Future Actions and Outcomes**

- **Interpreting Charts and Graphs**
- **Making Inferences**
- **Evaluating and Making Judgments**
- **Recognizing Propaganda**
- **Recognizing Author's Perspective and Purpose**
- **Distinguishing Between Fact and Opinion**

Using Context Clues; Using Word Parts (Objective 1)

The first objective tested by TAAS is students' ability to determine the meaning of written words. The lessons in these sections of the workbook reinforce strategic reading skills that will help students identify or infer the meaning of unfamiliar words.

- The lesson on context clues highlights seven different kinds of context clues—synonyms, antonyms, definition and restatement, description, example, comparison, and contrast—to teach students about the kinds of information that might appear in a passage with an unfamiliar word. In the practice sections, students read a passage and use different clues to help them define challenging words.

- The lesson on word parts helps students apply their prior linguistic knowledge to unfamiliar words. It defines the words *prefix* and *suffix*, and offers definitions of affixes that frequently appear on the TAAS. Similarly, it reviews base words and roots and demonstrates how their meanings can be modified by adding prefixes and suffixes. The practice pages provide grade-level-appropriate challenging words and ask students to construct each word's meaning from their knowledge of word parts.

Recognizing Supporting Details; Understanding Sequential Order; Identifying the Main Idea; Summarizing (Objectives 2 & 3)

The TAAS will ask students to identify main ideas and details.

- The lesson on recognizing supporting details clarifies this distinction and reinforces it with various graphic aids. Each practice page asks students to identify details from a passage that has clearly stated main ideas, so that they can observe the difference between main ideas and details in a sample text.

- The lesson on sequential order encourages students to look for clues that indicate the order of events in a passage. The practice section asks students to use time clues to arrange events in a passage on a time line.

- The lesson on main ideas addresses both stated and implied main ideas and provides examples for students to use. The practice gives students the opportunity to identify each type of main idea and arrange its characteristics in a graph.

- Drawing upon this groundwork, the lesson on summarizing explains that a summary presents the main ideas and important details of a passage, but leaves out less important details. Each practice section provides clearly stated main ideas and a substantial amount of information that should be omitted from a summary, so students have the opportunity to evaluate the importance of relevant details.

Perceiving Cause-and-Effect Relationships; Predicting Probable Future Actions and Outcomes (Objective 4)

The TAAS will ask students to identify causes and/or effects in a reading passage. Students must rely on reading strategies that help them identify causal relationships.

- The lesson on cause-and-effect relationships outlines three reading strategies: looking for *key words* that indicate causal relationships, looking for *reasons* behind events, and identifying *consequences*. Students will practice diagraming causal relationships.

- The lesson on predicting outcomes also helps students perceive relationships among pieces of information in written texts. Students will be asked to consider carefully all the details in a passage and to apply principles from their own experience to predict what will happen next. The practice pages require that they apply their knowledge to predict future outcomes.

Interpreting Charts and Graphs (Objectives 2, 5)

The TAAS measures students' ability to understand and to interpret information presented in a variety of written forms, including charts, graphs, diagrams, and tables. Naturally, these forms, which present information visually, require different kinds of analyses than do other types of written communication.

- This lesson aims to familiarize students with the various ways in which information can be presented visually. The exercises are designed to enhance their ability to shift from analyzing prose passages to analyzing graphic organizers.

Making Inferences (Objective 5)

The TAAS assesses students' ability to infer meanings in written texts.

- This lesson helps students read between the lines and apply their prior knowledge to reading selections. The lesson encourages students to look for clues as they read to help them infer meanings.

Evaluating and Making Judgments (Objective 5)

In order to interpret written information correctly, students must be able to distinguish between a well-supported judgment and a poorly supported one.

- This lesson helps students think critically when they encounter judgments and supporting evidence in a passage. It also prepares students to make judgments of their own. Students are encouraged to assess facts as they read.

Recognizing Propaganda (Objective 6)

Determining the validity of information requires students to recognize propaganda.

- In this lesson, students are presented with blatant propaganda and instructed as to how to analyze it.

Recognizing Author's Perspective and Purpose (Objective 6)

The TAAS assesses students' ability to determine the validity of information in a reading passage. To do this, students must be able to identify the author's perspective.

- In this lesson, students learn that an author's purpose is his or her reason for writing. They also learn that the author's perspective is the lens through which he or she views a subject and that this viewpoint incorporates the author's assumptions, biases, and opinions. They also learn to look for evidence of perspective in the judgments expressed in a passage, including those that an author tries to "pass off" as statements of fact. The lesson recommends that students collect clues from the passage to identify the author's perspective.

Distinguishing Between Fact and Opinion (Objective 6)

Portions of the TAAS require students to identify statements as either fact or opinion.

- This lesson explores the difference between fact and opinion. The model passage provides opinions and facts for students to identify. Students are encouraged to use a chart as a tool to help them distinguish between categories of information.

Writing Skills

The Writing Skills section of the workbook guides students through the various steps of writing an essay: brainstorming for main ideas and elaboration, organizing information and making a draft, proofreading, and revising. Lessons in the Writing Skills section address the skills below and are followed by two sections of Guided Writing Practice.

- **Analyzing Prompts: Subject, Purpose, and Audience**
- **Planning a Composition**
- **Organizing Writing**
- **Following Language Conventions**

The first section asks students to analyze a prompt. Subsequent exercises build on that analysis, asking students to brainstorm ideas, elaborate on their chosen topics, and experiment with organizational patterns. By the end of the skills review, students will have created materials they may choose to include in their Composition Test Practice.

It is important to note that the writing samples in the individual lessons do not add up to a unified model essay at the end of the section. Rather, they demonstrate the multiple components of the writing process and a wide variety of possible approaches to a single subject.

Analyzing Prompts: Subject, Purpose, and Audience (Objective 1)

In order to write an effective TAAS essay, students must first correctly analyze the writing prompt provided on the exam. Essays that are off-topic or do not fit the required purpose, mode, or audience usually receive very low scores.

- To ensure that students properly analyze the prompt, this lesson divides the prompt into its components: subject, purpose, and audience. Students examine the annotated models and identify these components in several practice prompts.

- The purpose of the essay component of the Grade 8 TAAS Writing test is one of three: persuasive; informative: classification; or informative: how-to. The audience may be any group of people. As does TAAS, the lesson on analyzing prompts requires students to consider a variety of purposes and audiences and to decide which is appropriate for a given prompt. Making this choice reinforces students' awareness that writing can have multiple purposes as well as helping to prepare students for the testing situation.

Organizing Writing (Objective 2)

This lesson teaches six types of logical organization that are useful in writing the types of composition included in the Grade 8 TAAS.

- **Main Idea and Elaboration**
- **Chronological Order**
- **Spatial Order**
- **Order of Degree**
- **Compare and Contrast**
- **Cause and Effect**

Writers of persuasive compositions generally use exposition to support judgments and description to describe a problem or circumstance that needs to be addressed. Thus, the organizational patterns associated with expository and descriptive writing—chronological, spatial, compare-and-contrast, and cause and effect—frequently appear in persuasive writing as well. Writers of classification essays often use a combination of two or more strategies, such as main idea and elaboration with the elaboration arranged in order of degree or in compare-and-contrast order. Writers of how-to compositions or process descriptions should use chronological order.

Planning and Generating Writing; Elaborating Ideas (Objective 4)

The error so many students make when taking an essay test is that they do not plan the points they wish to make. The lessons that correlate to Objective 4 give students practice brainstorming and elaborating on ideas to plan what to include in their essays.

- The first lesson guides students to produce main ideas and opposing views. It offers two brainstorming techniques—listing and creating a graphic organizer—to appeal to students' varied learning styles.

- The second lesson introduces students to various types of supporting details that appear in essays: facts, statistics, examples, quotations, and opinions. Students practice identifying supporting details in sample passages. Students will not be able to incorporate all these types of evidence in their TAAS essays, since they will not have access to secondary sources. However, we have included the full range of skills in this workbook to reinforce students' awareness of the different ways in which writers can support their ideas.

Following Language Conventions (Objectives 3, 5–7)

Although TAAS essays are scored holistically, part of the score depends on how well students follow the conventions of grammar, spelling, mechanics, and formal language.

- This lesson includes examples of common errors in grammar and mechanics, names each type of error, and offers sample corrections. Although the lesson is not exhaustive, it should help students identify the areas of grammar and mechanics in which their errors occur so they can review those areas on their own or with your assistance.

- The comments on appropriate language remind students that the TAAS writing assignment is a formal essay, thus discouraging them from using colloquialisms and slang.

Guided Writing Practice

The Guided Writing Practice helps students use the strategies of composition that they have learned in class and through practice in the Writing Skills section of *Preparing for TAAS*. This portion of the workbook includes sections on analyzing prompts, brainstorming main ideas, elaboration, organization, drafting, and revising. Students are encouraged to incorporate into their essays the ideas and strategies that they generated in the individual lessons of the Writing Skills section.

To assess how well they have met the objectives of the TAAS essay component, students may refer to the scored sample essays and Student Self-Evaluation questions that follow the Guided Writing Practice.

Instructional Materials: Anticipating TAAS 2003

In anticipation of the changes to Texas's testing program resulting from implementation of S.B. 103, a third section of this workbook includes lessons on skills, such as Speaking and Listening and Viewing and Representing skills, that may be tested beginning in 2003. As more about the new tests becomes known in the upcoming months and years, visit our Web site at mcdougallittell.com for updated TAAS preparation materials.

Speaking and Listening Skills

Two lessons address important speaking and listening TEKS not heretofore tested on TAAS. As with the Reading Skills lessons in the front of this workbook, these lessons include a page of instruction followed by a page for practice. On pages 155–157 of this Teacher's Edition, you will find scripts for reading aloud. For each lesson, there are separate scripts for Grades 6, 7, and 8. To have students complete the practice, ask them to listen carefully as you read the script.

- The lesson on interpreting a speaker's message highlights basic skills used by active listeners before, during, and after listening to a speaker.
- The lesson on distinguishing fact and opinion parallels the lesson on the corresponding reading skill.

Viewing and Representing Skills

- The lesson on interpreting advertisements focuses on persuasive techniques commonly used in print ads and other graphic presentations. There are separate practice pages for each grade level.

Composition Skills

Two additional modes of writing are taught.

- The lesson on business writing guides students through developing a process description and teaches the form and style appropriate to a business letter.
- The lesson on interpretive writing guides students as they write an interpretation of a poem. Two poems are provided for each grade level.

Table of Contents

PREPARING FOR TAAS: READING

PREPARING FOR TAAS: WRITING

COMPOSITION PRACTICE

Persuasive Writing

Informative Writing (Classification)

ANTICIPATING TAAS 2003

EXPECTED CHANGES TO TAAS

SPEAKING AND LISTENING SKILLS PRACTICE

Interpreting a Speaker's Message

Distinguishing Between a Speaker's Opinion and Fact

VIEWING AND REPRESENTING SKILLS PRACTICE

Interpreting and Analyzing Advertisements

COMPOSITION PRACTICE

Business Writing (Letter)

Interpretive Writing (Poetry)

Correlation of TAAS and TEKS Objectives
Grade 6 READING (2000–2001/2001–2002)

TAAS Objective	Related TEKS Objective(s)
TAAS Objective 1 The student will determine the meaning of words in a variety of written texts.	**TEKS Objective 6.9** *Reading/vocabulary development:* The student acquires an extensive vocabulary through reading and systematic word study.
TAAS Objective 2 The student will identify supporting ideas in a variety of written texts.	**TEKS Objective 6.10** *Reading/comprehension:* The student comprehends selections using a variety of strategies. **TEKS Objective 6.12** *Reading/text structures/literary concepts:* The student analyzes the characteristics of various types of texts (genres). **TEKS Objective 6.13** *Reading/inquiry/research:* The student inquires and conducts research using a variety of sources.
TAAS Objective 3 The student will summarize a variety of written texts.	**TEKS Objective 6.10** *Reading/comprehension:* The student comprehends selections using a variety of strategies.

TAAS Objective	Related TEKS Objective(s)
TAAS Objective 4 The student will perceive relationships and recognize outcomes in a variety of written texts.	**TEKS Objective 6.10** *Reading/comprehension:* The student comprehends selections using a variety of strategies. **TEKS Objective 6.11** *Reading/literary response:* The student expresses and supports responses to various types of texts.
TAAS Objective 5 The student will analyze information in a variety of written texts in order to make inferences and generalizations.	**TEKS Objective 6.10** *Reading/comprehension:* The student comprehends selections using a variety of strategies. **TEKS Objective 6.12** *Reading/text structures/literary concepts:* The student analyzes the characteristics of various types of texts (genres). **TEKS Objective 6.13** *Reading/inquiry/research:* The student inquires and conducts research using a variety of sources.
TAAS Objective 6 The student will recognize points of view, propaganda, and/or statements of fact and opinion in a variety of written texts.	**TEKS Objective 6.10** *Reading/comprehension:* The student comprehends selections using a variety of strategies. **TEKS Objective 6.2** *Reading/text structures/literary concepts:* The student analyzes the characteristics of various types of texts (genres).

Correlation of TAAS and TEKS Objectives
Grade 7 READING (2000–2001/2001–2002)

TAAS Objective	Related TEKS Objective(s)
TAAS Objective 1 The student will determine the meaning of words in a variety of written texts.	**TEKS Objective 7.9** *Reading/vocabulary development:* The student acquires an extensive vocabulary through reading and systematic word study.
TAAS Objective 2 The student will identify supporting ideas in a variety of written texts.	**TEKS Objective 7.10** *Reading/comprehension:* The student uses a variety of strategies to comprehend a wide range of texts of increasing levels of difficulty. **TEKS Objective 7.12** *Reading/text structures/literary concepts:* The student analyzes the characteristics of various types of texts (genres). **TEKS Objective 7.13** *Reading/inquiry/research:* The student inquires and conducts research using a variety of sources.
TAAS Objective 3 The student will summarize a variety of written texts.	**TEKS Objective 7.10** *Reading/comprehension:* The student uses a variety of strategies to comprehend a wide range of texts of increasing levels of difficulty.

TAAS Objective	Related TEKS Objective(s)
TAAS Objective 4 The student will perceive relationships and recognize outcomes in a variety of written texts.	**TEKS Objective 7.10** *Reading/comprehension:* The student uses a variety of strategies to comprehend a wide range of texts of increasing levels of difficulty. **TEKS Objective 7.11** *Reading/literary response:* The student expresses and supports responses to various types of texts.
TAAS Objective 5 The student will analyze information in a variety of written texts in order to make inferences and generalizations.	**TEKS Objective 7.10** *Reading/comprehension:* The student uses a variety of strategies to comprehend a wide range of texts of increasing levels of difficulty. **TEKS Objective 7.12** *Reading/text structures/literary concepts:* The student analyzes the characteristics of various types of texts (genres). **TEKS Objective 7.13** *Reading/inquiry/research:* The student inquires and conducts research using a variety of sources.
TAAS Objective 6 The student will recognize points of view, propaganda, and/or statements of fact and opinion in a variety of written texts.	**TEKS Objective 7.10** *Reading/comprehension:* The student uses a variety of strategies to comprehend a wide range of texts of increasing levels of difficulty. **TEKS Objective 7.12** *Reading/text structures/literary concepts:* The student analyzes the characteristics of various types of texts (genres).

Correlation of TAAS and TEKS Objectives
Grade 8 READING (2000–2001/2001–2002)

TAAS Objective	Related TEKS Objective(s)
TAAS Objective 1 The student will determine the meaning of words in a variety of written texts.	**TEKS Objective 8.9** *Reading/vocabulary development:* The student acquires an extensive vocabulary through reading and systematic word study.
TAAS Objective 2 The student will identify supporting ideas in a variety of written texts.	**TEKS Objective 8.10** *Reading/comprehension:* The student comprehends selections using a variety of strategies. **TEKS Objective 8.13** *Reading/inquiry/research:* The student inquires and conducts research using a variety of sources.
TAAS Objective 3 The student will summarize a variety of written texts.	**TEKS Objective 8.10** *Reading/comprehension:* The student comprehends selections using a variety of strategies.

TAAS Objective	Related TEKS Objective(s)
TAAS Objective 4 The student will perceive relationships and recognize outcomes in a variety of written texts.	**TEKS Objective 8.10** *Reading/comprehension:* The student comprehends selections using a variety of strategies. **TEKS Objective 8.11** *Reading/literary response:* The student expresses and supports responses to various types of texts.
TAAS Objective 5 The student will analyze information in a variety of written texts in order to make inferences and generalizations.	**TEKS Objective 8.10** *Reading/comprehension:* The student comprehends selections using a variety of strategies. **TEKS Objective 8.13** *Reading/inquiry/research:* The student inquires and conducts research using a variety of sources.
TAAS Objective 6 The student will recognize points of view, propaganda, and/or statements of fact and opinion in a variety of written texts.	**TEKS Objective 8.10** *Reading/comprehension:* The student comprehends selections using a variety of strategies. **TEKS Objective 8.12** *Reading/text structures/literary concepts:* The student analyzes the characteristics of various types of texts (genres).

Test-taking Strategies
ABOUT THE TAAS READING TEST

In Spring 2001 and 2002, the TAAS Reading test will be given to all Texas students in grades 1–8. In 2003 and following years, a new Reading test will be given at grades 1–9. For 2001 and 2002, in the reading section of the TAAS, you will be asked to read six passages. Each passage is followed by a series of multiple-choice questions testing your ability to understand and interpret the passage.

TEST-TAKING STRATEGIES

You can score well on the test if you practice your reading skills and use your test-taking smarts. The following strategies will help you do well on multiple-choice reading tests such as the TAAS:

1. Read the entire passage before answering the questions.

2. Reread a section carefully before answering questions about that section.

3. Answer general questions first. Look for questions with words such as *summary* or *main idea*.

4. If a question is too difficult, skip it, and come back later if you have time. Make a note so you can keep track of the questions you skipped.

5. Look for key words and phrases in each question—for instance, *best, implied,* or *evidence*—that will help you to determine exactly what the question is asking.

6. Read all the answer choices before choosing.

7. Eliminate answer choices that are obviously incorrect.

8. Mark your answer sheet neatly. As you select your answers, make sure that you fill in the answer bubbles completely. Erase all stray marks and wrong answers.

9. After you have finished, review your answer sheet to make sure that you have marked each answer in the correct line.

USING THIS BOOK

To help prepare for the reading test, *Preparing for TAAS* reviews 14 reading skills that will help you to succeed on the 2001 and 2002 TAAS.

Each lesson is divided into two parts. The first page, Understanding the Skill, demonstrates the skill and teaches the strategies that will help you to master it. This is followed by practice pages for grades 6, 7, and 8. The Practicing the Skill page provides guidelines for using the skill as well as a passage that you can use to practice what you have learned. Your teacher may assign one or more of these pages to help you prepare for a practice test or to use after a practice test if you need extra help with a particular skill.

For more information about TAAS in 2003 and beyond, visit our Web site: mcdougallittell.com.

READING SKILLS PRACTICE: READING OBJECTIVE 1
Using Context Clues

Good readers use a variety of strategies to understand unfamiliar words. For example, if a word has multiple meanings, is used in an unfamiliar way, or is just difficult, you may want to use context clues to figure out its meaning.

The context of a word is the part of the passage that surrounds it. By understanding the information around the targeted word—the **context clues**—you can work toward discovering the meaning of unfamiliar vocabulary. Types of context clues include:

- synonyms
- antonyms
- definition and restatement
- description
- example
- comparison
- contrast

Understanding the Skill

Step 1: Study the entire passage in which you find the unfamiliar word. Look for context clues that help you understand the meaning of the word you don't know. Sometimes a context clue will appear next to or near the unfamiliar word; other times you may find context clues for a word sprinkled throughout the passage. Notice the boxed clues in the passage below. These clues can help you understand the meaning of each boldface word.

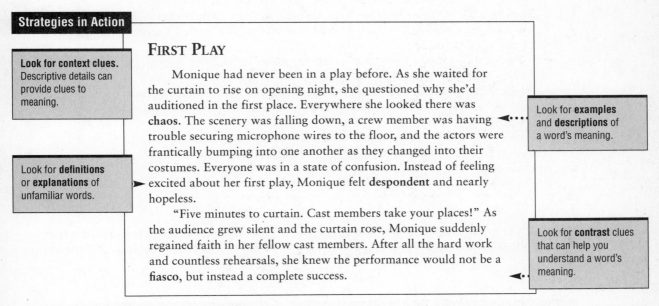

Strategies in Action

Look for context clues. Descriptive details can provide clues to meaning.

Look for definitions or **explanations** of unfamiliar words.

FIRST PLAY

Monique had never been in a play before. As she waited for the curtain to rise on opening night, she questioned why she'd auditioned in the first place. Everywhere she looked there was **chaos.** The scenery was falling down, a crew member was having trouble securing microphone wires to the floor, and the actors were frantically bumping into one another as they changed into their costumes. Everyone was in a state of confusion. Instead of feeling excited about her first play, Monique felt **despondent** and nearly hopeless.

"Five minutes to curtain. Cast members take your places!" As the audience grew silent and the curtain rose, Monique suddenly regained faith in her fellow cast members. After all the hard work and countless rehearsals, she knew the performance would not be a **fiasco,** but instead a complete success.

Look for **examples** and **descriptions** of a word's meaning.

Look for **contrast** clues that can help you understand a word's meaning.

Step 2: Make a list of unfamiliar words. List each unfamiliar word and its context clues. Include your previous knowledge about that word. Use these clues to determine the word's meaning.

Word	Context Clues	Best Guess at Meaning
chaos	"Confusion" is an example of this condition. "Nothing was in order" describes **chaos.**	disorganization or disorder
despondent	"Excited" is an antonym of **despondent**, which is less extreme than "hopeless."	discouraged
fiasco	"Complete success" is the opposite of **fiasco.**	failure

Practicing the Skill: Level 6

> **GUIDELINES FOR USING CONTEXT CLUES TO DETERMINE MEANING:**
>
> ■ Look for **synonyms** (words with similar meanings) or **antonyms** (opposites).
>
> ■ Recognize **descriptions** (phrases that elaborate on unfamiliar words).
>
> ■ Watch for **examples**: "The queen's raiment, *including her cape and an elaborate gown*, was made entirely of red silk."
>
> ■ Notice **definitions** or **explanations** (restatement of the idea in different words).
>
> ■ Watch for words or phrases that **compare** or **contrast** unfamiliar words with familiar words (*like, as, in the same way, but, unlike, on the contrary*).

Apply what you have learned. Refer to the guidelines above as you complete the exercises below. Use a separate sheet of paper if you need more room.

A. The following passage describes a young boy's audition for a spot in his school's orchestra. As you read, look for context clues that indicate the meaning of each underlined word.

THE AUDITION

John walked nervously into the audition room. There was only one spot open for violin in the school orchestra and there were still many students waiting in the hallway to try out for it. John reminded himself that panic wouldn't help him, only <u>composure</u> would get him through.

The boy before him had just come out. He had looked at John with a <u>haughty</u> grin as if to say, "I got in and you didn't."

John settled his violin under his chin and then looked at Mr. Scarlatti, the music teacher. Mr. Scarlatti was gazing <u>pensively</u> out the window as if he were deep in thought.

"Whenever you're ready," Mr Scarlatti mumbled.

John began to play and the music just flowed from his violin. When he finished, Mr. Scarlatti applauded. "That was a <u>stupendous</u> performance!" Mr. Scarlatti cried, "It was truly amazing!"

B. Fill in the chart with context clues from the passage. Use the clues to determine each word's meaning. When you have finished, check a dictionary to see whether you have interpreted each word's meaning correctly.

Word	Context Clues	Best Guess at Meaning
composure		
haughty		
pensively		
stupendous		

Practicing the Skill: Level 7

GUIDELINES FOR USING CONTEXT CLUES TO DETERMINE MEANING:

- Look for **synonyms** (words with similar meanings) or **antonyms** (opposites).

- Recognize **descriptions** (phrases that elaborate on unfamiliar words).

- Watch for **examples**: "The queen's raiment, *including her cape and an elaborate gown*, was made entirely of red silk."

- Notice **definitions** or **explanations** (restatement of the idea in different words).

- Watch for words or phrases that **compare** or **contrast** unfamiliar words with familiar words (*like, as, in the same way, but, unlike, on the contrary*).

Apply what you have learned. Refer to the guidelines above as you complete the exercises below. Use a separate sheet of paper if you need more room.

A. The following passage describes a brother and a sister as they explore an island on a lake. As you read, look for context clues that indicate the meaning of each underlined word.

THE SECRET ISLAND

Early one morning, Max and Amy snuck outside and rowed to the small island across from their family's cabin on the lake. Their mother had told them to help her clean the cabin, but Max and Amy couldn't resist going to the island. Exploring it would be an exciting break from the <u>tedious</u> chores their mother had in mind.

"Look!" Amy pointed to a huge tree whose branches were all twisted and <u>gnarled</u>.

"We're kings!" Max said. Max started climbing and Amy followed. The tree had lots of cracks and a huge <u>crevice</u> where they could put their hands and feet.

Amy stopped climbing. She was afraid that she might slip and <u>plummet</u> to the ground.

"This is our kingdom!" Max cried from the tree's top, but suddenly he stopped grinning.

"What do you see?" Amy said.

"Mom standing on our dock," Max said. "And boy does she look mad!"

B. Fill in the chart with context clues from the passage. Use the clues to determine each word's meaning. When you have finished, check a dictionary to see whether you have interpreted each word's meaning correctly.

Word	Context Clues	Best Guess at Meaning
tedious		
gnarled		
crevice		
plummet		

Practicing the Skill: Level 8

GUIDELINES FOR USING CONTEXT CLUES TO DETERMINE MEANING:

- Look for **synonyms** (words with similar meanings) or **antonyms** (opposites).
- Recognize **descriptions** (phrases that elaborate on unfamiliar words).
- Watch for **examples**: "The queen's raiment, *including her cape and an elaborate gown,* was made entirely of red silk."

- Notice **definitions** or **explanations** (restatement of the idea in different words).
- Watch for words or phrases that **compare** or **contrast** unfamiliar words with familiar words (*like, as, in the same way, but, unlike, on the contrary*).

Apply what you have learned. Refer to the guidelines above as you complete the exercises below. Use a separate sheet of paper if you need more room.

A. The following passage describes England's Industrial Revolution. As you read, look for context clues that indicate the meaning of each underlined word.

THE INDUSTRIAL REVOLUTION

Prior to the 1750s and the first Industrial Revolution, England's economy was based on cottage industry: workers purchased or grew their own raw materials, made the goods at home, and sold the goods themselves. This <u>primitive</u> system was sufficient until cotton cloth suddenly became in great demand. Small-scale production was too slow and too costly to meet the demands of the country. England needed a faster, more advanced way to produce cotton cloth. A major change was <u>imminent</u>, but few could imagine how great the changes would be.

In 1733, English weaver John Kay introduced the flying shuttle, an invention which allowed a weaver to produce cloth twice as fast as before. His <u>initiative</u> to speed production was a huge success. Other inventions followed, including the spinning jenny, the water-powered frame, and the spinning mule. Soon after, large buildings were built to house the machines, and workers were hired as machine operators. Cottage industry began to dwindle as the new factory system quickly emerged, dramatically changing not only England's cotton business but its entire economy and its traditional ways of life.

B. Fill in the chart with context clues from the passage. Use the clues to determine each word's meaning. When you have finished, check a dictionary to see whether you have interpreted each word's meaning correctly.

Word	Context Clues	Best Guess at Meaning
primitive		
imminent		
initiative		

READING SKILLS PRACTICE: READING OBJECTIVE 1
Using Word Parts

When you read, you often encounter new and unfamiliar words. One way to determine the meaning of unfamiliar words is to look them up in a dictionary or glossary. Often, however, you can figure out the meaning of a word by breaking it into parts.

Understanding the Skill

Step 1: Identify word parts as you read. Word parts include **base words**, **roots**, **prefixes**, and **suffixes**. A base word is a complete word to which prefixes or suffixes may be added. For example, *trust* is the base word of *distrust*. A root is similar to a base word except that it cannot stand alone. For instance, *psych* is the root of *psychology*. **Prefixes** are added before a root or base word (*non–, re–*). **Suffixes** are added after it (*–able, –ize*).

It is also helpful to recognize **word families**. Words with the same root form a **word family**: *dialogue* and *logical* share the root *log* ("word" or "reason"). Use familiar words to help you understand new words.

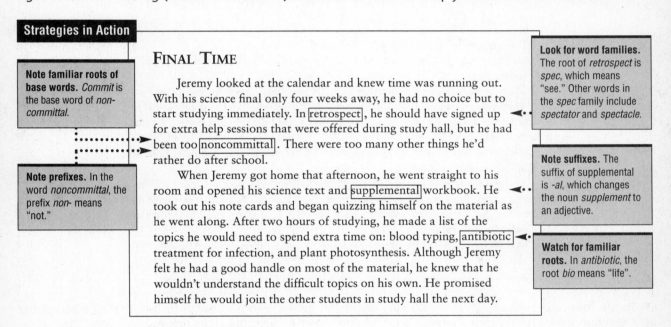

Strategies in Action

Note familiar roots of base words. *Commit* is the base word of *noncommittal.*

Note prefixes. In the word *noncommittal*, the prefix *non-* means "not."

FINAL TIME

Jeremy looked at the calendar and knew time was running out. With his science final only four weeks away, he had no choice but to start studying immediately. In retrospect, he should have signed up for extra help sessions that were offered during study hall, but he had been too noncommittal. There were too many other things he'd rather do after school.

When Jeremy got home that afternoon, he went straight to his room and opened his science text and supplemental workbook. He took out his note cards and began quizzing himself on the material as he went along. After two hours of studying, he made a list of the topics he would need to spend extra time on: blood typing, antibiotic treatment for infection, and plant photosynthesis. Although Jeremy felt he had a good handle on most of the material, he knew that he wouldn't understand the difficult topics on his own. He promised himself he would join the other students in study hall the next day.

Look for word families. The root of *retrospect* is *spec*, which means "see." Other words in the *spec* family include *spectator* and *spectacle.*

Note suffixes. The suffix of *supplemental* is *-al*, which changes the noun *supplement* to an adjective.

Watch for familiar roots. In *antibiotic*, the root *bio* means "life".

Step 2: Break a new word into parts. When you come across a new word, try to break it into its parts. If you can define the parts, you can combine the definitions to create a definition of the whole word. For example, separate the word *unmanageable* into its parts: *un-*, *manage*, and *-able*. You know *un-* means "not." To *manage* means "to control," and *-able* means "can be." Combining them gives "cannot be controlled," which is a good definition of *unmanageable*.

Word	Word Parts	Meaning
noncommittal	prefix: *non–* (not) base word: *commit* suffix: *–al* (of or characterized by)	a lack of commitment to a particular opinion or course of action
antibiotic	prefix: *anti–* (against) root word: *bio* (life) suffix: *–ic* (of or related to)	a substance that can destroy life or stop the growth of microorganisms
supplemental	base word: *supplement* suffix: *–al*	serving to provide additional information
retrospect	prefix: *retro-* (back) root: *spec* (see)	a review, survey, or looking back of things in the past

Practicing the Skill: Level 6

> **GUIDELINES FOR USING WORD PARTS TO DETERMINE THE MEANINGS OF UNFAMILIAR WORDS:**
>
> ■ Break unfamiliar words into parts.
>
> ■ Identify word parts—base words, roots, prefixes, and suffixes.
>
> ■ Make notes about the word parts you understand.
>
> ■ Use your knowledge of the word parts to determine the meaning of the whole word.
>
> ■ Use a chart to organize your notes about word parts and new vocabulary.
>
> ■ Relate new words to word families you already know.

Apply what you have learned. Refer to the guidelines above as you complete the exercises below. Use a separate sheet of paper if you need more room.

A. Read the following passage that describes a girl who is late for school. As you read, break the underlined words into parts. Look for familiar base words, roots, prefixes, and suffixes.

EVERYBODY HAS A BAD DAY

"I'm going to be late for school!" Beth cried.

Her father was driving her and they were stuck in traffic. Up ahead, a car was being towed away.

"That car broke down," her father said. "What a <u>misfortune</u> for the driver."

"That won't mean much to Mr. Copley," Beth said. Mr. Copley, the principal of her school, was nice most of the time, but he was a strict <u>disciplinarian</u> when it came to students being late.

"Everybody has a bad day once in awhile," Beth's father said, but Beth didn't think Mr. Copley would accept her excuse as <u>legitimate</u>.

At school, Beth went straight to Mr. Copley's office. Maybe Mr. Copley will be <u>compassionate</u> if I just explain what happened, Beth thought. She knocked on his door and saw that Mr. Copley was still wearing his hat and coat. She started to explain and Mr. Copley began to smile.

"Everybody has a bad day once in awhile," he said. "It was my car that broke down!"

B. Relate the word parts to words you already know. Put the meanings of the parts together to determine a definition for each underlined word. Use this information to fill in the chart below.

Word	Word Parts	Word Meaning
misfortune		
disciplinarian		
legitimate		
compassionate		

Practicing the Skill: Level 7

GUIDELINES FOR USING WORD PARTS TO DETERMINE THE MEANINGS OF UNFAMILIAR WORDS:

- Break unfamiliar words into parts.
- Identify word parts—base words, roots, prefixes, and suffixes.
- Make notes about the word parts you understand.

- Use your knowledge of the word parts to determine the meaning of the whole word.
- Use a chart to organize your notes about word parts and new vocabulary.
- Relate new words to word families you already know.

Apply what you have learned. Refer to the guidelines above as you complete the exercises below. Use a separate sheet of paper if you need more room.

A. Read the following passage about a young girl trying to build a secret clubhouse. As you read, break the underlined words into parts. Look for familiar base words, roots, prefixes, and suffixes.

HIDING FROM BROCK

For weeks now, Sarah had been trying to find a place for a secret clubhouse, one that would be safe from her little brother Brock. The garage, the cellar, even the tree out back had all been <u>inadequate</u> for what she needed. Brock had always found her.

"What are you doing?" Brock would say.

No matter what Sarah told Brock, he always had another question. His curiosity was <u>unappeasable</u>. Besides, once Brock found her, he usually broke or spilled something.

"Mom, he ruins everything!" Sarah complained, hoping that Brock would be sent to his room, but Brock had been given <u>impunity</u>. "He's only seven," Mom said, "be patient."

One day, Sarah found a huge box at the back of the attic. She crept inside as quietly as she could. "He'll never find me," Sarah thought. But then she heard him.

"Let me in!" Brock cried.

<u>Resistance</u> was of no use. Sarah let Brock come inside.

B. Relate the word parts to words you already know. Put the meanings of the parts together to determine a definition for each underlined word. Use this information to fill in the chart below.

Word	Word Parts	Word Meaning
inadequate		
unappeasable		
impunity		
resistance		

Using Word Parts, continued

Practicing the Skill: Level 8

> **GUIDELINES FOR USING WORD PARTS TO DETERMINE THE MEANINGS OF UNFAMILIAR WORDS:**
>
> ■ Break unfamiliar words into parts.
>
> ■ Identify word parts—base words, roots, prefixes, and suffixes.
>
> ■ Make notes about the word parts you understand.
>
> ■ Use your knowledge of the word parts to determine the meaning of the whole word.
>
> ■ Use a chart to organize your notes about word parts and new vocabulary.
>
> ■ Relate new words to word families you already know.

Apply what you have learned. Refer to the guidelines above as you complete the exercises below. Use a separate sheet of paper if you need more room.

A. Read the following passage about a special birthday celebration. As you read, break the underlined words into parts. Look for familiar base words, roots, prefixes, and suffixes.

BIRTHDAY SURPRISE

Jessica knew she was in for a treat when her grandparents said they had something special for her birthday. Every year they gave her a unique and thoughtful gift. Last year they gave her tickets to her favorite musical. She not only had great seats, but she had the <u>privilege</u> of going backstage to meet the cast. The fact that she had seen the show twice already was <u>inconsequential</u>—each time was more wonderful than the last.

When the package arrived the day before her birthday, Jessica couldn't wait to open it. After much pleading with her parents, she tore open the box. Inside was a framed autographed photograph of her favorite actor. She couldn't believe it! She had been <u>infatuated</u> with this actor for years! The frame came with a certificate of <u>authenticity</u> which proved that the signature was real. Jessica wondered how next year's gift could possibly be any better.

B. Relate the word parts to words you already know. Put the meanings of the parts together to determine a definition for each underlined word. Use this information to fill in the chart below.

Word	Word Parts	Word Meaning
privilege		
inconsequential		
infatuated		
authenticity		

READING SKILLS PRACTICE: READING OBJECTIVE 2
Recognizing Supporting Details

The facts and examples that relate to the main idea of a passage and prove it to be true are called **supporting details.** Authors often use facts selectively to make an argument more persuasive. They may also use certain details simply to make their writing more interesting. As a reader, you must be able to recognize which points are central to the main idea of a piece of writing and which are there primarily to increase the reader's interest.

Understanding the Skill

Step 1: Recognize details as you read. The following passage describes the game of lacrosse. As you read the passage, notice the details that support the main idea.

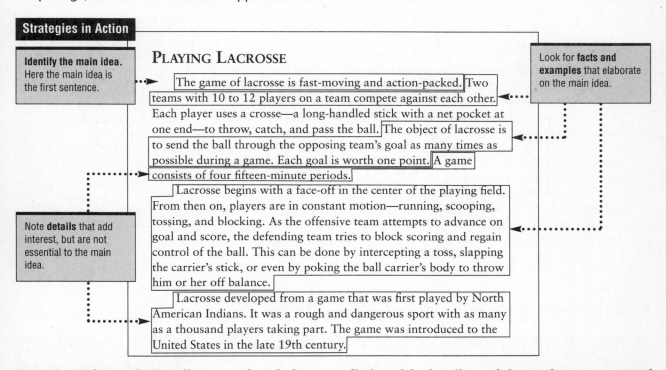

Strategies in Action

Identify the main idea. Here the main idea is the first sentence.

Note **details** that add interest, but are not essential to the main idea.

Look for **facts and examples** that elaborate on the main idea.

PLAYING LACROSSE

The game of lacrosse is fast-moving and action-packed. Two teams with 10 to 12 players on a team compete against each other. Each player uses a crosse—a long-handled stick with a net pocket at one end—to throw, catch, and pass the ball. The object of lacrosse is to send the ball through the opposing team's goal as many times as possible during a game. Each goal is worth one point. A game consists of four fifteen-minute periods.

Lacrosse begins with a face-off in the center of the playing field. From then on, players are in constant motion—running, scooping, tossing, and blocking. As the offensive team attempts to advance on goal and score, the defending team tries to block scoring and regain control of the ball. This can be done by intercepting a toss, slapping the carrier's stick, or even by poking the ball carrier's body to throw him or her off balance.

Lacrosse developed from a game that was first played by North American Indians. It was a rough and dangerous sport with as many as a thousand players taking part. The game was introduced to the United States in the late 19th century.

Step 2: Make a cluster diagram that helps you distinguish details and facts that are central to the purpose of the text.

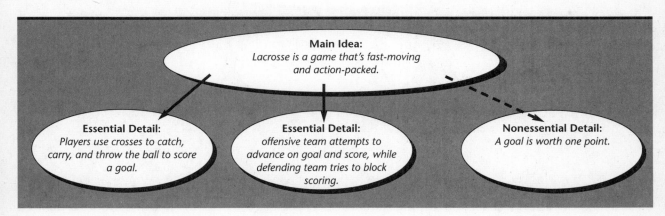

Main Idea:
Lacrosse is a game that's fast-moving and action-packed.

Essential Detail:
Players use crosses to catch, carry, and throw the ball to score a goal.

Essential Detail:
offensive team attempts to advance on goal and score, while defending team tries to block scoring.

Nonessential Detail:
A goal is worth one point.

Practicing the Skill: Level 6

GUIDELINES FOR RECOGNIZING SUPPORTING DETAILS:

- Determine the text's main idea.
- Look for important facts and examples— those that support the main idea.
- Recognize details that add interest but are not essential to the main idea.
- Use a cluster diagram to distinguish details that are central to the purpose of the text.

Apply what you have learned. Refer to the guidelines above as you complete the exercises below. Use a separate sheet of paper if you need more room.

A. The following passage describes how nursing home residents can benefit from having pets. Read through the letter, then answer the questions. The questions will help you determine the supporting details.

PETS WELCOME!

I disagree completely with Bailey Mumford's article, *Nursing Homes, No Pets Allowed*. I think the many advantages that animals bring to senior citizens living in elderly housing facilities and nursing homes outweigh any disadvantages. I know this for a fact because my grandmother lives in a nursing home. If my grandmother and her friends were allowed to keep pets, they would be less lonely and bored. Pets replace loneliness with companionship and boredom with interest. I know of some nursing homes where animals visit residents regularly. These pet visits help residents "come alive" and build their self-esteem.

I've read about scientific studies that prove pets help people relax, lower stress levels, and help prolong life. Pets make their owners laugh and forget their troubles. A pet is devoted, nonjudgmental, and eager to please—no matter what the person's age or physical health. Life in a nursing home is not always easy, but a pet provides enormous physical and emotional rewards, and will make all the difference for my grandmother and her friends.

1. What is the main idea of this selection?
2. List the details that support the idea that pets are beneficial to nursing home residents?
3. What details support the idea that pets help to prolong life?
4. How does the detail that pets make their owners laugh and forget their troubles support the main idea of the passage? Explain.

B. Use your answers to the questions above to help you fill in the web diagram.

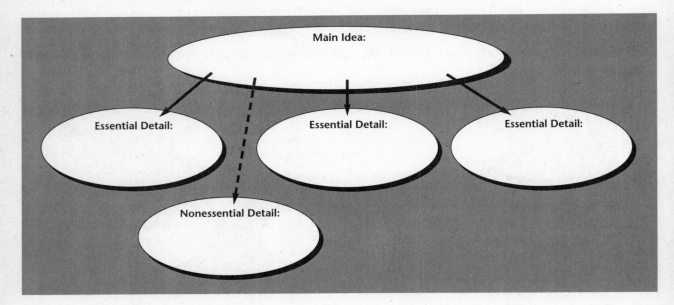

Practicing the Skill: Level 7

GUIDELINES FOR RECOGNIZING SUPPORTING DETAILS:

■ Determine the text's main idea.

■ Look for important facts and examples—those that support the main idea.

■ Recognize details that add interest but are not essential to the main idea.

■ Use a cluster diagram to distinguish details that are central to the purpose of the text.

Apply what you have learned. Refer to the guidelines above as you complete the exercises below. Use a separate sheet of paper if you need more room.

A. The following passage describes the world's three main climate zones. Read through the passage, then answer the questions. The questions will help you determine the supporting details.

CLIMATE ZONES

Every place on earth has its own climate. Climate is defined by the regular weather patterns that an area has, measured over a long time. Climate is affected by a number of factors including distance from the equator, ocean temperatures and currents, winds, altitude, and many other factors.

Scientists recognize that there are 12 major kinds of climate. Most of the different climates fall within three climate zones. The tropical zone is closest to the equator. This area has hot climates all year long and high rainfall. The temperate zone lies between the poles and the tropics. The climate in these areas is warm and dry in the summer and cold and wet in the winter. The polar zone includes areas below the Antarctic Circle and above the Arctic Circle. There, the winters are very cold and there often is snow during the summers.

Climate affects people's way of life no matter where they live. Only 7 percent of the Earth's land surface has a temperate climate. Yet, nearly half the world's population lives in these areas.

1. What is the main idea of this selection?
2. What details support the idea that different factors affect climate?
3. What details support the idea that there are different climate zones?
4. Does the fact that 7 percent of the Earth's land surface has a temperate climate support the main idea of this passage? Explain.

B. Use you answers to the questions above to help you fill in the Web diagram.

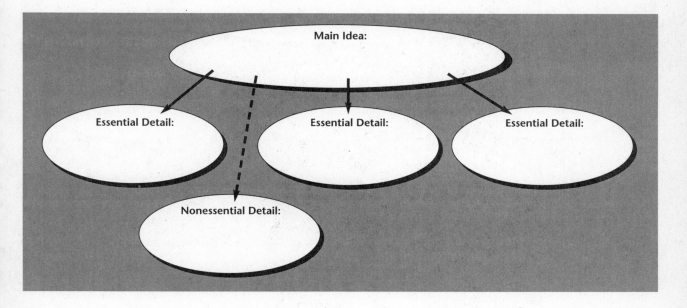

Practicing the Skill: Level 8

GUIDELINES FOR RECOGNIZING SUPPORTING DETAILS:

■ Determine the text's main idea.

■ Look for important facts and examples—those that support the main idea.

■ Recognize details that add interest but are not essential to the main idea.

■ Use a cluster diagram to distinguish details that are central to the purpose of the text.

Apply what you have learned. Refer to the guidelines above as you complete the exercises below. Use a separate sheet of paper if you need more room.

A. The following passage describes how we see a rainbow. Read through the passage, then answer the questions. The questions will help you determine the supporting details.

SIGHTING A RAINBOW

A rainbow is an arch of beautiful colors that appears in the sky under certain conditions. Most often, it is visible when the sun shines after a brief rain shower. A rainbow forms in the part of the sky that is opposite the sun. The sun's ray is bent as it enters the water droplet and is separated into different colors. As it passes through the droplet's inner surface it is reflected. Many drops can make a rainbow. In addition to the weather, other conditions must be right for a rainbow to occur—the sun's position in the sky and the time of day. This explains why rainbows are usually seen in the late afternoon when the sun is close to the horizon.

A more rare sighting is a double rainbow. This may occur when the sun's light is reflected twice within each water droplet. The secondary arch usually appears less intense than the primary arch. A rainbow is always a wonder to see whether it appears in the sky or in the spray of a garden sprinkler on a hot summer's afternoon.

1. What is the main idea of this selection?
2. List the details that support the idea that rainbows are usually seen after a brief period of rain.
3. What details support the idea that there other conditions that must occur in order to see a rainbow?
4. How does the detail that double rainbows are rarely seen support the main idea of the passage? Explain.

B. Use your answers to questions above to help you fill in the web diagram.

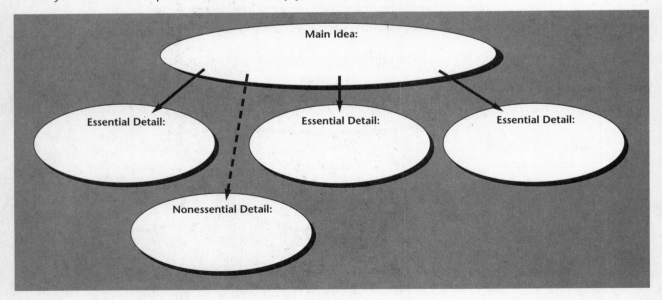

Main Idea:

Essential Detail: Essential Detail: Essential Detail:

Nonessential Detail:

READING SKILLS PRACTICE: READING OBJECTIVE 2

Understanding Sequential Order

Sequential order, or chronological order, is the order in which events happen in time. It is essential for a reader to understand the order in which the events described in a passage take place. Since writers do not always write about events in the exact order in which they happened, it is important to be able to determine when events occurred relative to one another.

Understanding the Skill

Step 1: Look for time clues. The following passage describes the history of comics in the United States. As you read the passage, search for words and phrases that indicate a sequence of events.

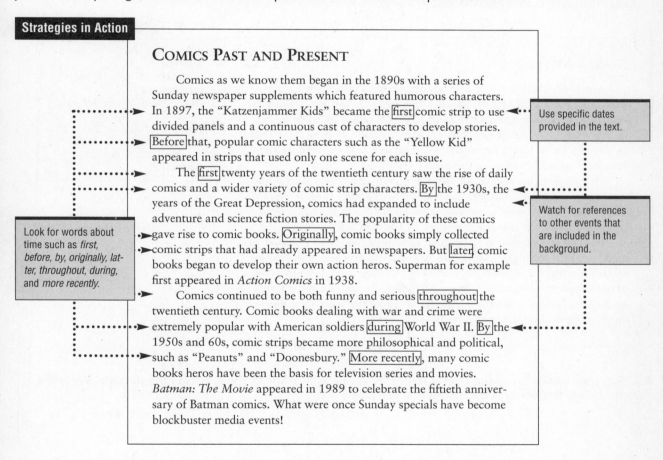

Strategies in Action

COMICS PAST AND PRESENT

Comics as we know them began in the 1890s with a series of Sunday newspaper supplements which featured humorous characters. In 1897, the "Katzenjammer Kids" became the first comic strip to use divided panels and a continuous cast of characters to develop stories. Before that, popular comic characters such as the "Yellow Kid" appeared in strips that used only one scene for each issue.

The first twenty years of the twentieth century saw the rise of daily comics and a wider variety of comic strip characters. By the 1930s, the years of the Great Depression, comics had expanded to include adventure and science fiction stories. The popularity of these comics gave rise to comic books. Originally, comic books simply collected comic strips that had already appeared in newspapers. But later, comic books began to develop their own action heros. Superman for example first appeared in *Action Comics* in 1938.

Comics continued to be both funny and serious throughout the twentieth century. Comic books dealing with war and crime were extremely popular with American soldiers during World War II. By the 1950s and 60s, comic strips became more philosophical and political, such as "Peanuts" and "Doonesbury." More recently, many comic books heros have been the basis for television series and movies. *Batman: The Movie* appeared in 1989 to celebrate the fiftieth anniversary of Batman comics. What were once Sunday specials have become blockbuster media events!

Sidebar notes:

Use specific dates provided in the text.

Watch for references to other events that are included in the background.

Look for words about time such as *first, before, by, originally, latter, throughout, during,* and *more recently.*

Step 2: Order events on a time line. Write the dates below the line and the events above the line.

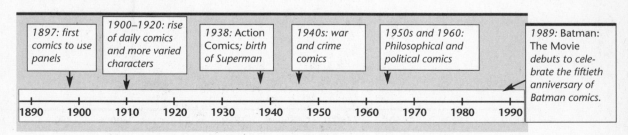

1897: first comics to use panels

1900–1920: rise of daily comics and more varied characters

1938: Action Comics; birth of Superman

1940s: war and crime comics

1950s and 1960: Philosophical and political comics

1989: Batman: The Movie debuts to celebrate the fiftieth anniversary of Batman comics.

1890 1900 1910 1920 1930 1940 1950 1960 1970 1980 1990

Practicing the Skill: Level 6

GUIDELINES FOR UNDERSTANDING SEQUENTIAL ORDER:

- ■ Use specific dates provided in the text.
- ■ Look for words about time such as *first, then, before, during, later, now, after, ultimately, already,* and *by that time.*

- ■ Watch for references to other events that are included in the background.
- ■ If the events are complex, make a time line of them.

Apply what you have learned. Refer to the guidelines above as you complete the exercises below. Use a separate sheet of paper if you need more space.

A. Read the passage below, which describes the events in the life of Maria Mitchell. Use the questions to help place events in sequential order.

MARIA MITCHELL

Maria Mitchell, the first woman astronomer in the United States, was born August 1, 1818, on the island of Nantucket in Massachusetts. For the first sixteen years of her life, Maria was taught at home by her father, who believed that girls should receive an education equal to that of boys. In 1835, Maria became an assistant at a teacher's college and a year later opened a school of her own.

One night in the autumn of 1847, Maria discovered a comet while looking through her four-inch telescope on her parent's roof. It was an achievement for which she received a gold medal from the king of Denmark. Later, the comet was named, "Miss Mitchell's Comet."

In 1848 she was voted as the first woman astronomer to become a member of the prestigious American Academy of Arts and Sciences. She served as professor of astronomy at Vassar College from 1865 to 1888. Maria was a well respected teacher. At Vassar, she focused her research on the sun, Jupiter, and Saturn. After having to retire from the college due to poor health, Maria died on June 28, 1889.

---

1. What specific dates are mentioned in the text?

2. In what year did Maria Mitchell open her own school?

3. When did Maria Mitchell discover a comet?

4. What year did Maria Mitchell become the first woman member of the American Academy of Arts and Sciences?

B. Using your responses to the questions above, create a time line of the events in the passage. Write the dates below the line and the events above the line.

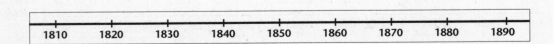

| 1810 | 1820 | 1830 | 1840 | 1850 | 1860 | 1870 | 1880 | 1890 |

Practicing the Skill: Level 7

GUIDELINES FOR UNDERSTANDING SEQUENTIAL ORDER:

- Use specific dates provided in the text.
- Look for words about time such as *first, then, before, during, later, now, after, ultimately, already,* and *by that time.*

- Watch for references to other events that are included in the background.
- If the events are complex, make a time line of them.

Apply what you have learned. Refer to the guidelines above as you complete the exercises below. Use a separate sheet of paper if you need more space.

A. Read the passage below, which describes the events in the life of Ella Fitzgerald. Use the questions to help place events in sequential order.

ELLA FITZGERALD

    Jazz great Ella Fitzgerald was born on April 25, 1917, in Newport News, Virginia. She was orphaned at the age of 15. Ella started on the road to success when she was still a teenager. She was scheduled to appear as a dance contestant in a talent competition, but she decided to sing instead. That decision proved to be an important move—she was heard by a musician in the famous Chick Webb Band and was asked to sing with them for one night. The one night launched her into a career of stardom, as she become one of the nation's greatest jazz and pop vocalists of all time.

    In 1938 Fitzgerald recorded a song called "A Tisket-A Tasket," one that earned her international fame and became one of her standards. In the 1940s, she perfected a style of singing known as "scat singing," a technique where she used her voice to imitate the sounds of instruments, such as trumpets and saxophones. Although she had no formal vocal training, Fitzgerald was among the best performers in show business. She is still referred to as "The First Lady of Song" for her contributions to the music world. Ella Fitzgerald died in 1996. Over her 60-year career, Ella recorded more than 250 albums.

1. What specific dates are mentioned in the text?
2. In what year was Ella Fitzgerald orphaned?
3. According to the passage, when did Ella Fitzgerald perfect the technique of "scat singing?"
4. How old was Ella Fitzgerald when she died?

B. Using your responses to the questions above, create a timeline of the events in the passage. Write the dates below the line and the events above the line.

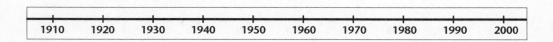

Practicing the Skill: Level 8

> **GUIDELINES FOR UNDERSTANDING SEQUENTIAL ORDER:**
>
> ■ Use specific dates provided in the text.
>
> ■ Look for words about time such as *first, then, before, during, later, now, after, ultimately, already,* and *by that time.*
>
> ■ Watch for references to other events that are included in the background.
>
> ■ If the events are complex, make a time line of them.

Apply what you have learned. Refer to the guidelines above as you complete the exercises below. Use a separate sheet of paper if you need more space.

A. Read the passage below, which describes events in the life of Helen Keller. Use the questions to help place events in sequential order.

HELEN KELLER

Helen Keller was an extraordinary woman who overcame incredible difficulties to become one of the most famous people in this country's history. She was born healthy on June 27, 1880, but an illness when she was about 19 months old left her both blind and deaf. One result of this illness was that communication became very difficult for Keller. As she grew older, she also grew more and more frustrated when her family did not immediately understand what she wanted, so she began to throw temper tantrums to get her way. Before she turned seven, her parents found a young woman from the Perkins School of the Blind, Annie Sullivan, to help tudor their young daughter. By spelling letters with her fingers into Helen Keller's hand, Annie Sullivan was able to show Keller that letters connect into words that have meanings, and that words are related to objects in the world.

Annie Sullivan remained Helen Keller's teacher, helping Keller graduate with honors from Radcliffe College in 1904. After Sullivan married, she continued as Keller's friend and companion, assisting Keller in her constant work for other people with similar disabilities and challenges to Keller's own. Keller was granted many awards and honorary degrees during a long life. In 1964 she received the Presidential Medal of Freedom and in the following year she was elected to the Women's Hall of Fame at the New York World's Fair. Helen Keller deserved all the fame and awards that her life and work inspired. She died on June 1, 1968 three weeks shy of her 88th birthday.

> 1. What specific dates are mentioned in the text?
> 2. According to this passage, in what year did Annie Sullivan begin to work as Helen Keller's tutor?
> 3. In what year did Helen Keller graduate from college?
> 4. In what year was Helen Keller elected to the Women's Hall of Fame?

B. Using your responses to the questions above, create a time line of the events in the passage. Write the dates below the line and the events above the line.

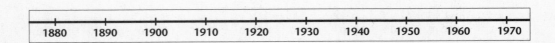

READING SKILLS PRACTICE: READING OBJECTIVE 3
Identifying the Main Idea

The **main idea** of a reading passage is the principal message that the writer wants to convey. Sometimes, the main idea is clearly **stated** in a **topic sentence**. Other times, the main idea is **implied** rather than explicitly stated. When the main idea is implied, clues in the text must be used to find the main idea.

Understanding the Skill

Step 1: Identify the main idea as you read. Read the following passage on the work and training of archaeologists. Notice how the main idea is stated directly in the first paragraph. In the second paragraph, notice the clues that can help you determine the implied main idea.

Strategies in Action

Stated Main Idea. The **topic sentence** is often the first sentence of a paragraph. It is supported by the rest of the paragraph.

Implied Main Idea: Clue 1. Look for shifts in focus. In this example, the focus of the passage moves from an explanation of what archaeologists do, to an overview of education in this field of study.

THE ARCHAEOLOGIST

(1) An archaeologist studies the past by investigating the remains of human cultures. These remains may include pieces of pottery, tools, bones, fossils, buildings, and artwork. By analyzing the remains, the archaeologist pieces together a picture of what life was once like. He or she may be able to determine what people did for work, or the presence of specific plants and animals in a given area. Most archaeologists are employed in three main fields: teaching, museum work, and government service.

(2) All professional archaeologists are college graduates. Many major in anthropology, the study of human culture, and take courses in history and science for background knowledge. Many take courses to get an in-depth understanding of specific cultures. Students also spend a good portion of their training gaining hands-on experience at excavation sites and in laboratories. If you're a person who likes working with your hands, are interested in solving mysteries, and like the idea of an outdoor classroom, a career in archaeology might be for you.

Implied Main Idea: Clue 2. Notice examples. Generalizing from examples can help you draw basic conclusions about the main idea. In this case, three sentences describe the education that is necessary for becoming a professional archaeologist.

Implied Main Idea: Clue 3. Notice the end result. Much of the paragraph leads to a final statement or result.

Step 2: Identify supporting details. Make a diagram listing supporting statements and text clues that point to the main idea of each paragraph.

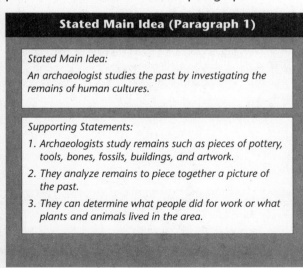

Stated Main Idea (Paragraph 1)	Implied Main Idea (Paragraph 2)
Stated Main Idea: *An archaeologist studies the past by investigating the remains of human cultures.*	*Text Clues:* *1. All professional archaeologists are college graduates.* *2. Many archaeologists major in anthropology and take history and science courses.* *3. Archaeologists need in-depth knowledge of specific cultures.* *4. Students spend time working in the field.*
Supporting Statements: *1. Archaeologists study remains such as pieces of pottery, tools, bones, fossils, buildings, and artwork.* *2. They analyze remains to piece together a picture of the past.* *3. They can determine what people did for work or what plants and animals lived in the area.*	*Implied Main Idea:* *A career as an archaeologist requires a great amount of training and offers many interesting challenges.*

Practicing the Skill: Level 6

GUIDELINES FOR IDENTIFYING THE MAIN IDEA:

■ Identify the topic sentence, if there is one.

■ Look for shifts in the narrative that may indicate a change in focus.

■ Recognize key events, which often lead to the main idea.

■ Notice the outcome, which may signal the main idea.

■ Make a diagram to help determine the main idea.

Apply what you have learned. Refer to the guidelines above as you complete the exercises below. Use a separate sheet of paper if you need more space.

A. The following paragraphs are about chocolate. In one of the paragraphs, the main idea is stated, and in the other it is implied. Read the paragraphs carefully, and look for the main idea in each.

MAKE MINE CHOCOLATE

(1) It's hard to imagine life without chocolate, but there was a time when chocolate candy was unheard of. When chocolate was brought to Europe from Mexico by the Spanish explorers around 1500, it was in the form of a bitter drink. It was so expensive that only the very wealthy could afford it. As time went on, other countries began growing cacao (the plant that bears the cocoa beans), eventually causing the price to drop. Once cacao was more affordable, people started experimenting with chocolate, such as by adding milk to make milk chocolate. Chocolate production began in the United States in 1765 in Dorchester, Massachusetts, and today the United States has the world's largest chocolate manufacturing industry.

(2) Chocolate is a popular gift that can be given on almost any occasion. It is especially popular on holidays such as Valentine's Day and Mother's Day, when it is given as a token of love and affection. Easter baskets and Christmas stockings often are stocked with chocolate formed into holiday shapes. Children may receive chocolate any time as a reward or treat. And what wedding anniversary would be complete without a bouquet of roses and a box of fancy chocolates?

B. Based on whether the main idea is stated or implied, choose the appropriate diagram for each paragraph and fill in the details.

Paragraph with Stated Main Idea
Stated Main Idea:
Supporting Statements: 1. 2.

Paragraph with Implied Main Idea
Text Clues: 1. 2. 3.
Implied Main Idea:

Identifying the Main Idea, continued

Practicing the Skill: Level 7

> **GUIDELINES FOR IDENTIFYING THE MAIN IDEA:**
>
> - Identify the topic sentence, if there is one.
> - Look for shifts in the narrative that may indicate a change in focus.
> - Recognize key events, which often lead to the main idea.
> - Notice the outcome, which may signal the main idea.
> - Make a diagram to help determine the main idea.

Apply what you have learned. Refer to the guidelines above as you complete the exercises below. Use a separate sheet of paper if you need more space.

A. The following paragraphs are about rafting down the Colorado River through the Grand Canyon. In one of the paragraphs, the main idea is stated, and in the other it is implied. Read the paragraphs carefully, and look for the main idea in each.

RAFTING THE COLORADO

(1) Millions of tourists head to the Grand Canyon each year. For those with a sense of adventure, taking a rafting trip through the canyon on the Colorado River is a great way to experience this natural wonder. As you travel down the Colorado River, your guides will point out rock formations and explain the canyon's geological history. Being inside the canyon gives you an amazing perspective on the canyon's formation over millions of years. Although most of your day will be spent on the raft, there are many stops along the way. You can hike, swim in natural pools, explore hidden waterfalls, or relax on riverside sandbars used for campsites—none of which can be enjoyed by the less adventurous tourists who stay above on the canyon's ridge.

(2) Unless you are a very experienced rafter, you should take a guided trip that provides equipment and meals. Depending upon your skill and abilities, you can choose either a small raft powered by oars or paddles or a larger raft with a motor. Because the Colorado River is over 200 miles long, a typical trip lasts 6–8 days, alternating between floating lazily on calm, peaceful waters and zooming through turbulent rapids.

B. Based on whether the main idea is stated or implied, choose the appropriate diagram for each paragraph and fill in the details.

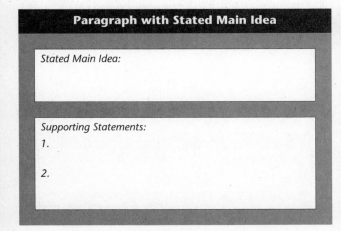

Paragraph with Stated Main Idea
Stated Main Idea:
Supporting Statements: 1. 2.

Paragraph with Implied Main Idea
Text Clues: 1. 2. 3.
Implied Main Idea:

Practicing the Skill: Level 8

> **GUIDELINES FOR IDENTIFYING THE MAIN IDEA:**
>
> - Identify the topic sentence, if there is one.
> - Look for shifts in the narrative that may indicate a change in focus.
> - Recognize key events, which often lead to the main idea.
>
> - Notice the outcome, which may signal the main idea.
> - Make a diagram to help determine the main idea.

Apply what you have learned. Refer to the guidelines above as you complete the exercises below. Use a separate sheet of paper if you need more space.

A. The following paragraphs are about the botanical art known as topiary. In one of the paragraphs, the main idea is stated, and in the other it is implied. Read the paragraphs carefully, and look for the main idea in each.

TOPIARY: A LIVING ART

(1) The garden art of training, pruning, and cutting live shrubs and trees into ornamental designs and figures is known as topiary. Topiary works best with thickly leafed evergreen shrubs such as cypress and yew. The plants can be clipped into shapes that serve as decorations for landscape gardening or can be made to resemble "live" statues. At Green Animals, a topiary garden in Portsmouth, RI, a playful monkey and a proud deer are only a couple of the creations on display.

(2) Topiary hasn't always been elaborate. Although it is not known when topiary art began, it is known that the Romans practiced topiary by shaping plants into geometric shapes such as pyramids and cones. Topiary became extremely popular and ornate in the 17th and 18th centuries, as people created detailed animal shapes such as giraffes and peacocks. In some cases, entire gardens have been sculpted into complex mazes, as seen at Hever Castle in Kent, England. Topiary is not so common today, and is usually found only in specialized private gardens, botanical displays, and formal parks.

B. Based on whether the main idea is stated or implied, choose the appropriate diagram for each paragraph and fill in the details.

Paragraph with Stated Main Idea
Stated Main Idea:
Supporting Statements: 1. 2.

Paragraph with Implied Main Idea
Text Clues: 1. 2. 3.
Implied Main Idea:

Name _____   Date _____

Summarizing

When you **summarize,** you create a shortened version of a selection. A summary presents the most important information—the main idea, crucial supporting details, and important facts or statistics—but it leaves out less important information. Summarizing is an important skill because it helps you remember critical information from your reading material.

Understanding the Skill

Step 1: Summarize as you read. The following passage describes some aspects of the giant panda's threatened extinction. Read the selection and identify the most important information.

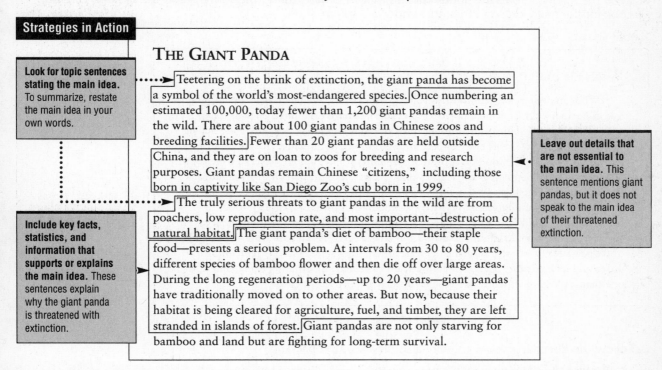

Strategies in Action

Look for topic sentences stating the main idea. To summarize, restate the main idea in your own words.

Include key facts, statistics, and information that supports or explains the main idea. These sentences explain why the giant panda is threatened with extinction.

THE GIANT PANDA

Teetering on the brink of extinction, the giant panda has become a symbol of the world's most-endangered species. Once numbering an estimated 100,000, today fewer than 1,200 giant pandas remain in the wild. There are about 100 giant pandas in Chinese zoos and breeding facilities. Fewer than 20 giant pandas are held outside China, and they are on loan to zoos for breeding and research purposes. Giant pandas remain Chinese "citizens," including those born in captivity like San Diego Zoo's cub born in 1999.

The truly serious threats to giant pandas in the wild are from poachers, low reproduction rate, and most important—destruction of natural habitat. The giant panda's diet of bamboo—their staple food—presents a serious problem. At intervals from 30 to 80 years, different species of bamboo flower and then die off over large areas. During the long regeneration periods—up to 20 years—giant pandas have traditionally moved on to other areas. But now, because their habitat is being cleared for agriculture, fuel, and timber, they are left stranded in islands of forest. Giant pandas are not only starving for bamboo and land but are fighting for long-term survival.

Leave out details that are not essential to the main idea. This sentence mentions giant pandas, but it does not speak to the main idea of their threatened extinction.

Step 2: Write a summary of the passage. Restate the main idea and key supporting information in your own words.

> The future for the giant panda is not very hopeful. There are many reasons why they may not survive; the most important is loss of habitat. Giant pandas eat a diet of bamboo while bamboo forests are being destroyed by logging and agricultural development.

Practicing the Skill: Level 6

GUIDELINES FOR SUMMARIZING:

- Look for topic sentences stating the main idea. Then restate the main idea in your own words.
- Include key facts, statistics, and information that support the main idea.

- Leave out details that are not essential to the main idea.

Apply what you have learned. Refer to the guidelines above as you complete the exercises below. Use a separate sheet of paper if you need more room.

A. Read the following passage about animals that hibernate during the winter. Read the passage carefully. Look for the main idea and the most important information.

WINTER SLEEP

While many birds fly south to warmer weather in the winter, some animals who live in northern climates must hibernate in order to survive. Animals such as bats, bears, skunks, and squirrels go into hibernation, or a sleep-like, dormant state during the winter months. This is not just because of the cold, but because the plants and berries they rely on for food disappear. Some animals, like the red squirrel, will stay in hibernation from September through March. Others, like the bear, may emerge from its den on warm days.

Hibernating animals must prepare for hibernation by eating enough food beforehand to build up a layer of fat. It is this fat reserve that allows the animal to survive. During the few months before a bear hibernates, it can gain up to 40 pounds of fat per week. Once the animal enters the hibernating state, its body temperature drops and its heart rate decreases dramatically. The ideal hibernating environment is one that is dark, quiet, and well-protected, such as burrows or caves.

B. Follow the directions below to write a summary of the passage.

1. Restate the main idea of this passage in your own words.

2. List all of the facts, statistics, and other information in the passage.

3. Read through your list, and underline the facts that directly support the main idea. You are deciding which information is important enough to include in a summary.

4. Using the main idea you wrote and the key information you have underlined, write a summary of the passage in your own words.

Summarizing, continued

Practicing the Skill: Level 7

GUIDELINES FOR SUMMARIZING:

■ Look for topic sentences stating the main idea. Then restate the main idea in your own words.

■ Include key facts, statistics, and information that support the main idea.

■ Leave out details that are not essential to the main idea.

Apply what you have learned. Refer to the guidelines above as you complete the exercises below. Use a separate sheet of paper if you need more room.

A. The following passage describes the parenting skills of the Emperor penguin. Read the passage carefully. Look for the main idea and the most important information.

THE EMPEROR PENGUIN

Unlike parenthood for many other families of the animal kingdom, parenthood for the Emperor penguin is a shared event. The male Emperor penguin is a model parent. He assumes sole care of the single egg's incubation while the female leaves for two months to search for food. In temperatures as low as -112°F, the male Emperor penguin cradles the egg on his feet under a fold of feathered abdominal skin. While the male waits for the female to return, he gathers with other males in a densely packed group called a huddle. The males press closely against each other to protect their eggs as they take turns braving the outer rim of the circle. Throughout this time, the male lives on his fat reserves. The male Emperor penguin loses over half of his original body weight as he is assaulted by 65-mph winds and freezing Antarctic temperatures.

Around the time the egg hatches, the female Emperor penguin returns to assist the male. She takes over the task of providing their young with much needed heat. Despite the chick's thick, wooly coat, the cold could kill it in under two minutes. Both parents take turns finding food to nourish their chick and to protect it from predators. Sadly, despite the parents' best efforts, only ten percent of Emperor penguin chicks survive to adulthood.

B. Follow the directions below to write a summary of the passage.

1. Restate the main idea of this passage in your own words.

2. List all of the facts, statistics, and other information in the passage.

3. Read through your list, and underline the facts that directly support the main idea. You are deciding which information is important enough to include in a summary.

4. Using the main idea you wrote and the key information you have underlined, write a summary of the passage in your own words.

Practicing the Skill: Level 8

GUIDELINES FOR SUMMARIZING:

- Look for topic sentences stating the main idea. Then restate the main idea in your own words.
- Include key facts, statistics, and information that support the main idea.

- Leave out details that are not essential to the main idea.

Apply what you have learned. Refer to the guidelines above as you complete the exercises below. Use a separate sheet of paper if you need more room.

A. The following passage describes some of the drawbacks for teenagers who attend school and work part-time. Read the passage carefully. Look for the main idea and the most important information.

TEENAGERS WHO WORK

Should teenagers work to pay for their own cars, CDs, clothes, and stereo equipment? Many families wrestle with this question. Sure, a teenager who works part-time may be learning firsthand the pride and sense of responsibility that paid work outside the home may bring. But research indicates that working 20 hours or more a week does not bode well for a teen's future.

Teens who work too much sacrifice sleep and exercise, cut back on their homework, let their grades slip, and spend less time with their family and friends. In one recent study, teenagers who worked 15 hours had lower grades, higher dropout rates, and were less likely to attend college. Many states limit the number of hours that 16– and 17-year-olds can work. In the future, Congress may grant the U.S. Department of Labor the authority to limit working hours during the school year for anyone under age 18. Until then, each family must decide whether a teen's work schedule is undermining his or her academic, social, or emotional development.

B. Follow the directions below to write a summary of the passage.

1. Restate the main idea of this passage in your own words.

2. List all of the facts, statistics, and other information in the passage.

3. Read through your list, and underline the facts that directly support the main idea. You are deciding which information is important enough to include in a summary.

4. Using the main idea you wrote and the key information you have underlined, write a summary of the passage in your own words.

READING SKILLS PRACTICE: READING OBJECTIVE 4
Perceiving Cause-and-Effect Relationships

A **cause** is the reason something happens or exists. An **effect** is the result of an action, event, or condition. Every narrative you read involves cause-and-effect relationships. Your ability to pick out these relationships helps you to understand the material you read.

Sometimes writers use signal words, such as *because, since, led to,* or *as a result,* to indicate a cause-and-effect relationship. Often, however, causes and effects are not so plainly stated but rather are implied in the text. Through active reading, you can recognize and infer cause-and-effect relationships from the order in which ideas are presented.

Understanding the Skill

Step 1: Identify causes and effects as you read. The following passage describes the Children's Movement for Peace, a peace advocacy group started by children and young adults in Colombia, South America.

Strategies in Action

Causes occur before effects. The Children's Movement for Peace recruited millions of children to vote in a special election.

Look for causes by looking for signal words. *As a result* of the mandate, a country-wide election was held.

CHILDREN'S MOVEMENT FOR PEACE

For many years, Colombia, South America, has suffered from civil war. In October, 1996, the Children's Movement for Peace began recruiting children who were living in the poorest and most violent neighborhoods of Colombia to vote in a special election. The election was known as the Children's Mandate for Peace and Rights. More than 2.7 million children aged 7 to 18 years were mobilized and asked to vote for their most important rights. The youth overwhelmingly voted for human rights for minors and the right to peace for their war-torn country.

The Children's Mandate had a huge impact on the Colombian nation. As a result of the mandate, a country-wide election was held. Over ten million adult Colombians turned out at the polls to support a peace referendum. The referendum included backing the Children's Mandate, condemning the guerrilla war in Colombia, and pledging their personal commitment for peace.

The Children's Movement for Peace was nominated for a Nobel Peace Prize for its successful effort to bring about the peace referendum.

Effect: Ask yourself questions about consequences of the events. Ask, "What resulted from the special election?" Answer: The youth voted for human rights for minors and the right to peace in their country.

Notice that an effect may be the cause of another event, resulting in a chain of events. The work of the Children's Movement for Peace was a cause leading to the peace referendum; the referendum, in turn, was a cause that led to a nomination for the Nobel Peace Prize.

Step 2: Make a cause-and-effect diagram. Summarize causes and effects in a chart.

cause	effect	cause	effect	cause	effect
Children's Movement for Peace rallies 2.7 billion youth.	In a special election Colombian children vote for human rights for minors and for peace in Colombia.	Colombians are excited about the children's crusade and desire for peace.	In a national election, adult Colombians vote to support a national peace referendum.	Adult Colombians support a national peace referendum.	The Children's Movement for Peace is nominated for a Nobel Peace Prize.

Practicing the Skill: Level 6

GUIDELINES FOR PERCEIVING CAUSE-AND-EFFECT RELATIONSHIPS:

■ Look for signal words like *because, since, led to,* or *as a result.*

■ Look for effects that cause other events, resulting in a chain of events.

■ To determine implied cause-and-effect relationships, ask yourself as you read "Why did _____ happen?" and "What happened because of _____?".

■ Use a chart to summarize causes and effects.

Apply what you have learned. Refer to the guidelines above as you complete the exercises below. Use a separate sheet of paper if you need more room.

A. The following passage describes different weather conditions. Read the passage, and then answer the questions.

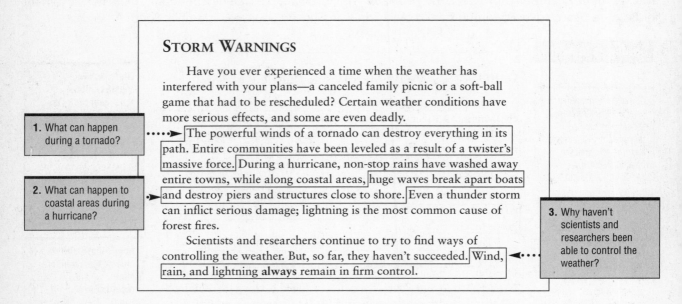

STORM WARNINGS

Have you ever experienced a time when the weather has interfered with your plans—a canceled family picnic or a soft-ball game that had to be rescheduled? Certain weather conditions have more serious effects, and some are even deadly.

1. What can happen during a tornado?

The powerful winds of a tornado can destroy everything in its path. Entire communities have been leveled as a result of a twister's massive force. During a hurricane, non-stop rains have washed away entire towns, while along coastal areas, huge waves break apart boats and destroy piers and structures close to shore. Even a thunder storm can inflict serious damage; lightning is the most common cause of forest fires.

2. What can happen to coastal areas during a hurricane?

Scientists and researchers continue to try to find ways of controlling the weather. But, so far, they haven't succeeded. Wind, rain, and lightning **always** remain in firm control.

3. Why haven't scientists and researchers been able to control the weather?

B. Use your answers to the questions above to help you fill in this chart. Note that you may need more (or fewer) boxes than those provided.

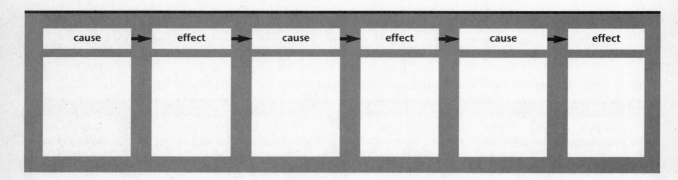

cause → effect → cause → effect → cause → effect

Perceiving Cause-and-Effect Relationships, continued

Practicing the Skill: Level 7

GUIDELINES FOR PERCEIVING CAUSE-AND-EFFECT RELATIONSHIPS:

■ Look for signal words like *because, since, led to,* or *as a result.*

■ Look for effects that cause other events, resulting in a chain of events.

■ To determine implied cause-and-effect relationships, ask yourself as you read "Why did _____ happen?" and "What happened because of _____?".

■ Use a chart to summarize causes and effects.

Apply what you have learned. Refer to the guidelines above as you complete the exercises below. Use a separate sheet of paper if you need more room.

A. The following passage describes food allergies. Read the passage, and then answer the questions.

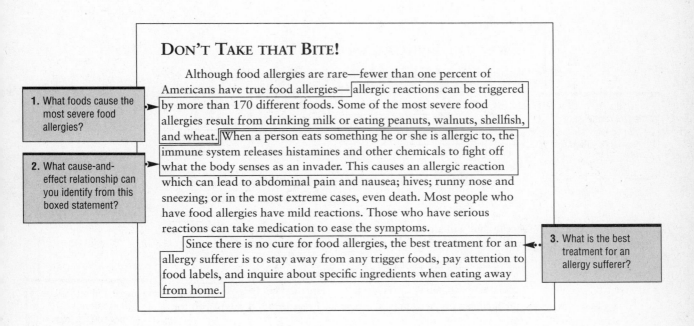

DON'T TAKE THAT BITE!

Although food allergies are rare—fewer than one percent of Americans have true food allergies— allergic reactions can be triggered by more than 170 different foods. Some of the most severe food allergies result from drinking milk or eating peanuts, walnuts, shellfish, and wheat. When a person eats something he or she is allergic to, the immune system releases histamines and other chemicals to fight off what the body senses as an invader. This causes an allergic reaction which can lead to abdominal pain and nausea; hives; runny nose and sneezing; or in the most extreme cases, even death. Most people who have food allergies have mild reactions. Those who have serious reactions can take medication to ease the symptoms.

Since there is no cure for food allergies, the best treatment for an allergy sufferer is to stay away from any trigger foods, pay attention to food labels, and inquire about specific ingredients when eating away from home.

1. What foods cause the most severe food allergies?

2. What cause-and-effect relationship can you identify from this boxed statement?

3. What is the best treatment for an allergy sufferer?

B. Use your answers to the questions above to help you fill in this chart. Note that you may need more (or fewer) boxes than those provided.

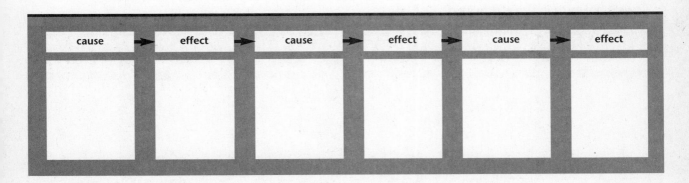

| cause | → | effect | → | cause | → | effect | → | cause | → | effect |

Practicing the Skill: Level 8

GUIDELINES FOR PERCEIVING CAUSE-AND-EFFECT RELATIONSHIPS:

■ Look for signal words like *because, since, led to,* or *as a result.*

■ Look for effects that cause other events, resulting in a chain of events.

■ To determine implied cause-and-effect relationships, ask yourself as you read "Why did _____ happen?" and "What happened because of _____?".

■ Use a chart to summarize causes and effects.

Apply what you have learned. Refer to the guidelines above as you complete the exercises below. Use a separate sheet of paper if you need more room.

A. The following passage describes the fundraising efforts on behalf of Central High. Read the passage, and then answer the questions.

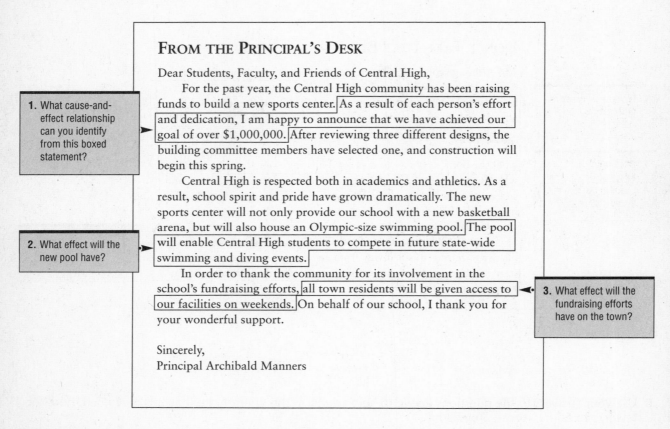

1. What cause-and-effect relationship can you identify from this boxed statement?

2. What effect will the new pool have?

3. What effect will the fundraising efforts have on the town?

FROM THE PRINCIPAL'S DESK

Dear Students, Faculty, and Friends of Central High,

For the past year, the Central High community has been raising funds to build a new sports center. As a result of each person's effort and dedication, I am happy to announce that we have achieved our goal of over $1,000,000. After reviewing three different designs, the building committee members have selected one, and construction will begin this spring.

Central High is respected both in academics and athletics. As a result, school spirit and pride have grown dramatically. The new sports center will not only provide our school with a new basketball arena, but will also house an Olympic-size swimming pool. The pool will enable Central High students to compete in future state-wide swimming and diving events.

In order to thank the community for its involvement in the school's fundraising efforts, all town residents will be given access to our facilities on weekends. On behalf of our school, I thank you for your wonderful support.

Sincerely,
Principal Archibald Manners

B. Use your answers to the questions above to help you fill in this chart. Note that you may need more (or fewer) boxes than those provided.

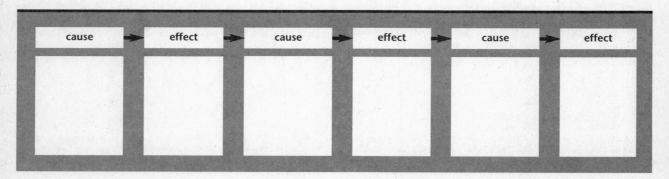

Name _____   Date _____

Predicting Probable Future Actions and Outcomes

Predicting involves speculating about the future. When making predictions, you use text clues to make reasonable guesses about what will happen at a future point based on what has already happened and on your prior knowledge of similar events. You can learn how to make logical predictions by combining what you already know with facts and other relevant information. You might make predictions about characters, events, or other details in a written work.

Understanding the Skill

Step 1: Identify facts and draw conclusions from the text. The following passage describes the decline of tiger populations throughout Asia. As you read, predict what might happen as a result of the events described. First, identify the facts presented in the text. Then draw conclusions based on the facts.

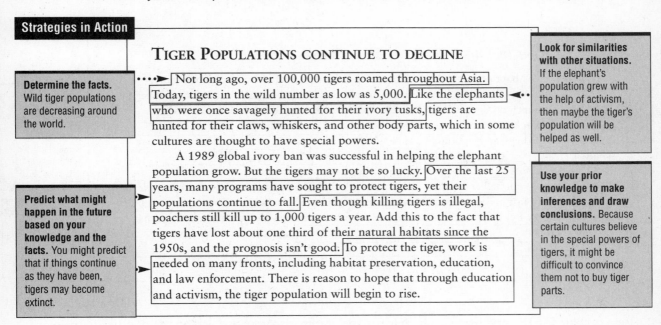

Strategies in Action

Determine the facts. Wild tiger populations are decreasing around the world.

Predict what might happen in the future based on your knowledge and the facts. You might predict that if things continue as they have been, tigers may become extinct.

TIGER POPULATIONS CONTINUE TO DECLINE

Not long ago, over 100,000 tigers roamed throughout Asia. Today, tigers in the wild number as low as 5,000. Like the elephants who were once savagely hunted for their ivory tusks, tigers are hunted for their claws, whiskers, and other body parts, which in some cultures are thought to have special powers.

A 1989 global ivory ban was successful in helping the elephant population grow. But the tigers may not be so lucky. Over the last 25 years, many programs have sought to protect tigers, yet their populations continue to fall. Even though killing tigers is illegal, poachers still kill up to 1,000 tigers a year. Add this to the fact that tigers have lost about one third of their natural habitats since the 1950s, and the prognosis isn't good. To protect the tiger, work is needed on many fronts, including habitat preservation, education, and law enforcement. There is reason to hope that through education and activism, the tiger population will begin to rise.

Look for similarities with other situations. If the elephant's population grew with the help of activism, then maybe the tiger's population will be helped as well.

Use your prior knowledge to make inferences and draw conclusions. Because certain cultures believe in the special powers of tigers, it might be difficult to convince them not to buy tiger parts.

Step 2: Make a graphic that summarizes the information you have gathered.

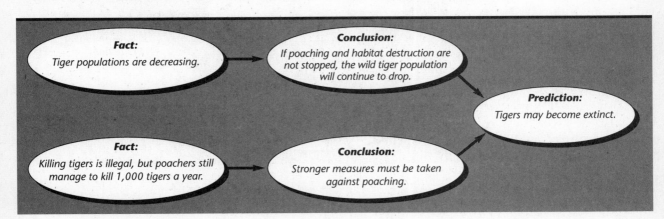

Fact: Tiger populations are decreasing.

Conclusion: If poaching and habitat destruction are not stopped, the wild tiger population will continue to drop.

Prediction: Tigers may become extinct.

Fact: Killing tigers is illegal, but poachers still manage to kill 1,000 tigers a year.

Conclusion: Stronger measures must be taken against poaching.

Predicting Probable Future Actions and Outcomes, continued

Practicing the Skill: Level 6

GUIDELINES FOR PREDICTING PROBABLE FUTURE ACTIONS AND OUTCOMES:

■ Determine the facts about the situation.

■ Look for similarities with other situations.

■ Use your own knowledge and experience to make inferences and draw conclusions from the facts.

■ Use facts and conclusions to make a prediction about the future.

■ Use a chart to summarize the information that led to your prediction.

Apply what you have learned. Refer to the guidelines above as you complete the exercises below. Use a separate sheet of paper if you need more room.

A. The following passage describes a deer and her fawn as they flee from hunters. Read the passage, and then answer the questions.

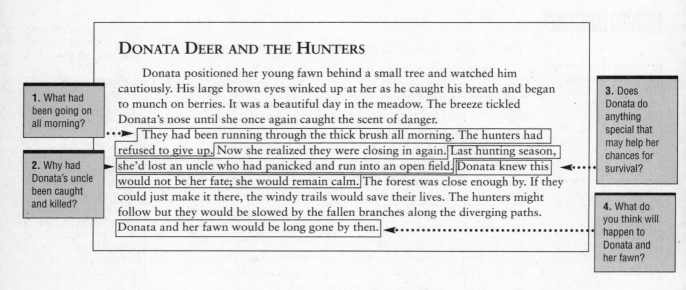

DONATA DEER AND THE HUNTERS

Donata positioned her young fawn behind a small tree and watched him cautiously. His large brown eyes winked up at her as he caught his breath and began to munch on berries. It was a beautiful day in the meadow. The breeze tickled Donata's nose until she once again caught the scent of danger.

They had been running through the thick brush all morning. The hunters had refused to give up. Now she realized they were closing in again. Last hunting season, she'd lost an uncle who had panicked and run into an open field. Donata knew this would not be her fate; she would remain calm. The forest was close enough by. If they could just make it there, the windy trails would save their lives. The hunters might follow but they would be slowed by the fallen branches along the diverging paths. Donata and her fawn would be long gone by then.

1. What had been going on all morning?

2. Why had Donata's uncle been caught and killed?

3. Does Donata do anything special that may help her chances for survival?

4. What do you think will happen to Donata and her fawn?

B. Use a graphic like the one below to help focus and summarize your answers to the questions above.

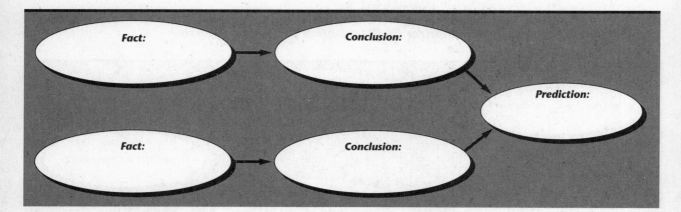

Fact:

Conclusion:

Prediction:

Fact:

Conclusion:

Practicing the Skill: Level 7

GUIDELINES FOR PREDICTING PROBABLE FUTURE ACTIONS AND OUTCOMES:

- Determine the facts about the situation.
- Look for similarities with other situations.
- Use your own knowledge and experience to make inferences and draw conclusions from the facts.
- Use facts and conclusions to make a prediction about the future.
- Use a chart to summarize the information that led to your prediction.

Apply what you have learned. Refer to the guidelines above as you complete the exercises below. Use a separate sheet of paper if you need more room.

A. The following passage describes the final seconds of a basketball game. Read the passage, and then answer the questions.

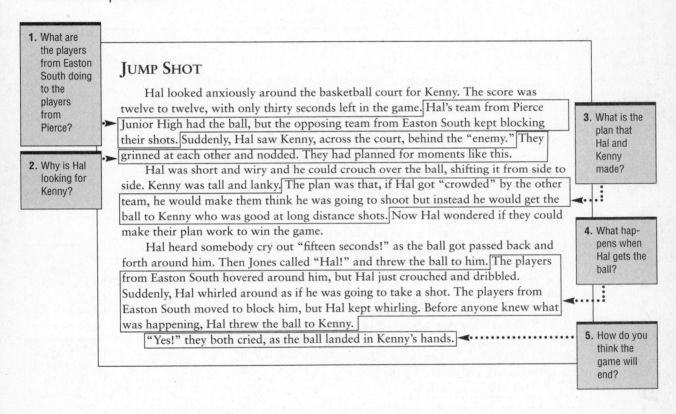

1. What are the players from Easton South doing to the players from Pierce?

2. Why is Hal looking for Kenny?

3. What is the plan that Hal and Kenny made?

4. What happens when Hal gets the ball?

5. How do you think the game will end?

JUMP SHOT

Hal looked anxiously around the basketball court for Kenny. The score was twelve to twelve, with only thirty seconds left in the game. Hal's team from Pierce Junior High had the ball, but the opposing team from Easton South kept blocking their shots. Suddenly, Hal saw Kenny, across the court, behind the "enemy." They grinned at each other and nodded. They had planned for moments like this.

Hal was short and wiry and he could crouch over the ball, shifting it from side to side. Kenny was tall and lanky. The plan was that, if Hal got "crowded" by the other team, he would make them think he was going to shoot but instead he would get the ball to Kenny who was good at long distance shots. Now Hal wondered if they could make their plan work to win the game.

Hal heard somebody cry out "fifteen seconds!" as the ball got passed back and forth around him. Then Jones called "Hal!" and threw the ball to him. The players from Easton South hovered around him, but Hal just crouched and dribbled. Suddenly, Hal whirled around as if he was going to take a shot. The players from Easton South moved to block him, but Hal kept whirling. Before anyone knew what was happening, Hal threw the ball to Kenny.

"Yes!" they both cried, as the ball landed in Kenny's hands.

B. Use a graphic like the one below to help focus and summarize your answers to the questions above.

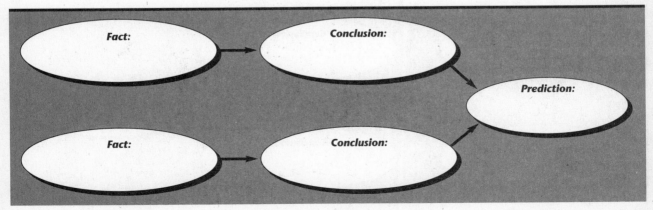

Fact: → Conclusion:

Prediction:

Fact: → Conclusion:

Practicing the Skill: Level 8

> ### GUIDELINES FOR PREDICTING PROBABLE FUTURE ACTIONS AND OUTCOMES:
>
> ■ Determine the facts about the situation.
>
> ■ Look for similarities with other situations.
>
> ■ Use your own knowledge and experience to make inferences and draw conclusions from the facts.
>
> ■ Use facts and conclusions to make a prediction about the future.
>
> ■ Use a chart to summarize the information that led to your prediction.

Apply what you have learned. Refer to the guidelines above as you complete the exercises below. Use a separate sheet of paper if you need more room.

A. The following describes a discussion between a brother and a sister. Read the passage, and then answer the questions.

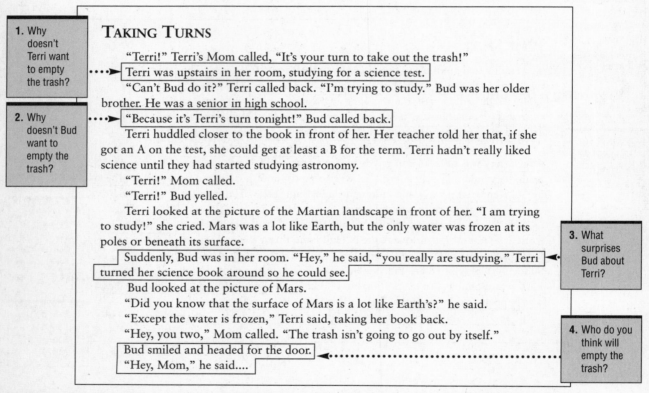

1. Why doesn't Terri want to empty the trash?

2. Why doesn't Bud want to empty the trash?

3. What surprises Bud about Terri?

4. Who do you think will empty the trash?

TAKING TURNS

"Terri!" Terri's Mom called, "It's your turn to take out the trash!"

Terri was upstairs in her room, studying for a science test.

"Can't Bud do it?" Terri called back. "I'm trying to study." Bud was her older brother. He was a senior in high school.

"Because it's Terri's turn tonight!" Bud called back.

Terri huddled closer to the book in front of her. Her teacher told her that, if she got an A on the test, she could get at least a B for the term. Terri hadn't really liked science until they had started studying astronomy.

"Terri!" Mom called.

"Terri!" Bud yelled.

Terri looked at the picture of the Martian landscape in front of her. "I am trying to study!" she cried. Mars was a lot like Earth, but the only water was frozen at its poles or beneath its surface.

Suddenly, Bud was in her room. "Hey," he said, "you really are studying." Terri turned her science book around so he could see.

Bud looked at the picture of Mars.

"Did you know that the surface of Mars is a lot like Earth's?" he said.

"Except the water is frozen," Terri said, taking her book back.

"Hey, you two," Mom called. "The trash isn't going to go out by itself."

Bud smiled and headed for the door.

"Hey, Mom," he said....

B. Use a graphic like the one below to help focus and summarize your answers to the questions above.

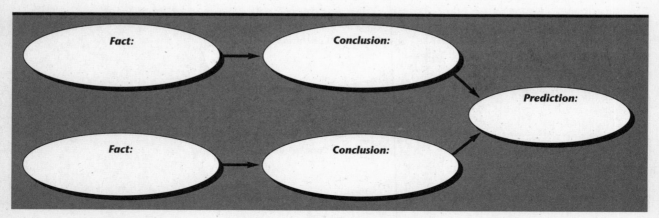

Name _____   Date _____

Interpreting Charts and Graphs

Graphs present numerical information in a visual manner. Writers use graphs to show comparisons, trends, physical relationships, changes, organization, and structure. **Line graphs** show changes over time, or trends. **Pie graphs** indicate relative proportions by showing how wedges of a circle relate to the whole. **Bar graphs** compare numbers or sets of numbers.

A **chart** or **table** is a systematic presentation of data in columns and rows. The data may be words or numbers. A **diagram** is an illustration that shows how something works or how its parts relate to one another. The simple structure of a chart, table, or diagram makes information easy to understand and remember.

Understanding the Skill

Step 1: Determine what the chart or graph is presenting or comparing. Many graphs and charts have a title that indicates the main point of the information being presented. Identify the title, determine the main idea, and then examine the other elements of the line graph, pie graph, bar graph, or chart to see how the information is being presented or compared.

Strategies in Action

A. Interpreting a Line Graph

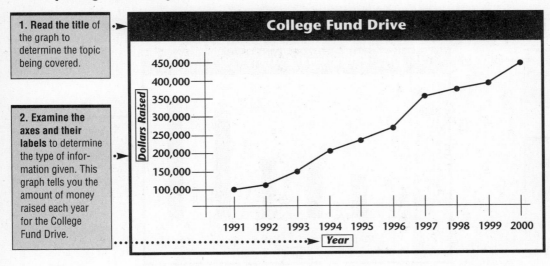

1. Read the title of the graph to determine the topic being covered.

2. Examine the axes and their labels to determine the type of information given. This graph tells you the amount of money raised each year for the College Fund Drive.

3. Analyze the data. The data of this graph show a trend: the amount of money raised for the College Fund Drive has steadily increased from 1991 to 2000.

B. Interpreting a Chart

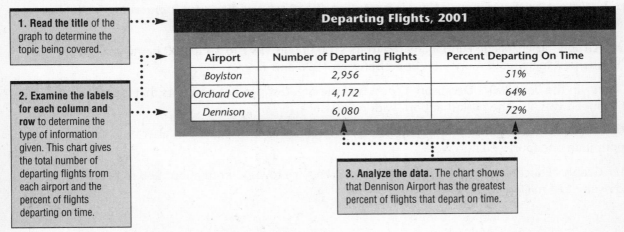

1. Read the title of the graph to determine the topic being covered.

2. Examine the labels for each column and row to determine the type of information given. This chart gives the total number of departing flights from each airport and the percent of flights departing on time.

3. Analyze the data. The chart shows that Dennison Airport has the greatest percent of flights that depart on time.

C. Interpreting a Pie Graph

1. Read the title of the graph to determine the topic being covered.

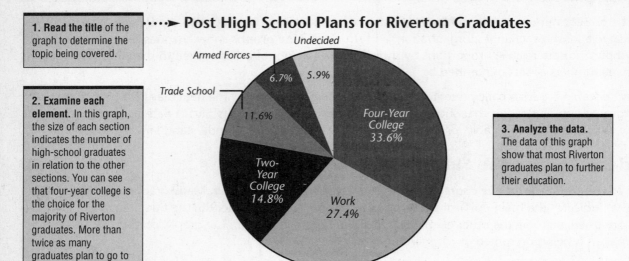

Post High School Plans for Riverton Graduates

2. Examine each element. In this graph, the size of each section indicates the number of high-school graduates in relation to the other sections. You can see that four-year college is the choice for the majority of Riverton graduates. More than twice as many graduates plan to go to a four-year college than a two-year college.

3. Analyze the data. The data of this graph show that most Riverton graduates plan to further their education.

D. Interpreting a Bar Graph

1. Read the title of the graph to determine the topic.

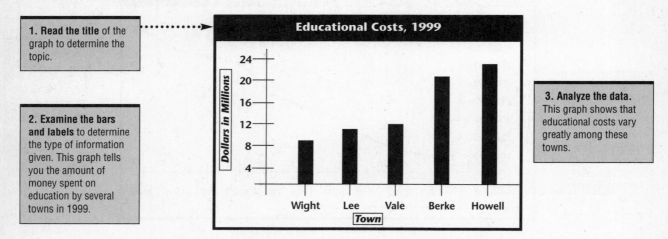

Educational Costs, 1999

2. Examine the bars and labels to determine the type of information given. This graph tells you the amount of money spent on education by several towns in 1999.

3. Analyze the data. This graph shows that educational costs vary greatly among these towns.

Step 2: Write a brief summary of the information the chart and line graph presents. The following are summaries of the chart and graphs shown above and on the previous page.

A. Line Graph - The College Fund increased from $100,000 in 1991 to $450,000 in the year 2000. The sharpest increase in money occurred between 1996 and 1997.

B. Chart - In the year 2001, Dennison Airport had the greatest percent of flights that departed on-time. It was also the busiest airport, with 6,080 departures.

C. Pie Graph - More than half of the graduates plan to continue their education after high school, and more than one fourth plan to work.

D. Bar Graph - Educational costs vary greatly among the five towns—from about $88 million in Wight to nearly $24 million in Howell.

Practicing the Skill: Level 6

Apply what you have learned. Refer to the guidelines above as you complete the exercises below. Write on a separate sheet of paper if you need more room.

A. Examine the line graph and the bar graph, and then answer the questions.

1. What is the topic of the line graph?

2. What does the horizontal axis represent?

3. What does the vertical axis represent?

4. What is the topic of the bar graph?

5. What does the length of each bar represent?

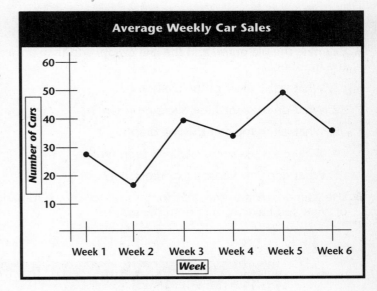

B. Use your answers to the questions above to write summaries of what you have learned from the graphs.

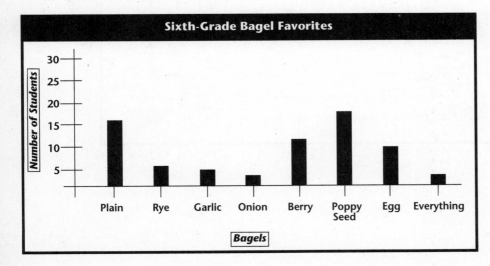

Practicing the Skill: Level 7

GUIDELINES FOR INTERPRETING CHARTS AND GRAPHS:

■ Read the title to identify the topic being covered.

■ Examine each element or category in the chart or graph.

■ Look for the main idea.

■ Analyze the data presented.

■ Summarize in a paragraph what you learned from the chart or graph.

Apply what you have learned. Refer to the guidelines above as you complete the exercises below. Write on a separate sheet of paper.

A. Examine the pie graph and the line graph, and then answer the questions.

1. What is the topic of the pie graph?

2. What do the individual slices represent?

3. What is the topic of the line graph?

4. What does the horizontal axis represent?

5. What does the vertical axis represent?

B. Use your answers to the questions above to write summaries of what you have learned from the graphs.

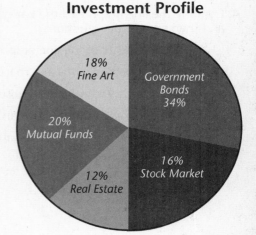

Investment Profile

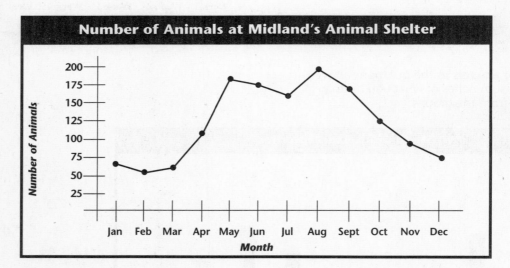

Practicing the Skill: Level 8

GUIDELINES FOR INTERPRETING CHARTS AND GRAPHS:

- Read the title to identify the topic being covered.
- Examine each element or category in the chart or graph.

- Look for the main idea.
- Analyze the data presented.
- Summarize in a paragraph what you learned from the chart or graph.

Apply what you have learned. Refer to the guidelines above as you complete the exercises below. Write on a separate sheet of paper.

A. Examine the pie graph and line graph, and then answer the questions.

1. What is the topic of the pie graph?
2. What do the individual slices represent?
3. What is the topic of the line graph?
4. What does the horizontal axis represent?
5. What does the vertical axis represent?

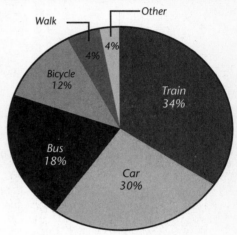

Means of Transport for James Middle School Teachers

Other
Walk
4%
4%
Train 34%
Bicycle 12%
Bus 18%
Car 30%

B. Use your answers to the questions above to write a summary of what you have learned from the graphs.

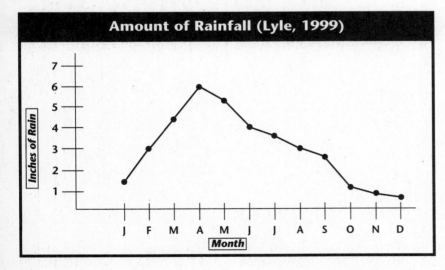

Amount of Rainfall (Lyle, 1999)

Inches of Rain

Month

READING SKILLS PRACTICE: READING OBJECTIVE 5
Making Inferences

Have you ever learned something by "reading between the lines" of a text? If you have, then you are already familiar with inferences. An **inference** is an idea that a reader deduces by examining the evidence, or facts, presented in a passage. Think of inferring as detective work: you gather clues from your reading and then make an educated guess as to what they imply.

Understanding the Skill

Step 1: Make inferences as you read. The following passage describes what it's like to climb Mount Everest. Identify the facts presented in the passage. Apply your own knowledge of the subject, as well as of the world in general, to make an inference about each fact.

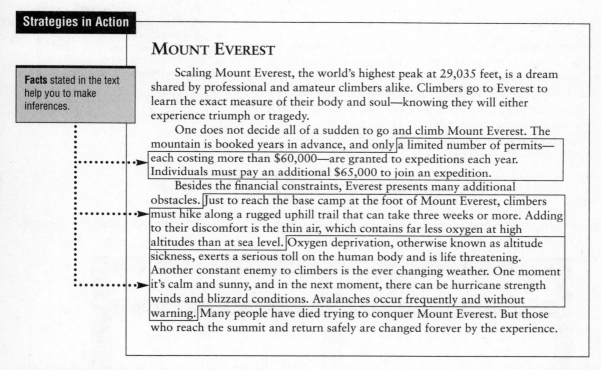

Strategies in Action	
Facts stated in the text help you to make inferences.	**MOUNT EVEREST** Scaling Mount Everest, the world's highest peak at 29,035 feet, is a dream shared by professional and amateur climbers alike. Climbers go to Everest to learn the exact measure of their body and soul—knowing they will either experience triumph or tragedy. One does not decide all of a sudden to go and climb Mount Everest. The mountain is booked years in advance, and only a limited number of permits—each costing more than $60,000—are granted to expeditions each year. Individuals must pay an additional $65,000 to join an expedition. Besides the financial constraints, Everest presents many additional obstacles. Just to reach the base camp at the foot of Mount Everest, climbers must hike along a rugged uphill trail that can take three weeks or more. Adding to their discomfort is the thin air, which contains far less oxygen at high altitudes than at sea level. Oxygen deprivation, otherwise known as altitude sickness, exerts a serious toll on the human body and is life threatening. Another constant enemy to climbers is the ever changing weather. One moment it's calm and sunny, and in the next moment, there can be hurricane strength winds and blizzard conditions. Avalanches occur frequently and without warning. Many people have died trying to conquer Mount Everest. But those who reach the summit and return safely are changed forever by the experience.

Step 2: Make a chart. In the chart, list the facts in the text and the inferences you can draw from them.

Facts	Inferences
Only a limited number of permits costing more than $60,000 are granted to expeditions each year. Individuals must also pay $65,000 to join an expedition.	Only wealthy people can afford to climb Mount Everest.
Just to reach the base camp at the foot of the mountain, climbers must hike along a rugged uphill trail that can take three weeks or more.	Climbers must be in excellent physical condition to climb Mount Everest.
Altitude sickness is life threatening. Avalanches occur frequently and without warning.	A climber risks his or her life when climbing Mount Everest.

Making Inferences, continued

Practicing the Skill: Level 6

GUIDELINES FOR MAKING INFERENCES:

- Identify and evaluate the facts stated in the text.

- Consider relevant information you already know.

- Use the facts, your prior knowledge, and common sense to make inferences.

- Use a chart to summarize the facts and your inferences.

Apply what you have learned. Refer to the guidelines above as you complete the exercises below. Use a separate sheet of paper if you need more room.

A. Read the following passage about a "driver," and then answer the questions.

THE DRIVER

Heather glanced at the speedometer. Ninety! The number startled her. She never traveled that fast. Heather grasped the wheel tightly and released the pressure off her right foot. All of a sudden, she heard a siren blaring through the open window. Heather looked in her rear-view mirror and noticed a flashing red light in the distance. As she stared in disbelief, the light grew brighter and larger, making its way towards her. Heather slowly steered herself into the break-down lane and came to a complete stop.

1. What do the first few sentences suggest about where the driver is and what she is doing?
2. Why might the flashing red light and siren be following Heather?
3. What might happen to Heather when she stops?

B. Use your answers to the questions above as you fill in the chart with facts and inferences from the passage.

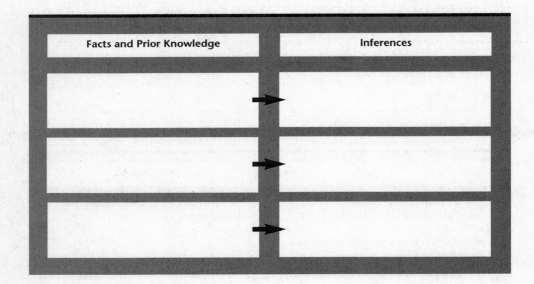

Facts and Prior Knowledge	Inferences

Making Inferences, continued

Practicing the Skill: Level 7

GUIDELINES FOR MAKING INFERENCES:

■ Identify and evaluate the facts stated in the text.

■ Consider relevant information you already know.

■ Use the facts, your prior knowledge, and common sense to make inferences.

■ Use a chart to summarize the facts and your inferences.

Apply what you have learned. Refer to the guidelines above as you complete the exercises below. Use a separate sheet of paper if you need more room.

A. Read the following passage about the Winchester Mystery House and the woman who owned it. Then answer the questions.

THE WINCHESTER MYSTERY HOUSE

In 1884, Sarah Winchester, a widow, began a building project that remains today one of the largest and most bizarre houses ever built. According to reports, Sarah, the Winchester Rifle heiress, was told shortly after the death of her husband that she too would die unless she moved to the West and built a house. She was informed that the day construction stopped, she would die. Thus began a building project that continued uninterrupted 24-hours-a-day for the next 38 years. Work halted on the house the day after Sarah died in 1922.

The Winchester Mystery House, as it has become known, is located in San Jose, California. It has 160 rooms, approximately 10,000 windows, 950 doors, 47 fireplaces, 40 staircases, and many secret passageways. There are staircases that end at the ceiling, doors that open onto blank walls, and windows that are built into the floor. Each night Sarah slept in one of the forty different bedrooms. She never slept in the same bedroom two nights in a row.

1. What do the first three sentences of the passage suggest about the owner of the house, Sarah Winchester?
2. Why might the house feature so many oddities?
3. Why might Sarah Winchester not sleep in the same bedroom two days in a row?

B. Use your answers to the questions above as you fill in the chart with facts and inferences from the passage.

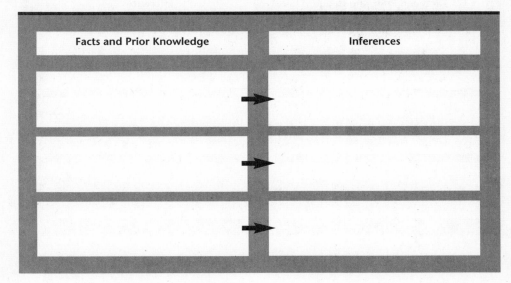

Facts and Prior Knowledge	Inferences

Practicing the Skill: Level 8

GUIDELINES FOR MAKING INFERENCES:

- Identify and evaluate the facts stated in the text.
- Consider relevant information you already know.

- Use the facts, your prior knowledge, and common sense to make inferences.
- Use a chart to summarize the facts and your inferences.

Apply what you have learned. Refer to the guidelines above as you complete the exercises below. Use a separate sheet of paper if you need more room.

A. The following passage describes an exciting and action-filled amusement ride. Read the passage carefully. Then answer the questions.

THE RIDE

As you hurtle toward the earth from a height of 225 feet, your stomach floats to your throat. Plunging downward, you hit the bottom of the drop. In the next moment you're weightless—suspended from your seat as you start the climb over the next hill. Soaring at speeds up to 85 miles per hour, tumbling down sheer slopes, looping wildly, then crawling to the top of another nosebleed crest, you plummet once more to the bottom of a hill. You continue on with more twists, turns, curves, and loops. All the while you're screaming upside-down with cold-blooded terror. At last, it's over. You're back at the start—breathlessly wanting to ride again!

1. How do the first three sentences suggest the activity makes someone feel?
2. How does the activity make a person behave?
3. What is the activity and why would someone want to repeat it?

B. Use your answers to the questions above as you fill in the chart with facts and inferences from the passage.

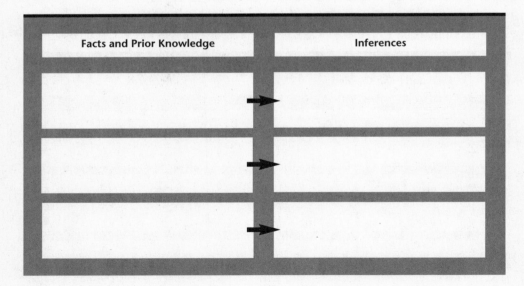

Facts and Prior Knowledge	Inferences

Name _____   Date _____

Evaluating and Making Judgments

On reading tests you will often be asked to make a judgment about material that you read. A **judgment** is an opinion formed by using logical thinking to evaluate facts. To make a valid judgment, you must first decide what you are making a judgment about. Next, develop standards, or **criteria,** for evaluating the text. You can establish criteria by determining whether a writer has supported his or her main idea with adequate facts and clear reasoning. Then, by comparing evidence from the text with your criteria, you will be able to make reasonable judgments of your own or to evaluate the judgments made by the writer.

Understanding the Skill

Step 1: Evaluate and make judgments as you read. The following passage describes the country of Iceland. Follow the steps below to evaluate the writer's judgment and judge for yourself whether Iceland is an ideal place to live.

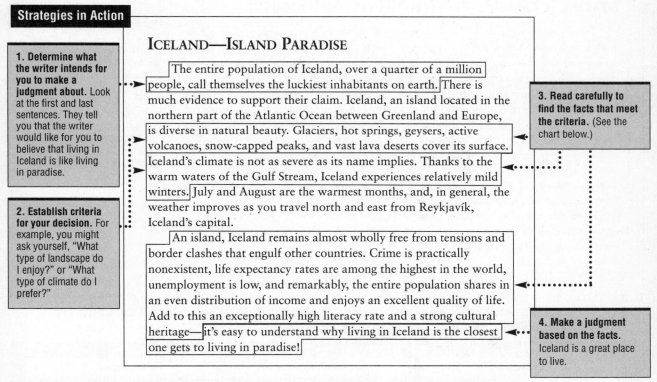

Strategies in Action

1. Determine what the writer intends for you to make a judgment about. Look at the first and last sentences. They tell you that the writer would like for you to believe that living in Iceland is like living in paradise.

2. Establish criteria for your decision. For example, you might ask yourself, "What type of landscape do I enjoy?" or "What type of climate do I prefer?"

ICELAND—ISLAND PARADISE

The entire population of Iceland, over a quarter of a million people, call themselves the luckiest inhabitants on earth. There is much evidence to support their claim. Iceland, an island located in the northern part of the Atlantic Ocean between Greenland and Europe, is diverse in natural beauty. Glaciers, hot springs, geysers, active volcanoes, snow-capped peaks, and vast lava deserts cover its surface. Iceland's climate is not as severe as its name implies. Thanks to the warm waters of the Gulf Stream, Iceland experiences relatively mild winters. July and August are the warmest months, and, in general, the weather improves as you travel north and east from Reykjavík, Iceland's capital.

An island, Iceland remains almost wholly free from tensions and border clashes that engulf other countries. Crime is practically nonexistent, life expectancy rates are among the highest in the world, unemployment is low, and remarkably, the entire population shares in an even distribution of income and enjoys an excellent quality of life. Add to this an exceptionally high literacy rate and a strong cultural heritage—it's easy to understand why living in Iceland is the closest one gets to living in paradise!

3. Read carefully to find the facts that meet the criteria. (See the chart below.)

4. Make a judgment based on the facts. Iceland is a great place to live.

Step 2: Summarize your findings in a chart to help you form your own judgments.

Criteria	Facts Meeting Criteria	Judgment
An ideal place to live should be diverse in physical beauty.	Iceland has glaciers, hot springs, geysers, active volcanoes, snow-capped peaks, and vast lava deserts.	
An ideal place to live should have a moderate climate: not too hot or too cold.	The warm waters of the Gulf Stream contribute to Iceland's mild winters and relatively warm summer months.	Iceland is a great place to live.
People living in an ideal place should enjoy an excellent quality of life.	Crime is rare; life expectancy is high, so people are probably healthy; literacy is high, so education is probably good; unemployment is low.	

Evaluating and Making Judgments, continued

Practicing the Skill: Level 6

> **GUIDELINES FOR EVALUATING AND MAKING JUDGMENTS:**
> - ■ Determine what the writer intends for you to make a judgment.
> - ■ Establish criteria or standards for your decision.
> - ■ Read carefully to identify and understand evidence—such as statistics, quotations, and examples—that meets the criteria.
> - ■ Use a chart to summarize the facts and form your own judgment.

Apply what you have learned. Refer to the guidelines above as you complete the exercises below. Use a separate sheet of paper if you need more room.

A. Read the following passage describing the environmental education program, "Roots & Shoots." Look for the facts that help you make a judgment about whether each individual effort to protect wildlife can make a difference.

MAKING A DIFFERENCE WITH "ROOTS & SHOOTS"

Have you ever seen a TV news report about protecting the world's wildlife and wished you could help? Maybe in the next breath you voiced, "How can I make a difference? I'm only one person." Some people never get past the wishing stage. But others are helping to save some animal species from extinction.

"Roots & Shoots" is an environmental education and humanitarian program for young people. "Roots & Shoots" was established by Jane Goodall, the well-known anthropologist, to promote care and concern for wild and domestic animals. "Roots & Shoots" has chapters in over 50 countries, and members range from pre-school through college ages. Members participate in activities that range from building birdhouses to helping local animal shelters solve the abandoned pet problem. Through "Roots & Shoots," young people in Tanzania can email their peers in Barcelona and Maine to share concerns and offer suggestions about improving conditions for animals. "Roots & Shoots" members in the United States recognize that children all around the world are concerned with protecting wildlife and that each individual effort makes a difference.

> **1.** How does the writer believe that young people can effect change?
> **2.** What criteria will you use to judge whether "Roots & Shoots" is a success?
> **3.** What statistics, quotations, and examples meet those criteria?
> **4.** Based on the information in this passage, what can you say about an individual's ability to make a difference?

B. If you have been instructed not to write in your workbook, copy the chart below onto a separate sheet of paper. Use the answers to the questions above to fill in the chart. Make a judgment about whether "Roots & Shoots" helps young people make a difference.

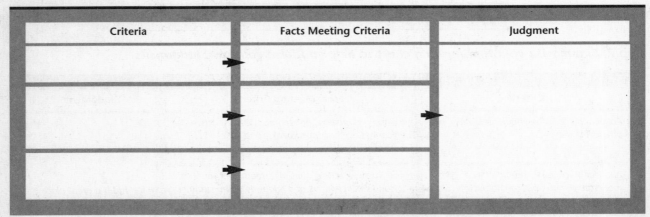

Criteria	Facts Meeting Criteria	Judgment

Evaluating and Making Judgments, continued

Practicing the Skill: Level 7

GUIDELINES FOR EVALUATING AND MAKING JUDGMENTS:

■ Determine what the writer intends for you to make a judgment.

■ Establish criteria or standards for your decision.

■ Read carefully to identify and understand evidence—such as statistics, quotations, and examples—that meets the criteria.

■ Use a chart to summarize the facts and form your own judgment.

Apply what you have learned. Refer to the guidelines above as you complete the exercises below. Use a separate sheet of paper if you need more room.

A. Read the following passage about email. Look for the facts that will help you make a judgment about whether email has advantages over other forms of communication.

THE EMAIL REVOLUTION

When was the last time you communicated with a friend or relative in another city or country? Did you mail a letter, talk via telephone long-distance, send a fax, or email him or her by computer? Email or "electronic mail" is causing a communications revolution among all age groups around the world. Considering how quickly we've adapted to this revolution, it is easy to see the many advantages email has over other forms of communication.

The first advantage is that email is convenient. Once you're in possession of an email address, you can use any computer connected to the Internet. Email is helping people renew and repair forgotten relationships, and in some cases it's helping to create new ones. Geographical distances and time zones no longer present barriers to long-lasting contact between family and friends. Go ahead, sleep through the night! You don't need to awaken in the middle of the night to telephone a friend half-way around the world. Just send an email. Email is immediate. It takes only minutes to complete. Email is inexpensive. Most of the time email is included in a service provider's contract at no additional charge.

Email is truly "environmentally friendly." No writing paper is used; no trees are cut down, nor forests destroyed. Nor are harmful pollutants expelled into the atmosphere by delivery vans, trains, or airplanes. With only an email account, you can communicate with the world in a quick, convenient, inexpensive, and environmentally sound way.

1. What does the writer think about email?
2. What criteria will you use to judge whether using email is more advantageous than other forms of communication?
3. What statistics, quotations, and examples meet those criteria?
4. Based on the information in this passage, do you feel email has more advantages than other methods of communication? Explain.

B. If you have been instructed not to write in your workbook, copy the chart below onto a separate sheet of paper. Use the answers to the questions above to fill in the chart. Make a judgment about whether email has more advantages than other forms of communication do.

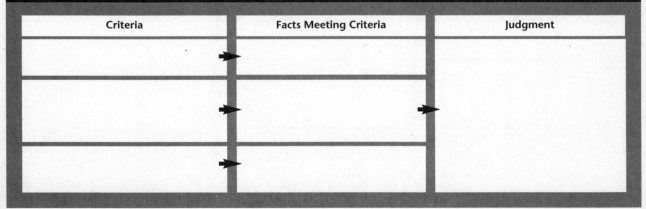

Criteria	Facts Meeting Criteria	Judgment

Practicing the Skill: Level 8

> **GUIDELINES FOR EVALUATING AND MAKING JUDGMENTS:**
>
> ■ Determine what the writer intends for you to make a judgment about.
>
> ■ Establish criteria or standards for your decision.
>
> ■ Read carefully to identify and understand evidence—such as statistics, quotations, and examples—that meets the criteria.
>
> ■ Use a chart to summarize the facts and form your own judgment.

Apply what you have learned. Refer to the guidelines above as you complete the exercises below. Use a separate sheet of paper if you need more room.

A. Read the following passage about the political and spiritual leader Mahatma Gandhi. Look for facts that will help you make a judgment about whether Mahatma Gandhi was a respected and effective leader.

MAHATMA GANDHI

Mohandas Karamchand Gandhi was born in India in 1869. Before he was shot to death in 1948, he helped to end British rule and win independence for India. Gandhi was one of the gentlest of men, a dedicated believer and follower of Hinduism, but he had an unbending iron will. Nothing could change his convictions. This combination of traits made him a respected and capable leader of India's nationalist movement. Some people thought he was a skilled politician. Others viewed him as a saint. Millions of followers called Gandhi Mahatma, meaning "great soul."

Gandhi was zealous in applying only non-violent methods, such as organizing massive labor strikes, disobeying unfair laws, and engaging in extended fasts to aid his cause. Gandhi applied these methods to successfully bring about Indian independence from British rule. But he also proved that ordinary people can challenge their government and rulers and change the course of their destiny through non-violent actions. The world will forever be indebted to Gandhi. After his death, his methods of non-violent civil disobedience were adopted by many protest movements throughout the world, including Martin Luther King, Jr. Gandhi will always be remembered as India's architect of freedom and champion of peace.

1. What does the writer think about Mahatma Gandhi?
2. What criteria will you use to judge whether Gandhi was a respected and effective leader?
3. What statistics, quotations, and examples meet those criteria?
4. Based on the information in this passage, what can you say about Gandhi as a respected and effective leader?

B. If you have been instructed not to write in your workbook, copy the chart below onto a separate sheet of paper. Use your answers to the questions above to fill in the chart. Make a judgment about whether Gandhi was an effective and respected leader.

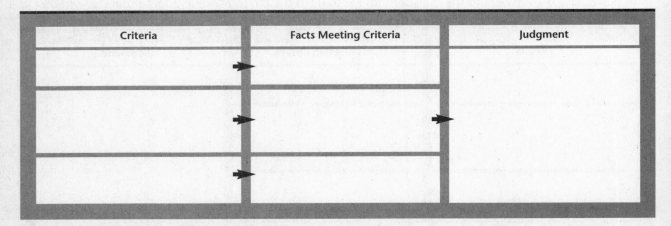

Criteria	Facts Meeting Criteria	Judgment

READING SKILLS PRACTICE BOOK: READING OBJECTIVE 6
Recognizing Propaganda

Propaganda is biased, or one-sided, information presented in an attempt to persuade people to believe a specific opinion or doctrine. The ability to recognize propaganda is important in evaluating the truth of what you read. Propaganda uses many techniques to persuade:

• Presenting half-truths, or only those facts that support the author's perspective.

• Using loaded language that appeals to the reader's emotions. Examples include vague terms (*conservative* and *liberal*), misused qualifiers (*every, all, none*), emotional connotations of words (*compulsive* versus *prompt*), and exaggerations.

• Applying stereotypes—unfairly attaching certain characteristics to all members of a group—that deny individual differences or appeal to the reader's own prejudices.

Understanding the Skill

Step 1: Identify propaganda as you read. The following passage is an ad for a community college. The chart that follows summarizes the elements of propaganda in the passage.

Strategies in Action

Stereotypes and loaded language are techniques of propaganda.

Exaggerated claims and half-truths should not be taken literally.

From the text of a television commercial:
    Are you tired of pushing a broom on the night shift? Do you feel envious of friends with good jobs? Without an education you can say farewell to a good future. But, once you earn an Associates Degree from Midville Community College, you'll start climbing the ladder of success. Our nationally ranked degree program can help you master all the skills for a successful career. Enroll now and discover that your dream job is within reach!
    Every professional on our staff will guarantee your success. With more night and weekend courses than any other community college in the area, we will design a program to suit your busy schedule. Once your enroll in classes, tuition assistance is almost assured. Your path to future happiness begins at our door. Let us walk with you toward your American dream.

It is important to read into the author's message and intention. The author uses exaggerated language in order to stir up emotion.

Step 2: Make a chart. List the stereotypes, exaggerated claims, emotional language, and other one-sided information the author uses to persuade the reader.

Stereotype	Exaggerated Claims and Emotional Language	Author's Intention
People who don't attend Midville Community College will be unable to secure a good job.	*"say farewell to a good future," "dream job is within reach," "guarantee your success," "future happiness begins at our door," "walk with you toward your American dream"*	*To convince the viewer that an Associates Degree from Midville Community College can guarantee a great job and provide happiness.*

Practicing the Skill: Level 6

GUIDELINES FOR RECOGNIZING PROPAGANDA:

- Identify any stereotypes.
- Recognize exaggerated claims.
- Recognize loaded language.
- Look for half-truths.

- Read into the author's message and intention.
- Use a chart to summarize the process of recognizing propaganda.

Apply what you have learned. Refer to the guidelines above as you examine the following excerpts for the elements of propaganda.

A. For the following passage, write the types of bias you identify, and make an inference about the author's message and intention. Use a chart to organize your thoughts. Record your answers on a separate sheet of paper.

VOTE FOR JOE

Elect Joe Maxon. He will change our city into a city that is safe and secure for ourselves and our children.

Frank Norman, his opponent, is a typical politician: he's against change that will help people. If Frank Norman is elected, our city will become a place where people are scared and children won't get a good education. Frank Norman has gone on record as saying that he is opposed to increasing the size of our police force. A small police force will turn our streets into safe havens for crime. Frank Norman has gone on record as saying that he's opposed to spending more money to improve our schools. He'll give our students an inferior education that won't prepare them for the future.

Joe Maxon will spend money to hire more police officers to make our streets safe. He'll hire more teachers and improve our schools so that our children will have a good education. Vote for Joe Maxon—a new kind of politician who wants only the kind of change that will help you and your children.

1. What stereotypes are mentioned in the passage?
2. List any examples of half-truths.
3. What are some examples of loaded, emotional language from the passage?
4. What is the author's intention in the passage?

B. Copy the chart onto your own paper. Use your answers to the questions above to fill in the chart.

Stereotype	Exaggerated Claims and Emotional Language	Author's Intention

Practicing the Skill: Level 7

GUIDELINES FOR RECOGNIZING PROPAGANDA:

- Identify any stereotypes.
- Recognize exaggerated claims.
- Recognize loaded language.
- Look for half-truths.

- Read into the author's message and intention.
- Use a chart to summarize the process of recognizing propaganda.

Apply what you have learned. Refer to the guidelines above as you examine the following excerpt for the elements of propaganda.

A. For the following passage, write the types of bias you identify, and make an inference about the author's message and intention. Use a chart to organize your thoughts. Record your answers on a separate sheet of paper.

WATCH OUT!

Did you know that every time you turn on your computer, you could connect to an epidemic? Every day, seemingly innocent messages appear on the screen which, when opened, can release viruses that crawl into your computer, eat up your files, invade your address books, and hide there until you, unknowingly, send them back out into the world to infect your friends' and colleagues' computers and destroy their data. You need to find and destroy these bugs. You need WATCHDOG.

WATCHDOG is a foolproof virus detection program that surpasses all others on the market in its ability to detect and destroy viruses. WATCHDOG can protect companies and businesses and save millions of dollars. WATCHDOG can protect hospitals and doctors' offices and save lives. Buy WATCHDOG for your home or office. Protect yourself.

1. What stereotypes are mentioned in the passage?
2. List any examples of half-truths.
3. What are some examples of loaded, emotional language from the passage?
4. What is the author's intention in the passage?

B. Copy the chart onto your own paper. Use your answers to the questions above to fill in the chart.

Stereotype	Exaggerated Claims and Emotional Language	Author's Intention

Practicing the Skill: Level 8

GUIDELINES FOR RECOGNIZING PROPAGANDA:

- ■ Identify any stereotypes.
- ■ Recognize exaggerated claims.
- ■ Recognize loaded language.
- ■ Look for half-truths.

- ■ Read into the author's message and intention.
- ■ Use a chart to summarize the process of recognizing propaganda.

Apply what you have learned. Refer to the guidelines above as you examine the following excerpts for the elements of propaganda.

A. For the following passage, write the types of bias you identify, and make an inference about the author's message and intention. Use a chart to organize your thoughts. Record your answers on a separate sheet of paper.

LET DOLPHINS LIVE!

Every time you bite into your tuna sandwich, you've helped kill another dolphin. Big business and lying politicians want you to believe that dolphins no longer die in the nets of the tuna fishermen, but that isn't so. Even one dolphin in those nets is too many, yet hauls containing dolphins are recorded "dolphin free."

Day after day, entire families of innocent dolphins are the sad victims of the fishing nets. The meager few that survive are so badly battered that nothing can ensure their survival in the open ocean. If we are to keep our lovable dolphins from becoming extinct, the cruel practices of these fishing fleets must be exposed. Only your compassion and action can save the few remaining dolphins.

1. What stereotypes are mentioned in the passage?
2. List any examples of half-truths.
3. What are some examples of loaded, emotional language from the passage?
4. What is the author's intention in the passage?

B. Copy the chart onto your own paper. Use your answers to the questions above to fill in the chart.

Stereotype	Exaggerated Claims and Emotional Language	Author's Intention

Name _____   Date _____

Recognizing Author's Perspective and Purpose

An author's **perspective** is the view from which he or she examines a subject. When you identify an author's perspective, you can uncover his or her attitudes, assumptions, and biases. For instance, a juvenile has a very different perspective on a proposed curfew for juveniles than does an adult, so they are likely to have different attitudes about the subject.

An author's **purpose** deals with his or her reasons for writing. A writer's purpose might be to inform, to influence or persuade, to express an opinion, or to entertain. Identifying an author's perspective and purpose is an important part of critical reading because it helps you determine the accuracy and intent of what you read.

Understanding the Skill

Step 1: Identify the author's perspective and purpose as you read. The following passage discusses rattlesnakes. As you read, look for the author's attitude toward rattlesnakes and her purpose for writing the piece.

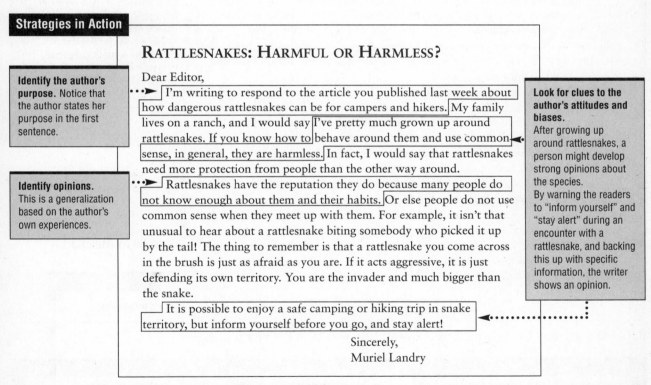

Strategies in Action

RATTLESNAKES: HARMFUL OR HARMLESS?

Identify the author's purpose. Notice that the author states her purpose in the first sentence.

Identify opinions. This is a generalization based on the author's own experiences.

Dear Editor,

I'm writing to respond to the article you published last week about how dangerous rattlesnakes can be for campers and hikers. My family lives on a ranch, and I would say I've pretty much grown up around rattlesnakes. If you know how to behave around them and use common sense, in general, they are harmless. In fact, I would say that rattlesnakes need more protection from people than the other way around.

Rattlesnakes have the reputation they do because many people do not know enough about them and their habits. Or else people do not use common sense when they meet up with them. For example, it isn't that unusual to hear about a rattlesnake biting somebody who picked it up by the tail! The thing to remember is that a rattlesnake you come across in the brush is just as afraid as you are. If it acts aggressive, it is just defending its own territory. You are the invader and much bigger than the snake.

It is possible to enjoy a safe camping or hiking trip in snake territory, but inform yourself before you go, and stay alert!

Sincerely,
Muriel Landry

Look for clues to the author's attitudes and biases.
After growing up around rattlesnakes, a person might develop strong opinions about the species.
By warning the readers to "inform yourself" and "stay alert" during an encounter with a rattlesnake, and backing this up with specific information, the writer shows an opinion.

Step 2: Summarize the author's perspective and purpose. In a chart, list key words, phrases, and details that reveal the author's opinion. Then summarize the author's perspective and her reasons for it. Finally, determine the author's purpose in writing the piece and how that might affect how you view the content.

Key Words, Phrases, and Details	Author's Perspective	Author's Purpose
• *in general, they are harmless* • *rattlesnakes need protection from people* • *many do not know enough about them* • *rattlesnakes are just as afraid as you are*	*People are far more dangerous to rattlesnakes than they are to people. A rattlesnake will only bite as a defensive action and not an aggressive one.*	*The author's purpose is to persuade the reader that rattlesnakes are not as dangerous as most people believe. This means that you have to question the facts that are presented. Are they balanced?*

Name _____ Date _____

Practicing the Skill: Level 6

> **GUIDELINES FOR RECOGNIZING AUTHOR'S PERSPECTIVE AND PURPOSE:**
>
> ■ Look for words or phrases that reveal the author's opinion about the subject.
>
> ■ Look for generalizations based on the author's own experiences.
>
> ■ Determine the author's purpose and how it might affect the content.
>
> ■ In a chart, summarize the author's perspective and the details that confirm it.

Apply what you have learned. Refer to the guidelines above as you complete the exercises below. Use a separate sheet of paper if you need more room.

A. The following passages describes the newly minted dollar coin. Read through the passage, and then answer the questions.

A NEW DOLLAR COIN

The U. S. Congress recently made the decision to mint a new dollar coin. Susan B. Anthony was on the head of the old dollar coin for twenty years. But only a few Americans ever saw one of those. The old coin was attractive to collectors or the odd person who stashed them away, thinking they might be valuable some day. However, the Susan B. Anthony dollar was always rare, and it never caught on for everyday use.

The main reason the old coin dollars never caught on was that they were too much like quarters. These two coins were almost exactly the same size, and both of them had a rough rim. This made it hard to tell them apart. If you had a quarter and a Susan B. Anthony dollar in your pocket, it was almost impossible to tell, just by feeling, which was which.

The new dollar has changed completely. First of all, it is not silver in color, but golden. It is also larger in size than any other coin today, and it has a distinctive edge. This is especially helpful for people who are blind or have trouble seeing. The new dollar is identified simply by a quick touch. Also, Susan B. Anthony has been replaced with a likeness of Sacajawea, the popular heroine who helped Lewis and Clark on their expedition to reach the Pacific Ocean. Sacajawea is the first Native American woman to appear on a coin minted in the United States. She certainly deserves this honor.

1. How does the author feel about the new dollar coin as compared to the older Susan B. Anthony dollar coin?

2. What words or phrases reveal the author's opinions?

3. What does the author feel about Sacajawea appearing on the new dollar coin?

4. How does the author's purpose affect how you view the content?

B. Use the answers to the questions above to help you fill in the chart.

Key Words, Phrases, and Details	Author's Perspective	Author's Purpose

Recognizing Author's Perspective and Purpose, continued

Practicing the Skill: Level 7

GUIDELINES FOR RECOGNIZING AUTHOR'S PERSPECTIVE AND PURPOSE:

■ Look for words or phrases that reveal the author's opinion about the subject.

■ Look for generalizations based on the author's own experiences.

■ Determine the author's purpose and how it might affect the content.

■ In a chart, summarize the author's perspective and the details that confirm it.

Apply what you have learned. Refer to the guidelines above as you complete the exercises below. Use a separate sheet of paper if you need more room.

A. The following passage describes the factors that contribute to healthy aging. Read through the passage, and then answer the questions.

HEALTHY AGING

Americans are living longer than they ever have before. In 1900, the average life expectancy, or average number of years a person lives, was 47. Today that average is 76, an increase of almost thirty years. Several factors have contributed to this change. Among them are the discovery of medicines that prevent or help heal diseases, better eating habits, and the right kinds of exercise. The genes we inherit also play a role, but probably not as big a role as people used to think. All of these factors have been mentioned often in discussions about healthy aging. One important factor, however, that needs more attention is social interaction—being with other people.

Just because people are living longer does not mean they are living better. According to recent research, social interaction not only insures that the elderly live longer. It actually improves the quality of their lives. For children, teenagers, and young adults, contact with older adults can also be beneficial. Most elderly people have more time than other adults. But it is not necessary that an older person be related to the younger as a family member. In general, contact with younger people makes the elderly feel more connected to life. And young people who reach out to someone much older may find that they are doing more than offering a gift of their time. They may have some fun and improve their own lives in the process.

1. What does the author think about the aging process?
2. According to the author, what is the critical factor that improves the quality of life?
3. What words or phrases reveal the author's opinions?
4. How does the author feel about older and younger generations spending time together?
5. How does the author's purpose affect how you view the content?

B. Use the answers to the questions above to help you fill in the chart.

Key Words, Phrases, and Details	Author's Perspective	Author's Purpose

Name _____ Date _____

Practicing the Skill: Level 8

GUIDELINES FOR RECOGNIZING AUTHOR'S PERSPECTIVE AND PURPOSE:

■ Look for words or phrases that reveal the author's opinion about the subject.

■ Look for generalizations based on the author's own experiences.

■ Determine the author's purpose and how it might affect the content.

■ In a chart, summarize the author's perspective and the details that confirm it.

Apply what you have learned. Refer to the guidelines above as you complete the exercises below. Use a separate sheet of paper if you need more room.

A. The following passage describes the benefits and uses of solar power. Read through the passage, and then answer the questions.

SOLAR POWER: ENERGY FOR TODAY AND TOMORROW?

Solar power is an energy source that is renewed every day the sun shines. Solar energy is the safest and cleanest form of energy that we have. Today's larger and more powerful solar energy systems can harness the sun's energy no matter what the weather. Other energy sources commonly in use do not have these advantages. Trees for wood fires take decades to grow, while oil, coal, and natural gas need thousands of years to develop. For too long a time, we have been relying almost exclusively on these limited resources, polluting and destroying our environment in the process.

In the United States, homes and cabins beyond the range of electric power lines use solar energy. Many ranchers and farmers have solar operated water pumps that provide water for their livestock. In other countries, solar energy is the basis of electrical power for whole villages, providing energy for everything from pumping water to cooking.

In the future, people will rely more on the sun for their home and business power needs. Refrigerators, air conditioners, computers, cell phones—even our cars—will all be solar operated. It is crucial that private energy companies as well as state and local governments invest in solar technology to insure that solar power becomes our primary energy source.

---

1. What does the author think about solar energy?
2. What words, phrases, and details reveal the author's opinions?
3. According to the author, what should be done with non-solar energy sources?
4. How does the author's purpose affect how you view the content?

B. Use the answers to the questions above to help you fill in the chart.

Key Words, Phrases, and Details	Author's Perspective	Author's Purpose

READING SKILLS PRACTICE: READING OBJECTIVE 6

Distinguishing Between Fact and Opinion

Facts are events, dates, statistics, or statements that can be proved. Facts can be checked for accuracy. Statements of **opinions** are judgments, beliefs, and feelings of the writer or speaker. Distinguishing statements of fact from opinions is an important element of critical reading, as it helps you to evaluate the accuracy of what you read.

Understanding the Skill

Step 1: Distinguish between facts and opinions as you read. The following passage describes the life of British author Lewis Carroll.

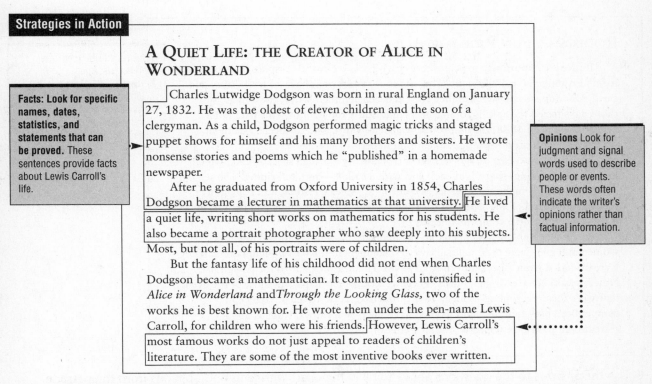

Strategies in Action

A QUIET LIFE: THE CREATOR OF ALICE IN WONDERLAND

Facts: Look for specific names, dates, statistics, and statements that can be proved. These sentences provide facts about Lewis Carroll's life.

Charles Lutwidge Dodgson was born in rural England on January 27, 1832. He was the oldest of eleven children and the son of a clergyman. As a child, Dodgson performed magic tricks and staged puppet shows for himself and his many brothers and sisters. He wrote nonsense stories and poems which he "published" in a homemade newspaper.

After he graduated from Oxford University in 1854, Charles Dodgson became a lecturer in mathematics at that university. He lived a quiet life, writing short works on mathematics for his students. He also became a portrait photographer who saw deeply into his subjects. Most, but not all, of his portraits were of children.

But the fantasy life of his childhood did not end when Charles Dodgson became a mathematician. It continued and intensified in *Alice in Wonderland* and *Through the Looking Glass,* two of the works he is best known for. He wrote them under the pen-name Lewis Carroll, for children who were his friends. However, Lewis Carroll's most famous works do not just appeal to readers of children's literature. They are some of the most inventive books ever written.

Opinions Look for judgment and signal words used to describe people or events. These words often indicate the writer's opinions rather than factual information.

Step 2: Organize facts and opinions in a chart. Summarize the factual information and the opinions expressed in the passage.

Facts	Opinions
• *Dodgson was born in England on January 27, 1832.* • *Dodgson was the oldest of 11 children.* • *Dodgson graduated Oxford University in 1854.* • *Dodgson lectured in mathematics.* • *Writing under the name of Lewis Carroll, Dodgson wrote* Alice in Wonderland *and* Through the Looking Glass.	• *Dodgson the photographer saw deeply into his subjects.* • *Dodgson's books appeal to adults as well as children.* • *Dodgson's books are among the most inventive books ever written.*

Distinguishing Between Fact and Opinion, continued

Practicing the Skill: Level 6

GUIDELINES FOR DISTINGUISHING BETWEEN FACT AND OPINION:

■ Look for specific names, dates, statistics, and statements that can be proved.

■ Note the writer's assertions, claims, hypotheses, and judgments.

■ Look for judgment words used to describe people and events.

■ Use a chart to organize facts and opinions.

Apply what you have learned. Refer to the guidelines above as you complete the exercises. Use a separate sheet of paper if you need more room.

A. Read the following passage about rodeo events, and then answer the questions.

RODEOS: A FUN RIDE FOR ALL

Rodeos are sporting contests where cowboys and cowgirls display their skills and form in roping and riding events. The origin of rodeos goes back to trail drives and cattle roundups in the 1800s. When they had finished their work, the cowboys of those days tested their skills roping steers and riding the wild or semi-wild horses called broncos. In 1888, the first rodeo was held before an audience. Since then, rodeos have become a form of paid entertainment.

Events fall into two categories. The first category is rough stock events, which include bronc riding—both bareback and with a saddle—and bull riding. The second category includes such timed events as calf roping, steer wrestling and roping, team roping, and barrel racing. Some of the timed events feature a single competitor. In others, several people compete as a team.

Previously, only men competed in the majority of rodeo events. However, women and girls were eventually allowed to compete in the barrel racing event. They were excluded from all other events, however. This was not fair to the cowgirls. Nowadays, there are all-girl rodeos. In these, women participate in most of the events that were formerly limited to men. Today, rodeos have achieved a balance in competition, now that men and women have their own shows. Rodeos are a recreational pastime enjoyed by the entire family.

1. Name at least three facts in the passage.
2. Identify an opinion or judgment the writer has made.
3. Name some judgment words the writer has used to describe persons or events.

B. Use the answers to the questions above to fill in the chart with facts and opinions from the passage.

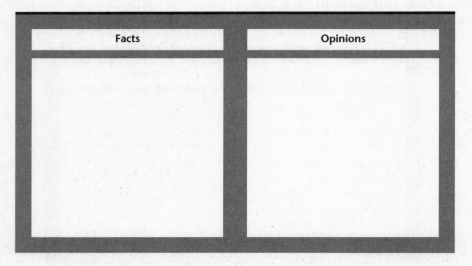

Facts	Opinions

Distinguishing Between Fact and Opinion, continued

Practicing the Skill: Level 7

GUIDELINES FOR DISTINGUISHING BETWEEN FACT AND OPINION:

■ Look for specific names, dates, statistics, and statements that can be proved.

■ Note the writer's assertions, claims, hypotheses, and judgments.

■ Look for judgment words used to describe people and events.

■ Use a chart to organize facts and opinions.

Apply what you have learned. Refer to the guidelines above as you complete the exercises. Use a separate sheet of paper if you need more room.

A. Read the following passage about the first non-stop helium balloon flight around the world, and then answer the questions.

AROUND THE WORLD IN 20 DAYS, PLUS 1

The *Breitling Orbiter 3* is a balloon fueled by helium and hot air and piloted by two adventurous and courageous men, Brian Jones and Bertrand Piccard. On March 20, 1999, it achieved one of the biggest goals in aviation history: flying non-stop around the world in a little over twenty days. Like the first people to land on the moon, Jones and Picard are true modern day heroes.

Before the success of the *Breitling Orbiter 3*, numerous other attempts to circle the globe by balloon had ended in failure. To fly around the world in a balloon was the last, great challenge in flying, and many people wanted to make history by doing it.

But the full crew of *Orbiter 3*—which included meteorologists and satellite experts, mapping the route for the pilots in the air—had learned a great deal from their earlier technical mistakes. In the end, though, the pilots on this flight were helped, not just by technical skill, but also by sheer luck. Almost all of the fuel had run out, and the heaters that kept Jones and Piccard warm at high altitiudes had quit, long before they finally landed. But the *Orbiter 3* was in the air longer than any balloon on record.

1. List at least three facts in the passage.
2. Identify an opinion or judgment the writer has made.
3. What are some judgment words the writer has used to describe persons or events.

B. Use the answers to the questions above to fill in the chart with facts and opinions from the passage.

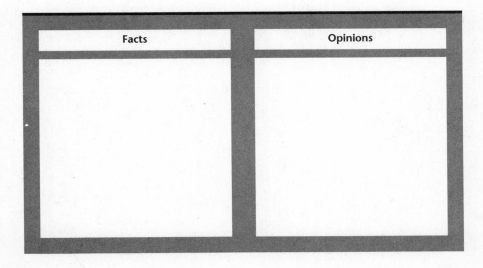

Facts	Opinions

Practicing the Skill: Level 8

> **GUIDELINES FOR DISTINGUISHING BETWEEN FACT AND OPINION:**
>
> ■ Look for specific names, dates, statistics, and statements that can be proved.
>
> ■ Note the writer's assertions, claims, hypotheses, and judgments.
>
> ■ Look for judgment words used to describe people and events.
>
> ■ Use a chart to organize facts and opinions.

Apply what you have learned. Refer to the guidelines above as you complete the exercises. Use a separate sheet of paper if you need more room.

A. Read the following passage about German author Friedrich Schiller. and then answer the questions.

FRIEDRICH SCHILLER: GERMAN AUTHOR WITH AN AMERICAN IDEA

What do cities as diverse as Cleveland, Omaha, St. Louis, New Orleans, San Francisco, and New York City share in common? One thing is a respect for the German writer Friedrich Schiller. A statue to honor the writer can be found in each of these cities. But why should a German poet and playwright be so important to people in the United States? An answer lies in an idea prized by Americans since this country's beginnings, the idea of freedom.

Schiller was inspired in his writings by the American Revolution and by the belief of the founding fathers that all people are created free and equal. At the time that Schiller was writing, this belief in human freedom was not generally accepted, either in his own country or in the rest of the world. Schiller's plays began to be produced in the United States almost a decade before his early death—he died in 1805 when he was only 45 years old. About 50 years after his death, Schiller was still much admired. Two important advocates were Abraham Lincoln and Frederick Douglass. For Douglass, the abolitionist who had formerly been a slave, Schiller was "the poet of freedom." Schiller is certainly worth remembering for the role he played in making his belief in human freedom a more popular and acceptable idea to all people.

1. List at least three facts in the passage.
2. Identify an opinion or judgment the writer has made.
3. What are some judgment words the writer has used to describe persons or events.

B. Use the answers to the questions above to fill in the chart with facts and opinions from the passage.

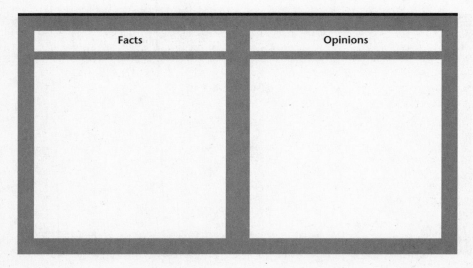

Facts	Opinions

Correlation of TAAS and TEKS Objectives
Grade 8 WRITING (2000–2001/2001–2002)[1]

TAAS Objective	Related TEKS Objective(s)
TAAS Objective 1 The student will respond appropriately in a written composition to the purpose/audience specified in a given topic.	**TEKS Objective 8.15** *Writing/purposes:* The student writes for a variety of audiences and purposes and in a variety of forms. **TEKS Objective 8.18** *Writing/processes:* The student selects and uses writing processes for self-initiated and assigned writing.
TAAS Objective 2 The student will organize ideas in a written composition on a given topic.	**TEKS Objective 8.15** *Writing/purposes:* The student writes for a variety of audiences and purposes and in a variety of forms. **TEKS Objective 8.18** *Writing/processes:* The student selects and uses writing processes for self-initiated and assigned writing.
TAAS Objective 3 The student will demonstrate control of the English language in a written composition on a given topic.	**TEKS Objective 8.15** *Writing/purposes:* The student writes for a variety of audiences and purposes and in a variety of forms. **TEKS Objective 8.16** *Writing/penmanship/capitalization/punctuation/spelling:* The student composes original texts, applying the conventions of written language, such as capitalization, punctuation, penmanship, and spelling, to communicate clearly. **TEKS Objective 8.17** *Writing/grammar/usage:* The student applies standard grammar and usage to communicate clearly and effectively in writing. **TEKS Objective 8.18** *Writing/processes:* The student selects and uses writing processes for self-initiated and assigned writing.

[1] Students in eighth grade in 2000–2001 and 2001–2002 will take the **TAAS Writing** test as eighth-graders. Beginning in 2002–2003, the **TAAS Writing** test will be given in seventh grade.

TAAS Objective	Related TEKS Objective(s)
TAAS Objective 4 The student will generate a written composition that develops/ supports/ elaborates the central idea stated in a given topic.	**TEKS Objective 8.15** *Writing/purposes:* The student writes for a variety of audiences and purposes and in a variety of forms. **TEKS Objective 8.17** *Writing/grammar/usage:* The student applies standard grammar and usage to communicate clearly and effectively in writing. **TEKS Objective 8.18** *Writing/processes:* The student selects and uses writing processes for self-initiated and assigned writing.
TAAS Objective 5 The student will recognize appropriate sentence construction within the context of a written passage.	**TEKS Objective 8.17** *Writing/grammar/usage:* The student applies standard grammar and usage to communicate clearly and effectively in writing. **TEKS Objective 8.18** *Writing/processes:* The student selects and uses writing processes for self-initiated and assigned writing.
TAAS Objective 6 The student will recognize appropriate English usage within the context of a written passage.	**TEKS Objective 8.17** *Writing/grammar/usage:* The student applies standard grammar and usage to communicate clearly and effectively in writing.
TAAS Objective 7 The student will proofread for spelling, capitalization, and punctuation errors within the context of a written passage.	**TEKS Objective 8.16** *Writing/penmanship/capitalization/punctuation/spelling:* The student composes original texts, applying the conventions of written language, such as capitalization, punctuation, penmanship, and spelling, to communicate clearly. **TEKS Objective 8.17** *Writing/grammar/usage:* The student applies standard grammar and usage to communicate clearly and effectively in writing. **TEKS Objective 8.18** *Writing/processes:* The student selects and uses writing processes for self-initiated and assigned writing.

Preparing for TAAS: Writing

Test-taking Strategies
ABOUT THE TAAS WRITING TEST

In Spring 2001 and 2002, the TAAS Writing test will be given to all Texas students in grade 8. In 2003 and following years, a new Writing test will be given at grade 7. For 2001 and 2002, the TAAS Writing test is divided into two parts. The first part tests TAAS Objectives 5, 6, and 7 (see pp. 70–71). It provides several passages, each followed by a series of multiple-choice questions. There are three types of question:

- sentence structure questions (run-ons, fragments, sentence combining)
- usage questions (verb tense, pronoun case, agreement of subject and verb, agreement of pronoun and referent, commonly misused words)
- mechanics questions (spelling, capitalization, and punctuation)

The second part of the current TAAS Writing test tests TAAS Objectives 1–4 (see pp. 70–71). This part requires a written composition in response to a given "prompt" or instruction. This prompt will specify the subject, the purpose of the composition, and the audience for which your composition is intended. For the eighth-grade writing test, the purpose of the composition will be one of three types:

- persuasive
- informative: classification
- informative: how-to

TEST-TAKING STRATEGIES

You can score well on the test if you practice answering the types of questions asked in Part 1 and writing the types of composition tested in Part 2.

Strategies for TAAS WRITING: Part 1 To answer the multiple-choice questions in Part 1 of the Writing test, remember these strategies:

1. Read the entire passage before answering the questions.
2. Reread questions that are unclear to you.
3. If a question is too difficult, skip it, and come back later if you have time. Make a note so you can keep track of any questions you skipped.
4. Read all the answer choices before choosing.
5. Eliminate answer choices that are obviously incorrect.
6. Mark your answer sheet neatly. As you select your answers, make sure that you fill in the answer bubbles completely. Erase all stray marks and wrong answers.
7. After you have finished, review your answer sheet to make sure that you have marked each answer in the correct line.

Strategies for TAAS WRITING: Part 2 To write a successful composition for Part 2, make sure you take time to plan your writing. You should use all of the steps of the writing process. In particular, keep in mind the following strategies:

1. Before you begin, note whatever specific instructions you have received about time limits. Plan how much time to allow yourself for brainstorming, organizing, elaborating, drafting, revising, rewriting, and proofreading. As you are writing your composition, make sure that you budget your time carefully for the remaining steps.
2. Make certain that you understand exactly what the prompt is asking you to do.

3. Spend some time brainstorming. Jot down your ideas on a spare sheet of paper. Don't write in full sentences yet; just use key words and phrases.

4. Organize those ideas into an outline. Put the main idea of your composition at the top of the outline and supporting ideas below it.

5. Include an introduction and a conclusion.

6. As you write out your composition, write clearly and legibly.

7. Allow for some time after drafting your composition to review what you have written. Make sure that the main idea of each paragraph is clear and that the elaboration supports that main idea.

8. Proofread for spelling, capitalization, punctuation, and usage. If you have to erase and rewrite something, do so thoroughly and neatly.

USING THIS BOOK

The writing section of *Preparing for TAAS* reviews several writing skills that will help you succeed on the 2001 and 2002 TAAS. These skills are taught separately on pages 75–86.

You will use all of these skills together as you complete the exercises in two Guided Writing Practice sections. To help you evaluate your practice composition and improve your writing, you can compare your composition with the Scored Sample Student Responses. Your teacher may also have you use the Student Self-Evaluation form, either on your own or in pairs or small groups.

For more information about TAAS in 2003 and beyond, visit our Web site: mcdougallittell.com.

WRITING SKILLS PRACTICE: WRITING OBJECTIVE 1
Analyzing the Prompt: Subject, Purpose, and Audience

Understanding the Skill

Before you begin to write your essay, you need to determine three things:

Subject: WHAT are you writing about?

Purpose: WHY are you writing? (to inform, analyze, describe, state an opinion, persuade, or entertain.)

Audience: For WHOM are you writing?

In the writing you will do for the TAAS, your subject, purpose, and audience will be stated in the writing prompt. Sometimes a prompt is in the form of a question. More often it is a series of statements. Before you begin writing, carefully read the prompt you are given to make sure you understand what kind of essay you are to write.

Review the prompts that follow. Notice the key words that tell you what to do.

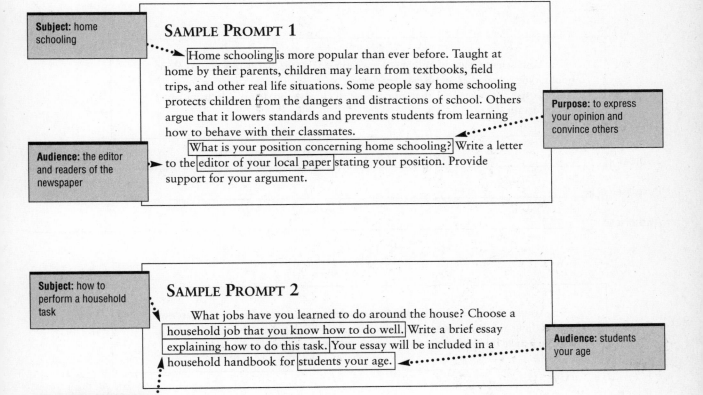

Subject: home schooling

Audience: the editor and readers of the newspaper

SAMPLE PROMPT 1

Home schooling is more popular than ever before. Taught at home by their parents, children may learn from textbooks, field trips, and other real life situations. Some people say home schooling protects children from the dangers and distractions of school. Others argue that it lowers standards and prevents students from learning how to behave with their classmates.

What is your position concerning home schooling? Write a letter to the editor of your local paper stating your position. Provide support for your argument.

Purpose: to express your opinion and convince others

Subject: how to perform a household task

SAMPLE PROMPT 2

What jobs have you learned to do around the house? Choose a household job that you know how to do well. Write a brief essay explaining how to do this task. Your essay will be included in a household handbook for students your age.

Audience: students your age

Purpose: to explain the steps in order

Practicing the Skill

Identify the subject, purpose, and audience in the following writing prompts. Use a separate sheet of paper if you have been instructed not to write in your workbook.

---

1. Suppose you want to bring home a new pet. Before you can bring the animal into the house, you need to get your family's permission. Decide what kind of pet you want to bring home. Then, write exactly what you would say to convince your family to permit you to bring home the animal.

Subject: _____

Purpose: _____

Audience: _____

---

2. Your science class is studying the weather. Your teacher wants you to write about a type of weather you have experienced, such as a thunderstorm or fog. Choose a specific experience that you can recall clearly, and describe it, using vivid sensory details.

Subject: _____

Purpose: _____

Audience: _____

---

3. You have been invited to write an article for your school yearbook describing the best thing about your school. Decide what you think is best about your school. Write an article in which you explain your opinion and give your reasons.

Subject: _____

Purpose: _____

Audience: _____

Name _____   Date _____

Exploring Ideas and Planning a Composition

Once you have discovered the subject, purpose, and audience of your assignment, you are ready to begin exploring ideas for your essay. For the TAAS, you will need to come up with ideas by yourself. The following strategies help you to explore ideas on your own.

Understanding the Skill

Strategies

- **Brainstorming:** List as many ideas as you can think of.

- **Freewriting:** As you think of your subject, write down whatever comes into your mind. Try doing this without lifting your pen from the paper.

- **Graphic Organizers:** Use concept webs, charts, and diagrams to help develop the content and structure of your written work.

Notice how one writer used a graphic organizer to explore her ideas for the following writing prompt.

> Movies are generally given ratings such as G (general audiences), PG-13 (some material may be unsuitable for children under 13), or R (under 17 not admitted without a parent) by the Motion Picture Association of America. However, many people think ratings shouldn't exist at all. Many young teens, for example, feel that they are mature enough to see an R-rated movie. But others say that ratings must remain in place to warn children and parents of a movie's harmful content.
>
> What is your position concerning movie ratings? Write a letter to the editor of your local paper stating your position. Provide support for your argument.

Should movie ratings be required for everyone under 17 years of age?	
Pro (Yes)	**Con (No)**
Movie ratings are a way to protect minors under the age of 17.	*Movie ratings dictate a false sense of morality.*
Movie ratings give society responsibility for determining acceptable content for teenagers.	*Movie ratings deny young adults personal choice and responsibility to make their own decisions.*
Movie ratings help to establish national moral guidelines.	*Movie ratings unduly influence a movie's commercial success.*

Some people generate ideas better when they see them in a pattern on a page. When you plan an essay, you might make a diagram like the one below.

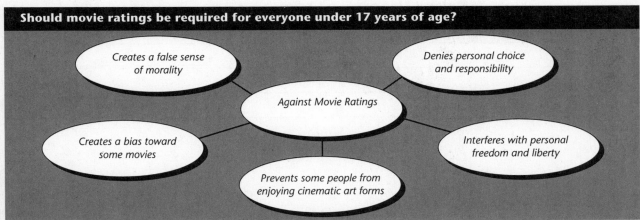

Should movie ratings be required for everyone under 17 years of age?

- Creates a false sense of morality
- Denies personal choice and responsibility
- Against Movie Ratings
- Creates a bias toward some movies
- Interferes with personal freedom and liberty
- Prevents some people from enjoying cinematic art forms

Exploring Ideas and Planning a Composition, continued

Practicing the Skill

Select one of the prompts on page 76 and review its subject, purpose, and audience. Use one of the strategies on page 77 to explore and plan your writing in response to the prompt you selected. If you have been instructed not to write in your book, use your own paper.

1. Use the space below to brainstorm, freewrite, or make a graphic organizer.

2. Decide which ideas from your brainstorming, freewriting, or graphic organizer you want to include in your written response. List them on the following lines. Use a separate sheet of paper if necessary.

   _____

   _____

   _____

   _____

   _____

WRITING SKILLS PRACTICE: WRITING OBJECTIVES 2 AND 4
Organizing and Elaborating Ideas

Understanding the Skill: Organizing Ideas

Organization is fundamental to any kind of writing. Poorly organized writing is easily misunderstood. A well–organized composition presents ideas in a logical order that the reader can easily follow. The following types of organization can be used regardless of the subject, audience, or purpose of a piece of writing.

Types of Logical Organization

Main idea and elaboration (supporting details)—statement of a main idea followed by supporting details

Chronological order—arrangement according to what happened first, second, third, and so on

Spatial order—organization according to how things are arranged in space (for example, a description of the buildings on a street that begins with the nearest building, then moves to the second nearest, and so on)

Order of degree—presents things according to importance, familiarity, complexity, etc.

Compare and contrast—organization that highlights similarities and differences

Cause and effect—shows how some ideas or events cause others

CHRONOLOGICAL ORDER

Chronological order arranges information or events in time. Writers often use chronological order in non-fiction, such as historical accounts, instructions, and directions, as well as in fiction.

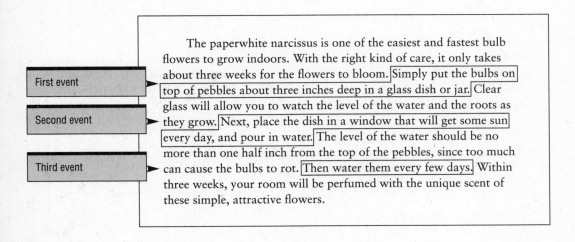

First event

Second event

Third event

The paperwhite narcissus is one of the easiest and fastest bulb flowers to grow indoors. With the right kind of care, it only takes about three weeks for the flowers to bloom. Simply put the bulbs on top of pebbles about three inches deep in a glass dish or jar. Clear glass will allow you to watch the level of the water and the roots as they grow. Next, place the dish in a window that will get some sun every day, and pour in water. The level of the water should be no more than one half inch from the top of the pebbles, since too much can cause the bulbs to rot. Then water them every few days. Within three weeks, your room will be perfumed with the unique scent of these simple, attractive flowers.

Organizing and Elaborating Ideas, continued

SPATIAL ORDER

Spatial order is an effective way to present physical descriptions. Examples of spatial order include right to left, top to bottom, near to far, largest to smallest, and longest to shortest.

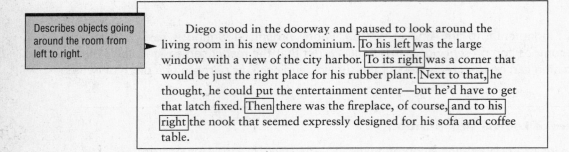

Describes objects going around the room from left to right.

> Diego stood in the doorway and paused to look around the living room in his new condominium. To his left was the large window with a view of the city harbor. To its right was a corner that would be just the right place for his rubber plant. Next to that, he thought, he could put the entertainment center—but he'd have to get that latch fixed. Then there was the fireplace, of course, and to his right the nook that seemed expressly designed for his sofa and coffee table.

ORDER OF DEGREE

Order of degree is used to present several elements that share common traits.

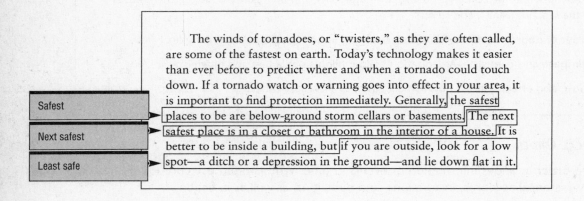

Safest

Next safest

Least safe

> The winds of tornadoes, or "twisters," as they are often called, are some of the fastest on earth. Today's technology makes it easier than ever before to predict where and when a tornado could touch down. If a tornado watch or warning goes into effect in your area, it is important to find protection immediately. Generally, the safest places to be are below-ground storm cellars or basements. The next safest place is in a closet or bathroom in the interior of a house. It is better to be inside a building, but if you are outside, look for a low spot—a ditch or a depression in the ground—and lie down flat in it.

Organizing and Elaborating Ideas, continued

COMPARE AND CONTRAST

Comparison and contrast can be used to illustrate the similarities and differences between ideas, information, qualities, people, or events.

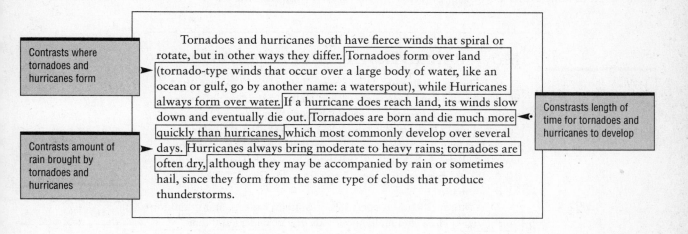

Contrasts where tornadoes and hurricanes form

Contrasts amount of rain brought by tornadoes and hurricanes

Tornadoes and hurricanes both have fierce winds that spiral or rotate, but in other ways they differ. Tornadoes form over land (tornado-type winds that occur over a large body of water, like an ocean or gulf, go by another name: a waterspout), while Hurricanes always form over water. If a hurricane does reach land, its winds slow down and eventually die out. Tornadoes are born and die much more quickly than hurricanes, which most commonly develop over several days. Hurricanes always bring moderate to heavy rains; tornadoes are often dry, although they may be accompanied by rain or sometimes hail, since they form from the same type of clouds that produce thunderstorms.

Contrasts length of time for tornadoes and hurricanes to develop

CAUSE AND EFFECT

Cause and effect shows how one event causes another event or how one idea leads to another idea. This is an effective way to organize information in any kind of writing.

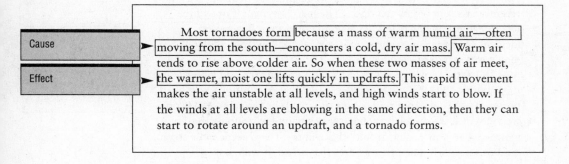

Cause

Effect

Most tornadoes form because a mass of warm humid air—often moving from the south—encounters a cold, dry air mass. Warm air tends to rise above colder air. So when these two masses of air meet, the warmer, moist one lifts quickly in updrafts. This rapid movement makes the air unstable at all levels, and high winds start to blow. If the winds at all levels are blowing in the same direction, then they can start to rotate around an updraft, and a tornado forms.

Understanding the Skill: Elaborating Ideas

Read the following paragraph. As you read, pay particular attention to the main idea nd the types of elaboration used to support it. Compare the types of elaboration highlighted below with those listed above.

MOVIE RATINGS PROTECT KIDS — *AND ADULTS*

Example: This anecdote illustrates the writer's point that many youths are insensitive to violence.

The other day I went to the movies. The movie I saw was rated PG-13 because there were some violent scenes in it. In one of those scenes, a car with people in it was blown up. When the car burst into flames, some kids sitting near me yelled out: "Awesome!" When the movie was over, I heard one of them say that there was a movie that was "way better" than the one they had just seen, but it was rated "R." "It's not fair we can't see it," he said to his friend. "Who says we're not mature?"

The Motion Picture Association of America says so, and I think they're right. These and many other kids do not understand that physical violence is dreadful, not "awesome." In a recent poll taken at Lothrop Junior High School, students were asked how they felt about the rising number of incidents of violence in the country; sixty eight percent replied that it didn't affect them at all, and seventy eight percent said that they saw nothing wrong with graphic violence in the movies.

Opinion: This states the writer's opinion.

Statistics: These facts are expressed as numbers.

"Movies and television have desensitized young people to violence," Dr. Ken Sahakian, guidance counselor at Lothrop, reported recently in a follow-up interview. "The ratings system is one of the few safeguards we have left." Sahakian noted that, in a recent incident of vandalism at the school, a slogan taken from an R-rated movie was scrawled on the wall.

Quotation: This is the counselor's exact statement.

Fact: This information can be verified.

"R" rated movies don't hold back on graphic sex and violence the way that "PG-13" rated movies do. Movie ratings are a way of protecting kids, parents, and society at large. The rating system is one way in which we can claim some responsibility for stopping the violence that is spreading around the country. There needs to be some kind of safeguard that either assures that an adult will take responsibility for what a kid sees or else sees to it that impressionable minds won't be exposed to that kind of movie.

Main idea: This explains what the essay is about.

Organizing and Elaborating Ideas, continued

Practicing the Skill

A. To practice organizing your ideas, first review the list of types of elaboration on p. 82. Then, look at the supporting details you came up with for the activity on p. 78. For each detail you have listed, decide which type of elaboration it is.

1. _____

   _____

   _____

   _____

2. _____

   _____

   _____

3. _____

   _____

   _____

   _____

B. Now review the organizational strategies discussed on pages 79–81. Choose an appropriate organization for your composition, and use it to arrange the details that you have listed above.

WRITING SKILLS PRACTICE: WRITING OBJECTIVES 3, 5, 6, AND 7
Following Language Conventions

To communicate clearly, it is important to use language and grammar that are appropriate to your audience. It will not matter how good your ideas are if your audience cannot understand you.

Understanding the Skill

Varieties of Standard English—Formal standard English is used in most writing. Informal English is used in casual speech and in some writing. Informal English is also called "colloquial language." Dialects are a part of colloquial language.

Language Conventions—Grammar, usage, mechanics, spelling, and paragraphing are important to conveying a clear message.

Read the following examples of text with errors, and study the corrections made to the language.

Error	Type of Error	Correction
I think that movie ratings make no **sence**.	spelling	I think that movie ratings make no **sense**.
Movie ratings which can often make or break a movie's commercial future are not based upon clear criteria, moral honesty, or a realistic consideration of viewers' maturity.	punctuation	Movie ratings, which can often make or break a movie's commercial future, are not based upon clear criteria, moral honesty, or a realistic consideration of viewers' maturity.
The Motion Picture Association of America should not be a **Moral Guardian** for young people.	capitalization	The Motion Picture Association of America should not be a **moral guardian** for young people.
If everyone **protested** the ratings system, there **will be** changes.	verb tense	If everyone **protests** the ratings system, there **will be** changes.
Every **person** should be able to make up **their** own mind.	pronoun-antecedent agreement	Every **person** should be able to make up **his or her** own mind.
Many young **people believes** that the current movie rating system is unfair.	subject-verb agreement	Many young **people believe** that the current movie rating system is unfair.
I think that movie ratings can be extremely superficial. Because they only look at movies from a limited point of view.	incomplete sentence	I think that movie ratings can be extremely superficial because they only look at movies from a limited point of view.
The movie rating system often makes young people angry, why don't more of them protest the system?	run-on sentence	The movie rating system often makes young people angry. **Why** don't more of them protest the system?
I would feel **more contentedly** if movie ratings were only advisory.	use of adjectives and adverbs	I would feel **more contented** if movie ratings were only advisory.

Following Language Conventions, continued

Practicing the Skill

Identify the errors in grammar, mechanics, and formal Standard English in the following sentences. Then revise the paragraph on the lines below, making all necessary corrections.

Movie Ratings should not preevent teenagers under the age of seventeen from seeing whatever movie they want. Too see. Its not fare. If a teenager wan'ts to see a movie that's rated "R." They should be alowed too. Teenagers under the age of seventeen have responsibly jobbs. They have to make judgements about alot of things, every day in order for them to keep those jobs. They should be able to pic there own movies. Otherwise, they wont never be alowed to grough up.

_____

_____

_____

_____

_____

_____

_____

_____

_____

_____

_____

_____

_____

_____

_____

_____

_____

_____

_____

_____

COMPOSITION PRACTICE: PERSUASIVE WRITING
Guided Writing Practice

Writing Prompt

Movies are generally given ratings such as G (general audiences), PG-13 (some material may be unsuitable for children under 13), or R (under 17 not admitted without a parent) by the Motion Picture Association of America. However, many people think ratings should not exist at all. Many young teens, for example, feel that they are mature enough to see an R-rated movie. But others say that ratings must remain in place to warn children and parents of a movie's harmful content.

What is your position concerning movie ratings? Write a letter to the editor of your local paper stating your position. Provide support for your argument.

In previous exercises you completed the first two steps in responding to the prompt—(1) identifying the subject, audience, and purpose of the writing, and (2) exploring ideas and planning the composition. In this section, you will complete these steps for the writing prompt about movie ratings, and develop your ideas and details into an essay, using the skills you have reviewed.

IDENTIFYING YOUR SUBJECT, AUDIENCE, AND PURPOSE

List the subject, audience, and purpose of your writing in response to the prompt shown here. Consult your work from page 76 of this workbook. Use a separate sheet of paper if necessary.

Subject: _____

Audience: _____

Purpose: _____

EXPLORING IDEAS AND PLANNING YOUR WRITING

On the following lines list the main idea of your writing. Then, rewrite it in the form of a thesis statement. A thesis statement is not simply the main idea, topic, or title of your essay. Instead, it is a sentence or two that summarize the central, dominant idea *and* purpose of your writing. A thesis statement gives readers a preview of ideas and purposes so that they know where the writing is headed.

Main Idea: _____

_____

_____

Thesis Statement: _____

_____

_____

Guided Writing Practice, continued

CREATING LOGICAL ORGANIZATION AND PROVIDING ELABORATION

Providing elaboration

List your key ideas and plans for elaboration below. Use a separate sheet of paper if necessary. Consult your work from page 83 of this workbook.

Key Idea: _____

Elaboration: _____

_____

_____

_____

_____

_____

Key Idea: _____

Elaboration: _____

_____

_____

_____

_____

Key Idea: _____

Elaboration: _____

_____

_____

_____

_____

Now review each key idea and the elaboration you have chosen. Make sure your elaboration actually supports the key idea.

Guided Writing Practice, continued

CREATING LOGICAL ORGANIZATION AND PROVIDING ELABORATION

Now work on organizing your writing.

First, review your key ideas and decide in which order you want to arrange them:

- chronologically
- spatially
- in order of importance
- in an order that compares and contrasts them
- in terms of causes and effects
- in some combination of the above

Then, write an outline below that provides an overview of your essay. Use a separate sheet of paper if necessary.

Guided Writing Practice, continued

DRAFTING YOUR WRITING—INTRODUCTION

Now you should begin writing a draft of your composition. Begin with an **introductory paragraph** that states the subject of your composition. It's important to catch your audience's attention early, so try to include an interesting anecdote or fact that will make the reader want to keep reading. Your introductory paragraph also needs to include a thesis statement—a sentence or two that summarize the main idea and purpose of your essay.

Write a first draft of your introduction below. You might try drafting two or more introductions and then deciding which you think is more effective. Use a separate sheet of paper if necessary.

Introduction 1

Introduction 2

DRAFTING YOUR WRITING—DEVELOPING KEY IDEAS

Continue working on your draft by **developing each of your key ideas** in order below. Use a separate sheet of paper if necessary. As you write, remember to do the following:

- Use language that is appropriate for your audience and purpose.

- Follow the rules of standard written English.

- Be sure your elaboration actually supports the key idea.

- Use appropriate transitions, such as *as a result, then, in contrast, for example, similarly,* and *furthermore* to connect ideas.

- Examine your arguments critically to ensure that they make sense.

Guided Writing Practice, continued

DRAFTING YOUR WRITING—CONCLUSION

Now, write a **concluding** paragraph for your composition. In the conclusion:

- restate the thesis of your essay in different words
- summarize the points you have made
- make a prediction
- call on your readers to take action

Write a first draft of your conclusion on the lines below. Use a separate sheet of paper if necessary. You might need to draft several versions of your conclusion before you write one that satisfies you. Review the drafts of your conclusions and choose the one you like best.

Conclusion 1

Conclusion 2

Conclusion 3

Guided Writing Practice, continued

USING APPROPRIATE AND GRAMMATICALLY CORRECT LANGUAGE

Review the draft of your composition and pay close attention to the language you used. Correct any errors in usage, grammar, and mechanics. Check for mistakes in paragraph structure. Make sure you used language appropriate to your subject, audience, and purpose. Then, write the final version of your composition below. Use a separate sheet of paper if necessary.

COMPOSITION PRACTICE: PERSUASIVE WRITING
Additional Prompts: Levels 6–8

Use the following prompts to complete the writing exercises in this book and to practice your composition skills.

Many schools issue required reading lists for students to complete over vacations. Some people think this is an excellent way to keep the minds of children active. But others say that vacations should give kids a break from school.

Write a letter to your principal about your opinion on required vacation reading.

Most schools require that students attend regular gym classes. Administrators believe that exercise promotes health and teaches valuable lessons. However, some kids say gym class is a waste of time and that school should be a place for book learning.

Write a letter to your school principal stating your views. Be sure to support your opinion.

Some schools use police dogs to sniff out drugs on campus. Lockers, book bags, and pocketbooks are all up for grabs. Many kids say these searches are an invasion of privacy. Others feel that they are necessary to protect the safety of all students.

What is your opinion on drug searches? Write an editorial article for your school paper stating your position.

In 1997, the Congress and President Clinton raised the minimum wage from $4.75 to $5.15. This meant that legally, an employer was required to pay at least this amount for each hour worked. Some people say this amount is still too low for people to live on. Others state that it is too high and that employers will cut more jobs in order to save money.

Is the minimum wage raise a good idea? Write an editorial article for your local newspaper stating your opinion on this subject.

Auto accidents are the leading cause of death for people ages 15-20. Some people argue that raising the legal driving age to 21 would solve the problem. They say young drivers are too immature and irresponsible to handle a vehicle. Many teens think raising the driving age would be unfair.

Should the legal driving age be raised? Write a letter to the editor of your local paper explaining your position.

For more persuasive writing prompts, visit our Web site: mcdougallittell.com.

COMPOSITION PRACTICE: PERSUASIVE WRITING
Scored Writing Samples: How TAAS Compositions are Scored

TAAS compositions are scored *holistically*. In holistic scoring, graders take into account the overall effect of the content and delivery rather than focusing primarily on grammar, punctuation, and spelling. They expect grammar, punctuation, and spelling to be correct, but they are mainly concerned with how effectively the overall message comes across. To do this, they focus on how well each composition meets several specific objectives.

Scores range from 1 (low) to 4 (high), although an essay may receive a "0" if it is off topic, indecipherable, or presents insufficient information. Sample essays with scores of 1–4 appear on pages 97–104. After each essay, a section appears in which the scored sample is analyzed according to the standards described here.

BASIC CRITERIA FOR EVALUATION

Topic All TAAS essays must address the topic presented in the prompt. An essay that is off-topic will receive a score of 0, no matter how well it is written.

Purpose If a TAAS essay addresses the topic in the prompt but fails to meet the purpose, it will receive a score of 1, even if the writing is effective. The ability to meet the purpose of the prompt is one of the basic skills the TAAS assesses. The writer's position should be clearly stated in the essay and supported with reasons.

ADDITIONAL CRITERIA FOR EVALUATION

The chart below demonstrates the characteristics of each score.

Score 0	Score 1	Score 2	Score 3	Score 4
Off topic Blank paper	Incorrect purpose, audience, or type of writing	Correct purpose, audience, and type of writing	Correct purpose, audience, and type of writing	Correct purpose, audience, and type of writing
Foreign language	Brief or vague	Some elaboration	Moderately well elaborated	Effective elaboration
Illegible Incoherent	Insufficient support Rambling	Some details	Clear, effective language	Consistent organization
Not enough content to score	Lack of language control Poor organization	Gaps in organization Limited language control	Organized (perhaps with brief digressions)	Sense of completeness, fluency

STANDARDS FOR A SCORE 4 COMPOSITION

Purpose	Expresses a definite position on the issue and attempts to persuade readers to agree with it.
Audience	Uses language, tone, and reasons that appeal to the specified audience.
Support	Provides several thoughtful reasons. Supports reasons with adequate elaboration (details, examples, etc.). Addresses opposing arguments convincingly.
Structure	Arranges main ideas and support according to logical patterns. Includes an introduction, conclusion, and appropriate transitions.
Fluency	Includes good word choice and sentence variety. Exhibits control of language.

COMPOSITION PRACTICE: PERSUASIVE WRITING

Student Self-Evaluation: A Persuasive Composition

The questions on this page will help you see how well your composition meets the objectives the evaluators are likely to look for. Become familiar with them so you can use them to evaluate your essay during the TAAS.

The Prompt

1. Does your response meet all the requirements stated in the prompt? Have you stated your position clearly and supported it with details? Have you raised and responded to opposing arguments?

2. Have you addressed the audience appropriately?

3. Does your essay fit the type of writing suggested in the prompt (letter to the editor, article to the school paper, and so on)?

Reasons

4. Do the reasons you offer really support your position?

5. Will your audience find your reasons convincing?

6. Have you stated your reasons clearly?

7. Have you given at least three reasons?

8. Have you supported your reasons with sufficient facts, examples, quotations, and other details?

9. Have you presented and responded to opposing arguments?

10. Is your reasoning sound? Have you avoided faulty logic?

Order and Arrangement

11. Have you included a strong introduction?

12. Have you included a strong conclusion?

13. Are the reasons arranged in a logical order?

Word Choice

14. Is the language of your essay appropriate for your audience?

15. Have you used precise, vivid words and persuasive language?

Fluency

16. Have you used sentences of varying lengths and structures?

17. Have you connected ideas with transitions and other devices?

18. Have you used correct spelling, punctuation, and grammar?

SCORED WRITING SAMPLES (SCORES 1–4)
Score 1 (lowest score)

PROMPT

> Home schooling is more popular than ever before. Taught at home by their parents, children may learn from textbooks, field trips, and other real life situations. Some people say home schooling protects children from the dangers and distractions of school. Others argue that it lowers standards and prevents students from learning how to behave with their classmates.
>
> What is your position concerning home schooling? Write a letter to the editor of your local paper stating your position. Provide support for your argument.

SAMPLE RESPONSE

Why would I want to go to school if I could stay home? School these days is nasty. Lots of adults I see went to school and they're not doing anything that great.

School is nasty and my parents know what to teech me the best for my education. I'll bet you a million dollars I like staying home better. I don't like sitting at a desk all day. Even when she lets us run around.

Why should teachers tell you what to do when you already have parents? All teachers want to do is to get you in trouble anyway.

Looking at Score 1

Purpose

The purpose is stated as "school is nasty." The author does not give a clear argument to support this position.

Audience

The language and tone are informal. The word "nasty" and expressions such as "I'll bet you a million dollars I like staying home better" are not appropriate for a formal essay.

Support

The writer does not consider that there are two sides to the issue. The support in all three paragraphs lacks development. The elaboration also veers off topic, becoming a dumping ground of personal opinions rather than a constructed argument. The most serious error in logic occurs in the last paragraph where the writer criticizes teachers' intentions. That line is a hasty generalization about teachers that is not supportive of the main idea.

Structure

The letter lacks an introduction and conclusion that state the writer's position and summarize the main points. The letter also lacks transitions to connect ideas.

Fluency

The effectiveness of the essay is further limited by numerous errors in spelling, grammar, and mechanics. Some sentences are run-on, and others are fragments.

Score 2

PROMPT

> Home schooling is more popular than ever before. Taught at home by their parents, children may learn from textbooks, field trips, and other real life situations. Some people say home schooling protects children from the dangers and distractions of school. Others argue that it lowers standards and prevents students from learning how to behave with their classmates.
>
> What is your position concerning home schooling? Write a letter to the editor of your local paper stating your position. Provide support for your argument.

SAMPLE RESPONSE

Lots of people have been talking about home schooling. My friends and I are talking about it, too. I think home schooling is a good idea. I'll tell you my reasons for thinking so in the rest of this essay.

Making kids go to school is unfair. This is a free country that protects kids rights to life, liberty and the persoot of happiness. If kids aren't happy in school, why should they be forced to go?

Second, home schooling would be safer. School is noisy. School is dangerous. At home, parents would be able to watch their kids at all times so they would know what was going on with them. They wouldn't worry as much.

My conclusion is that more kids should be home schooled. Parents would like it better. Kids would like it better. Everyone and anyone would be happier if more kids were home schooled. I hope this letter changes your mind.

Looking at Score 2

Purpose

The introduction states the writer's purpose and position.

Audience

The reasons and language are generally appropriate for the audience.

Support

Only two reasons are presented. The support for the first reason is vague. The support for the second reason is more concrete. However, both reasons are weak and the support is thin.

Structure

The essay is well organized.

Fluency

The grammar is correct but there are several errors in spelling and punctuation.

Score 3

PROMPT

> Home schooling is more popular than ever before. Taught at home by their parents, children may learn from textbooks, field trips, and other real life situations. Some people say home schooling protects children from the dangers and distractions of school. Others argue that it lowers standards and prevents students from learning how to behave with their classmates.
>
> What is your position concerning home schooling? Write a letter to the editor of your local paper stating your position. Provide support for your argument.

SAMPLE RESPONSE

I have had many conversations about whether students should be home schooled. Although I know others may disagree, I support home schooling.

The first reason I suport home schooling. It allows for differnt types of learning. Parents are able to teach their kids in whatever way they want to. I, for one, like to learn through field trips. My field trip to the aquarium was one of the funnest times I've had in a long time.

The second reason is that there are so many students in a class, some get lost in the crowd. Kids who need the most help misbehave and this hurts their learning. With home schooling, parents can spend more time with their kids. We need to let students learn at their own pace.

I realize many people don't think home schooling is a good idea because they say that students won't learn how to work with others. Maybe so, but the good outweighs the bad. Besides, students would be learning to work with their parents. This is a more valuable skill.

In conclusion, I understand why so many people are against home schooling, but I think it is a good option anyway.

Scored Writing Samples, continued

Looking at Score 3

━━━━━━━━━━━━━━━━━━━━━━━━━━━━━━━━━━━━━━

Purpose

The purpose is stated clearly in the introduction.

Audience

The language and reasons are appropriate to the audience.

Support

The first reason is strong and fairly well supported, although the example is a bit of a digression.

The second reason is well stated, although the support is not as clearly stated as it could be.

The essay would be improved by the inclusion of a third reason.

The writer addresses an opposing argument.

Structure

The paper includes a clearly stated introduction and a conclusion. The conclusion would be more effective if it included a summary of the writer's reasons for his or her opinion.

Each argument is presented in a separate, cohesive paragraph. The writer uses some transitions to connect the paragraphs.

Fluency

The writer varies sentence structure and length and uses some persuasive language. Occasional sentence fragments and misspellings interrupt the fluency of the writing.

Scored Writing Samples, continued

Score 4 (highest score)

PROMPT

Home schooling is more popular than ever before. Taught at home by their parents, children may learn from textbooks, field trips, and other real life situations. Some people say home schooling protects children from the dangers and distractions of school. Others argue that it lowers standards and prevents students from learning how to behave with their classmates.

What is your position concerning home schooling? Write a letter to the editor of your local paper stating your position. Provide support for your argument.

SAMPLE RESPONSE

As an eighth grader in a public school, I am concerned about today's classroom conditions. While I agree that the lessons learned in school are valuable, many kids would do better in a home schooling situation. I believe the benefits would outweigh the costs.

The first reason I support home schooling is that it allows parents the freedom to teach what they want to. Parents know their kids better than anyone. Parents don't have to rely on textbooks. They can create real life learning experiences built around their children's natural interests. This means that children will want to learn.

Home schooling works for another reason. Parents can teach kids at their own pace. It is no secret that many of today's classrooms are overcrowded. Kids with learning problems and kids who excel often get lost in the crowd. Low achieving students become frustrated and they decide they don't like learning. High performance kids often become bored because the class is moving too slow. With home schooling, parents can provide individualized attention.

Finally, I think one of the best arguments for home schooling is that it prevents kids from having to deal with peer pressure. Many kids aren't strong enough to turn away from the influence of other students. Home schooling gives those kids more time to develop the skills they need to become strong and healthy adults. Although some might say that school gives kids the skills necessary to deal with the pressures of drugs and violence, I disagree. I think parents can teach these lessons better at home.

At first glance, home schooling seems like an unfair solution, but it is not. Kids do better when they learn at their own pace in a calm, safe environment. They should be protected while they're young, so that they will grow into healthy, productive adults. I think the lessons learned in school can be learned just as well at home.

Looking at Score 4

Purpose

The purpose is stated clearly in the introductory paragraph. The writer identifies herself as one who is invested in the outcome of this issue.

Audience

The writer uses language and reasons appropriate for readers of a newspaper editorial.

Support

Throughout the essay the author's reasons are directly stated and supported with facts and details. The writer acknowledges opposing views and argues her points effectively.

Structure

This essay is well-organized. The author moves from one point to the next and directs the reader to each point. She includes a strong introduction, good transitions and sequence of ideas, and a strong conclusion.

Fluency

The author demonstrates a mastery of standard English usage. Her sentences vary in length and structure. She helps the reader follow her ideas by using transitional words and phrases.

COMPOSITION PRACTICE: INFORMATIVE WRITING (CLASSIFICATION)
Guided Writing Practice

Writing Prompt

> There are good things and bad things about having to do weekly chores.
>
> Write a composition for your teacher explaining both what is good about having to do chores and what is bad about it. Be sure to write about your ideas in detail.

In previous exercises you completed the first two steps in responding to the prompt—(1) identifying the subject, audience, and purpose of the writing, and (2) exploring ideas and planning the composition. In this section, you will complete these steps for the writing prompt about weekly chores, and develop your ideas and details into an essay, using the skills you have reviewed.

IDENTIFYING YOUR SUBJECT, AUDIENCE, AND PURPOSE

List the subject, audience, and purpose of your writing in response to the prompt shown here. Use a separate sheet of paper if necessary.

Subject: _____

Audience: _____

Purpose: _____

EXPLORING IDEAS AND PLANNING YOUR WRITING

On the following lines list the main idea of your writing. Then, rewrite it in the form of a thesis statement. A thesis statement is not simply the main idea, topic, or title of your essay. Instead, it is a sentence or two that summarize the central, dominant idea *and* purpose of your writing. A thesis statement gives readers a preview of ideas and purposes so that they know where the writing is headed.

Main Idea: _____

_____

_____

Thesis Statement: _____

_____

_____

Guided Writing Practice, continued

CREATING LOGICAL ORGANIZATION AND PROVIDING ELABORATION

Providing elaboration

List your key points and plans for elaboration below. Use a separate sheet of paper if necessary.

Key Idea: _____

Elaboration: _____

_____

_____

_____

_____

_____

Key Idea: _____

Elaboration: _____

_____

_____

_____

Key Idea: _____

Elaboration: _____

_____

_____

_____

Now review each key point and the elaboration you have chosen and choose two to include in the body of your essay. Make sure your elaboration actually supports the key idea and that you have covered both sides of the issue.

CREATING LOGICAL ORGANIZATION AND PROVIDING ELABORATION

Now work on organizing your writing.

First, review your key ideas and decide how you want to arrange them. Group them in paragraphs by similar characteristics. Be sure to present both sides of the issue and that you support both sides with facts and examples.

Then, write an outline below that provides an overview of your essay. Use a separate sheet of paper if necessary.

DRAFTING YOUR WRITING—INTRODUCTION

Now you should begin writing a draft of your composition. Begin with an **introductory paragraph** that states the subject of your composition—in this case, good and bad things about doing chores. It's important to catch your audience's attention early, so try to include an interesting anecdote or fact that will make the reader want to keep reading. Your introductory paragraph also needs to include a thesis statement—a sentence or two that summarize the main idea and purpose of your essay.

Write a first draft of your introduction below. You might try drafting two or more introductions and then deciding which you think is more effective. Use a separate sheet of paper if necessary.

Introduction 1

Introduction 2

Guided Writing Practice, continued

DRAFTING YOUR WRITING—DEVELOPING KEY IDEAS

Continue working on your draft by **developing each of your key ideas** in order below. Use a separate sheet of paper if necessary. As you write, remember to do the following:

- Use language that is appropriate for your audience and purpose.

- Follow the rules of standard written English.

- Be sure your elaboration actually supports the key idea.

- Use appropriate transitions, such as *as a result, then, in contrast, for example, similarly,* and *furthermore* to connect ideas.

DRAFTING YOUR WRITING—CONCLUSION

Now, write a **concluding** paragraph for your composition. In the conclusion:

- restate the thesis of your essay in different words
- summarize the points you have made

Write a first draft of your conclusion on the lines below. Use a separate sheet of paper if necessary. You might need to draft several versions of your conclusion before you write one that satisfies you. Review the drafts of your conclusions and choose the one you like best.

Conclusion 1

Conclusion 2

Conclusion 3

Guided Writing Practice, continued

USING APPROPRIATE AND GRAMMATICALLY CORRECT LANGUAGE

Review the draft of your composition and pay close attention to the language you used. Correct any errors in usage, grammar, and mechanics. Check for mistakes in paragraph structure. Make sure you used language appropriate to your subject, audience, and purpose. Then, write the final version of your composition below. Use a separate sheet of paper if necessary.

COMPOSITION PRACTICE: INFORMATIVE WRITING (CLASSIFICATION)
Additional Prompts: Levels 6–8

Use the following prompts to complete the writing exercises in this book and to practice your composition skills.

There are good things and bad things about owning a home computer.

Write a composition for your teacher explaining both what is good about owning a home computer and what is bad about it. Be sure to write about your ideas in detail.

There are good things and bad things about being a boy or girl (choose one).

Write a composition for your teacher explaining both what is good about being a boy or girl (choose one) and what is bad about it. Be sure to write about your ideas in detail.

There are good things and bad things about owning a car.

Write a composition for your teacher explaining both what is good about owning a car and what is bad about it. Be sure to write about your ideas in detail.

There are good things and bad things about being an actor or actress.

Write a composition for your teacher explaining both what is good about being an actor or actress and what is bad about it. Be sure to write about your ideas in detail.

There are good things and bad things about being rich.

Write a composition for your teacher explaining both what is good about being rich and what is bad about it. Be sure to write about your ideas in detail.

For more informative writing prompts, visit our Web site: mcdougallittell.com.

COMPOSITION PRACTICE: INFORMATIVE WRITING (CLASSIFICATION)
Scored Writing Samples: How TAAS Compositions are Scored

TAAS compositions are scored *holistically*. In holistic scoring, graders take into account the overall effect of the content and delivery rather than focusing primarily on grammar, punctuation, and spelling. They expect grammar, punctuation, and spelling to be correct, but they are mainly concerned with how effectively the overall message comes across. To do this, they focus on how well each composition meets several specific objectives.

Scores range from 1 (low) to 4 (high), although an essay may receive a "0" if it is off topic, indecipherable, or presents insufficient information. Sample essays with scores of 1–4 appear on pages 115–122. After each essay, a section appears in which the scored sample is analyzed according to the standards described here.

BASIC CRITERIA FOR EVALUATION

Topic All TAAS essays must address the topic presented in the prompt. An essay that is off-topic will receive a score of 0, no matter how well it is written.

Purpose If a TAAS essay addresses the topic in the prompt but fails to meet the purpose, it will receive a score of 1, even if the writing is effective. The ability to meet the purpose of the prompt is one of the basic skills the TAAS assesses. The writer must present what is good and what is bad about the specified topic.

ADDITIONAL CRITERIA FOR EVALUATION

The chart below demonstrates the characteristics of each score.

Score 0	Score 1	Score 2	Score 3	Score 4
Off topic Blank paper	Incorrect purpose, audience, or type of writing	Correct purpose, audience, and type of writing	Correct purpose, audience, and type of writing	Correct purpose, audience, and type of writing
Foreign language	Brief or vague	Some elaboration	Moderately well elaborated	Effective elaboration
Illegible Incoherent	Insufficient support Rambling	Some details	Clear, effective language	Consistent organization
Not enough content to score	Lack of language control Poor organization	Gaps in organization Limited language control	Organized (perhaps with brief digressions)	Sense of completeness, fluency

STANDARDS FOR A SCORE 4 COMPOSITION

Purpose	Expresses clear explanations of both sides of an issue.
Audience	Uses language, tone, and reasons that appeal to an objective adult audience.
Support	Provides at least three reasons for each side. Supports reasons with adequate elaboration (details, examples, etc.). Addresses opposing arguments convincingly.
Structure	Arranges main ideas and support according to logical patterns. Includes an introduction, conclusion, and appropriate transitions.
Fluency	Includes good word choice and sentence variety. Exhibits control of language.

COMPOSITION PRACTICE: INFORMATIVE WRITING (CLASSIFICATION)
Student Self-Evaluation: An Informative Composition

The questions on this page will help you see how well your composition meets the objective the evaluators are likely to look for. Become familiar with them so you can use them to evaluate your essay during the TAAS.

The Prompt
1. Does your response meet all the requirements stated in the prompt? Have you stated your purpose clearly and supported it with details? Have you addressed both sides of the topic?
2. Have you addressed the audience appropriately?

Support
3. Do the reasons you offer really support your key ideas?
4. Will your audience find your points convincing?
5. Have you stated your reasons clearly?
6. Have you elaborated on your main points?
7. Have you supported your points with sufficient facts, examples, quotations, and other details?
8. Have you presented and developed both sides of the topic?
9. Is your reasoning sound? Have you avoided faulty logic?

Order and Arrangement
10. Have you included a strong introduction?
11. Have you included a strong conclusion?
12. Are the points well organized and arranged in a logical order?

Word Choice
13. Is the language of your essay appropriate for your audience?
14. Have you used precise, vivid words and persuasive language?

Fluency
15. Have you used sentences of varying lengths and structures?
16. Have you connected ideas with transitions and other devices?
17. Have you used correct spelling, punctuation, and grammar?

WRITING SAMPLES (SCORES 1–4)
Score 1 (lowest score)

PROMPT

> There are good things and bad things about owning a dog.
>
> Write a composition for your teacher explaining both what is good about owning a dog and what is bad about it. Be sure to write about your ideas in detail.

SAMPLE RESPONSE

Dog's are good to have from when you are little. One good thing is that its fun. Another good thing is that it keeps you company. There are some bad things about owning a dog like dogs can be a pain. There is a lot of stuff to clean up after it.

I like the good things about owning a dog. You know you can have a lot of fun and I like that. I like the other things about a dog like it keeps you company.

But there are some things about owning a dog like dog are messy and a lot of people don't want to clean up after him.

So in conclusion, there are a lot of good things about owning a dog and a lot of bad things about owning a dog.

Scored Writing Samples, continued

Looking at Score 1

Purpose

The purpose is stated as "Dogs are good to have from when you are little." The author does not state that she will present both the good and bad things about having a dog.

Audience

The language and tone are informal. The statement "dogs can be a pain" is not appropriate for a formal essay.

Support

The writer presents a few general points (dogs are fun, they keep you company, they can be messy) at the beginning of the response but then simply repeats them, adding little information. This repetition weakens the logical progression of thought.

Structure

The letter lacks clearly defined paragraphs which state and support both sides of the issue. The writer does not organize the body of the essay by sorting information into groups based on qualities or characteristics. The conclusion fails to summarize the main points. The letter also lacks transitions to connect ideas.

Fluency

The effectiveness of the essay is further limited by numerous errors in spelling, grammar, and mechanics. Some sentences are run-on, and others are fragments.

Score 2

PROMPT

> There are good things and bad things about owning a dog.
>
> Write a composition for your teacher explaining both what is good about owning a dog and what is bad about it. Be sure to write about your ideas in detail.

SAMPLE RESPONSE

Have you ever thought about bying a dog? Having a dog can have its good and bad points. If you want to have a dog, you have to be responsible. I am sure there are some things I must clarify before you think about getting a dog.

First, one of the good things about dogs is that you always have someone to play with. You are never alone. The fact is that most dogs don't care about the weather. You can play outside on a snowy day in December or on a rainy Summer morning. A dog will even run beside you if you need help getting in shape. A dog can be your very own Personal traner. But as you know, good things can turn bad.

One of the bad things about dogs is that dogs can bite. No one likes a dog that bites. Especially me

You have the internal power to decide if you are ready for a dog. After writing this I have decided not to get a dog. With this in mind, you should recieve enough information to see both good and bad things about having a dog. I hope my assistance has helped you.

Looking at Score 2

Purpose

The introduction states the writer's purpose. She states that she will present both the good and bad things about having a dog.

Audience

The reasons and language are generally appropriate for the audience.

Support

The writer achieves minimal success by presenting a number of ideas (you can have fun with a dog, you always have someone to play with, dogs can bite you), some of which are specifically extended but only one of which is somewhat elaborated (dogs don't care about the weather). The writer doesn't elaborate about the bad points of having a dog.

Structure

Although the response is controlled and organized, the level of elaboration is list-like.

Fluency

The grammar is correct but there are several errors in spelling and punctuation.

Score 3

PROMPT

> There are good things and bad things about owning a dog.
>
> Write a composition for your teacher explaining both what is good about owning a dog and what is bad about it. Be sure to write about your ideas in detail.

SAMPLE RESPONSE

Have you ever dreamt of having a dog? I have always wondered what it would be like to have a furry friend by my side at all times. Still, I suppose there are good and bad things about owning a dog.

Some good things are that dogs are lifetime companions who will protect you. Your never alone. Wherever you go, you can always feel safe if your dog is at your side. And you'll be able to go more places at more times. For example, you can go for a walk at night or play Frisbee in the rain because dogs don't care about the time of day or the weather. They are just happy to be with you. Also, dogs can also save lives. I read about an elderly woman who had a stroke. Her dog barked until someone called for help. Yet with all the protection a dog can offer you, something else may come along as well.

Having a dog can have bad points. Sure there's the protection, but a dog might go overboard and bite someone who isnt really trying to hurt you. What if your just wrestling with your friend? Your dog might think you are in danger and he might attack your friend. Your frend could sue you and you'd have to pay for the hospital bills. This would be a very hard situation because you could lose the dog and the friend at the same time. This would not be an easy situation for anyone.

I suppose that having a dog has its "up-sides" and "down-sides" but everything else in life does too. Yet, if I had to choose between having a dog and not having one, I would definitely go for the dog.

Looking at Score 3

Purpose

The introduction states the writer's purpose.

Audience

The reasons and language are generally appropriate for the audience.

Support

The writer develops two moderately supported main ideas (dogs offer protection, dogs can be dangerous). She includes supporting details that are concise and specific.

Structure

The response is controlled and well organized because the writer moves smoothly from one idea to the next. The first paragraph about protection is a good example of this development and control. Overall, this response is a good attempt to present what is good and bad about having a dog.

Fluency

The grammar is correct but there are some errors in spelling and punctuation. This does not represent a "polished" piece of writing.

Score 4 (highest score)

PROMPT

> There are good things and bad things about owning a dog.
>
> Write a composition for your teacher explaining both what is good about owning a dog and what is bad about it. Be sure to write about your ideas in detail.

SAMPLE RESPONSE

Many people believe that owning a dog is all fun and games, but the animal many call "man's best friend" can cause problems as well.

Imagine this. You want to go running. It's dark out. You look around outside. You've made a commitment to yourself to run every day. But is your safety worth the risk? Well, one good way to get around this is to get a dog. For decades, television has celebrated dogs like Lassie who save the day by helping their owners solve crimes, do chores, and generally feel better. This isn't so far from reality. Dogs help you take care of yourself both physically and mentally. Running with a dog provides a good cardiovascular workout and you don't even have to worry about safety if you choose to run at night. A dog is like a personal protection service. Instead of an alarm which robbers might know how to disengage, a dog simply has to do what is natural, and that's bark. There have been many stories over the years about dogs who saved their owners' lives. For example, just last month in my neighborhood, a Doberman pinscher cornered two teenagers who broke into an elderly neighbor's basement. Dogs have other advantages as well. They can give you love and affection. Studies with the elderly have shown that people do better when they have something to love. Just ask any dog owner—only a dog can look up at you with wet brown eyes and lick your wounds when you're feeling blue.

While dogs can enrich your life, they can also make it more difficult. Dogs, like children, cost a lot of money. There are required visits to the veterinarian, costly shots, and check ups. There are also injuries and illnesses that involve operations, medicines, and boarding at kennels. Each of these things costs more than you'd think and very few people carry pet insurance to cover the costs. More money goes to dog food, shampoos, sprays, and grooming costs. Then, there can be damage to your property or to the property of others. Dogs are notorious for chewing up shoes, carpeting, furniture, and lawns. Can you imagine getting ready for a party and finding that your brand new leather boots are ripped to shreds? Your crooked canine might be crouching under the table, but the cute wide-eyed expression won't pay for what has been ruined. Further, if your dog bites another dog or person, you are responsible. Hospital bills are high and people are generally unwilling to let this serious situation fall to the wayside. You are the owner. You have to pay.

So having a dog can bring both good things and bad things. I feel that the good things outweigh the bad things when I think about all the advantages of having a dog. Would you enjoy having "man's best friend" at your side?

Looking at Score 4

Purpose

The introduction states the writer's purpose.

Audience

The reasons and language are generally appropriate for the audience.

Support

This thorough response is characterized by well-developed reasons that offer a thoughtful perspective (the elderly do better when they have something to love). In addition, particularly apt word choices contribute to the richness of the details (Your crooked canine might be crouching under the table, but the cute wide-eyed expression won't pay for what has been ruined.)

Structure

The response is controlled and well organized. The writer achieves a sense of order and completeness by presenting specifically elaborated ideas. The organizational strategy provides a clear link between ideas.

Fluency

The grammar is correct with few errors in spelling and punctuation. This represents a "polished" piece of writing.

Anticipating TAAS 2003

Changes to TAAS

The state assessment program in Texas is changing as a result of Senate Bill 103, which was passed during the 1999 legislative session. Both the schedule and the content of the tests will be changing.

New TAAS tests will be administered beginning in the 2002–2003 school year for grades 6–11. The main purpose of the content changes is for the TAAS to more closely reflect the TEKS. The new TAAS test will have new objectives that are expected to encompass a greater portion of the TEKS. However, the final TAAS objectives have not been approved as of this printing. You will see some new lessons in this sampler that reflect content, such as the viewing and representing TEKS, that is not currently tested on the TAAS test but which may be tested in the future.

Students who are in eighth grade in the 2000–2001 school year—the Class of 2005—will be the first students who are required to pass the revised Exit Level TAAS test before they graduate. Beginning in 2003, the Writing test will be given in seventh grade instead of eighth. Students who are in sixth grade in the 2001–2002 school year—the Class of 2006—will be required to take the new Writing test when they are in seventh grade, the following year. The chart below shows which tests will be given to students in grades 6–8 for the next few years.

School Year	Class of 2005 (8th Graders 2000–2001)	Class of 2006 (7th Graders 2000–2001)	Class of 2007 (6th Graders 2000–2001)	Class of 2008 (5th Graders 2000–2001)
2000–2001	**Grade:** 8 **Test:** Grade 8 TAAS—Reading, Writing, Mathematics, Social Studies, Science	**Grade:** 7 **Test:** Grade 7 TAAS—Reading, Mathematics	**Grade:** 6 **Test:** Grade 6 TAAS—Reading, Mathematics	
2001–2002		**Grade:** 8 **Test:** Grade 8 TAAS—Reading, Writing, Mathematics, Social Studies, Science	**Grade:** 7 **Test:** Grade 7 TAAS—Reading, Mathematics	**Grade:** 6 **Test:** Grade 6 TAAS—Reading, Mathematics
2002–2003			**Grade:** 8 **Test:** New Grade 8 Assessment (S.B. 103)—Reading, Mathematics, Social Studies	**Grade:** 7 **Test:** New Grade 7 Assessment (S.B. 103)—Reading, Writing, Mathematics
2003–2004				**Grade:** 8 **Test:** New Grade 8 Assessment (S.B. 103)—Reading, Mathematics, Social Studies

Preparing for TAAS 2003

The materials on the following pages can help you to review and strengthen several skills that may be tested on the new TAAS, including speaking and listening skills, viewing and representing skills, business writing, and interpretive writing. From time to time, visit our Web site at mcdougallittell.com for updated TAAS preparation materials and to learn about the new tests.

Name _____ Date _____

Interpreting a Speaker's Message

You can interpret a speaker's message by becoming an active listener.

Understanding the Skill
In order to convey a message effectively and to emphasize certain ideas, speakers use **nonverbal** and **verbal** cues. Some nonverbal and verbal cues are written below.

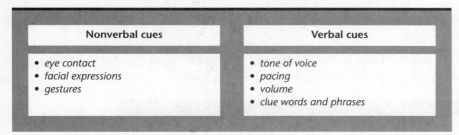

Nonverbal cues	Verbal cues
• eye contact • facial expressions • gestures	• tone of voice • pacing • volume • clue words and phrases

A. Use these strategies before, during, and after listening to help you interpret a speaker's message.

Before Listening

- **Determine your purpose.** Are you listening to enjoy or appreciate something, to gain information, to understand another's point of view, or to solve a problem?

- **Know your barriers.** What do you already know about the speaker? Do you have opinions that prevent you from keeping an open mind?

- **Block out distractions and focus on the speaker.** Keep your eyes and attention on the speaker.

During Listening

- **Listen for the main ideas and restate them in your own words.** Which ideas are presented first or last? Which are repeated several times? Which are presented in a loud voice or with forceful gestures? Note statements such as "My point is…"

- **Look for relationships between ideas.** Look for words that indicate comparisons and contrasts, such as *similarly, but* and *on the other hand.* Pay attention to words that indicate causes and effects, such as: *because, if… then,* and *as a result.*

- **Read body language.** How does the speaker use body language to emphasize a point? What effect does this have on the message?

After Listening

- **Ask questions for clarification.** Ask for explanations of points that confuse you. Indicate if you don't agree with something or if you need more information.

- **Draw conclusions and make judgments.** Do you agree with the speaker? Why or why not?

B. Make a chart to help you keep track of what you hear and your thoughts about it.

Before Listening	
• barriers	*I don't like dogs. I was bitten by a dog once. This might be a barrier. I need to keep an open mind if I am to learn anything new.*
During Listening	
• relationships	*Dogs need exercise, therefore, dogs should be allowed in the park without a leash.*
After Listening	
• questions	*Is dog exercise more important than safety from dog bites?*

C. Practice active listening as your teacher reads a speech about dogs.

Practicing the Skill: Levels 6–8

GUIDELINES FOR INTERPRETING A SPEAKER'S MESSAGE

■ Block out distractions and know your own barriers.

■ Identify the speaker's nonverbal and verbal cues and notice how they affect the message.

■ Look for the relationships between ideas.

■ Look for the main idea and restate it in your own words.

■ Ask questions to clarify ideas.

Apply what you have learned. Refer to the guidelines above as you complete the exercise. Use a separate sheet of paper if you need more room.

Listen as your teacher reads a speech. Notice the verbal and nonverbal cues to identify the speaker's message and draw conclusions about it. Fill out the chart below as you listen.

Before Listening	
• *purpose*	
• *barriers*	
During Listening	
• *main idea*	
• *nonverbal cues*	
• *verbal cues*	
• *comparisons*	
After Listening	
• *questions*	
• *conclusions*	
• *causes*	

SPEAKING AND LISTENING SKILLS PRACTICE
Distinguishing Between a Speaker's Opinion and Fact

Understanding the Skill

When you listen to a speech, it is important that you are able to tell which statements are facts and which are opinions. Use the chart to guide you.

Facts	Opinions
• *events*	• *judgments*
• *dates*	• *beliefs*
• *statistics*	• *feelings of the writer or speaker*
• *statements that can be proved*	• *cannot be proved*
• *can be checked for accuracy*	

Distinguish between a speaker's opinion and fact. The following passage describes a fear of public speaking. Think about which statements are opinions and which are facts.

SPEAKING TO YOUR FEAR

In a famous study, 80% of those interviewed named public speaking as their biggest fear. Researchers have compiled a list of symptoms that often accompany this fear. Symptoms include sweaty palms, increased heart rate, nervous jitters, and nausea. Some people also report feeling "spacey" while others find they cannot stop laughing. Laughing is the worst symptom because it's so embarrassing.

In the last ten years, many special programs and classes have been developed to help people overcome their fear of public speaking. If a person can't get over this fear, he or she isn't trying hard enough. How do I know this? Because I myself have done it! In 1996, I overcame my fear of public speaking. Getting over the fear is actually easy. The truth is, I never thought that entertaining a crowd with jokes and stories could actually be fun, but it is!

Facts: Look for specific names, dates, statistics, and statements that can be proved.

Opinions: Look for judgment and signal words used to describe people or events. These words often indicate the writer's opinions rather than factual information.

Organize facts and opinions in a chart.

Facts	Opinions
• *In a famous study, 80% of those interviewed named public speaking as their biggest fear.*	• *Laughing is the worst symptom, because it's so embarrassing.*
• *Symptoms include sweaty palms, increased heart rate, nervous jitters, and nausea.*	• *If a person can't get over this fear, he or she isn't trying hard enough.*
• *In the last ten years, many special programs and classes have been developed to help people overcome this fear.*	• *Getting over the fear is actually easy.*
• *In 1996, I overcame my fear of public speaking.*	

Practicing the Skill: Levels 6–8

GUIDELINES FOR DISTINGUISHING BETWEEN A SPEAKER'S OPINION AND FACT:

■ Listen for specific names, dates, statistics, and statements that can be proved.

■ Not the speaker's assertions, claims, hypotheses, and judgments.

■ Listen for judgment words used to describe people and events.

■ Use a chart to organize facts and opinions.

Apply what you have learned. Refer to the guidelines above as you complete the exercises. Use a separate sheet of paper if you need more room.

A. Listen as your teacher reads about an important author. Pay attention to distinguishing fact and opinion. Fill out the chart below as you listen.

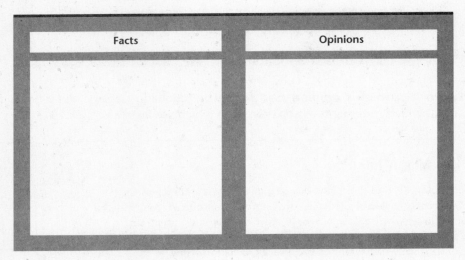

Facts	Opinions

B. Use the notes you made in your chart to answer the questions.

1. Name at least three facts in the passage.

_____

_____

_____

2. Identify two opinions or judgments the writer has made.

_____

_____

3. Name some judgment words the writer has used to describe persons or events.

_____

_____

VIEWING AND REPRESENTING SKILLS PRACTICE
Interpreting and Analyzing Advertisements

All advertisements seek to influence you, or affect how you think about something. Images and words you see in a newspaper or magazine ad have been carefully chosen to appeal to a **target audience**, a specific group of consumers. While parts of most advertisements are fair and factual, some contain messages that are **biased**, or unfairly weighted toward one point of view. Others use **loaded language**—words that have strong positive or negative feelings attached to them.

Interpreting and analyzing advertising means looking for the feeling, image, or idea that a company or group is trying to "sell" you. Political ads want to "sell" you on their ideas or their candidate, while consumer ads want to sell you a product. Smart consumers are able to separate the feeling from the product itself before they choose whether to buy.

Understanding the Skill

Step 1: Identify underlying messages and draw conclusions from the text. Examine the words and images in the advertisement below. Then draw conclusions based on what they represent.

Evaluate the sponsor What do you know about this company?

Determine the purpose Advertisements are intended to sway an audience. This ad tries to get you to eat at Birthday Burger.

Look for associations the ad wants you to make Determine the feeling or image the company is trying to sell you. Are the messages based on fact or opinion? Do they use loaded language?

Recognize the methods used to achieve the purpose Large type and images grab your attention, while the company might want you to overlook the small type. This ad also features a time-sensitive coupon, which implies that you should rush in to get the most savings.

Identify the target audience In this ad, pictures of children identify the target audience. The coupon probably appeals to parents.

Step 2: Make a chart. In the chart, list the language or images used in the ad and the associations you can draw from them.

Images and Words	Target Audience	Associations
illustration of kids with party hats eating at Birthday Burger	children	fun, happy, friends, celebration **Message:** You'll be happy if you eat at Birthday Burger.
"Where It's Your Birthday Every Day"	children	special day, birthday **Message:** You'll feel special if you eat at Birthday Burger.
coupon	parents of children	discount, save money, good deal **Message:** You'll save money if you buy these burgers soon, so don't pass up the deal.

Practicing the Skill: Level 6

GUIDELINES FOR ANALYZING ADVERTISEMENTS:

- Determine the purpose of the ad.
- Identify the target audience.
- Identify loaded language and bias.
- Evaluate the sponsor.

- Recognize the methods used to sell the product.
- Use a chart to analyze images, words and their associations, and hidden messages.

Apply what you have learned. Refer to the guidelines above as you analyze the following advertisement.

A. For the following advertisement, write the types of images and words used as well as their associations. Then make an inference about the target audience. Use a chart to organize your thoughts. Record your answers on a separate sheet of paper.

1. Who is the sponsor and what is the purpose of the ad?
2. Who is the target audience?
3. What are some examples of loaded or biased language?
4. What methods does the sponsor use to sell the product or service?
5. List any examples of association the ad might be conveying.

B. Copy the chart onto your own paper. Use your answers to the questions above to fill in the chart.

Images and Words	Target Audience	Associations

Practicing the Skill: Level 7

GUIDELINES FOR ANALYZING ADVERTISEMENTS:

- Determine the purpose of the ad.
- Identify the target audience.
- Identify loaded language and bias.
- Evaluate the sponsor.

- Recognize the methods used to sell the product.
- Use a chart to analyze images, words and their associations, and hidden messages.

Apply what you have learned. Refer to the guidelines above as you analyze the following advertisement.

A. For the following advertisement, write the types of images and words used as well as their associations. Then make an inference about the target audience. Use a chart to organize your thoughts. Record your answers on a separate sheet of paper.

1. Who is the sponsor and what is the purpose of the ad?
2. Who is the target audience?
3. What are some examples of loaded or biased language?
4. What methods does the sponsor use to sell the product or service?
5. List any examples of association the ad might be conveying.

B. Copy the chart onto your own paper. Use your answers to the questions above to fill in the chart.

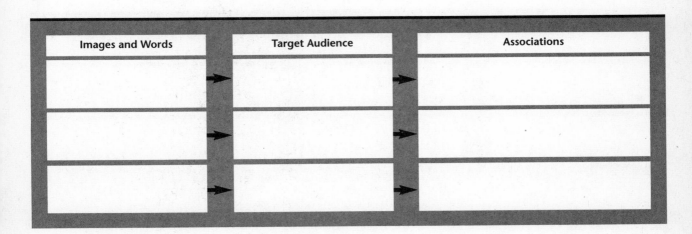

Images and Words	Target Audience	Associations

Practicing the Skill: Level 8

GUIDELINES FOR ANALYZING ADVERTISEMENTS:

- Determine the purpose of the ad.
- Identify the target audience.
- Identify loaded language and bias.
- Evaluate the sponsor.

- Recognize the methods used to sell the product.
- Use a chart to analyze images, words and their associations, and hidden messages.

Apply what you have learned. Refer to the guidelines above as you analyze the following advertisement.

A. For the following advertisement, write the types of images and words used as well as their associations. Then make an inference about the target audience. Use a chart to organize your thoughts. Record your answers on a separate sheet of paper.

1. Who is the sponsor and what is the purpose of the ad?
2. Who is the target audience?
3. What are some examples of loaded or biased language?
4. What methods does the sponsor use to sell the product or service?
5. List any examples of association the ad might be conveying.

B. Copy the chart onto your own paper. Use your answers to the questions above to fill in the chart.

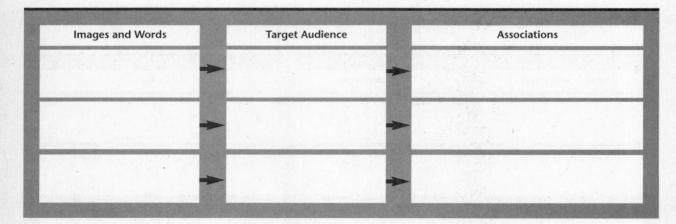

Images and Words	Target Audience	Associations

COMPOSITION PRACTICE: BUSINESS WRITING (LETTER)
Guided Writing Practice

Writing Prompt

You and your family are going on a trip for two weeks. You have hired someone to come to your home to take care of a pet while you are away. Write a business letter to the pet sitter in which you explain one of the jobs the sitter must do.

In previous exercises you completed the first two steps in responding to the prompt—(1) identifying the subject, audience, and purpose of the writing, and (2) exploring ideas and planning the composition. In this section, you will complete similar steps for the business writing prompt, and develop your ideas into a business letter, using the skills you have reviewed.

IDENTIFYING YOUR SUBJECT, AUDIENCE, AND PURPOSE

List the subject, audience, and purpose of your writing in response to the prompt shown here. Consult your work from page 76 of this workbook. Use a separate sheet of paper if necessary.

Subject: _____

Audience: _____

Purpose: _____

FOCUSING YOUR BUSINESS LETTER

On the following lines write a clear statement of your topic in which you identify the process you will describe. When you describe a process, remember to focus on a single activity. Present the steps in logical order, and use transitional words to signal the start of each new step.

Topic Sentence: _____

_____

_____

CREATING LOGICAL ORGANIZATION AND PROVIDING ELABORATION

Providing elaboration

List the steps you will discuss and your plans for elaboration below. Consult your work from pages 82–83 of this workbook. Use a separate sheet of paper if necessary.

Step: _____

_____

_____

Materials: _____

_____

_____

Step: _____

_____

_____

Materials: _____

_____

_____

Step: _____

_____

_____

Materials: _____

_____

_____

Now review each step and the materials you have chosen to make sure you have not left anything out.

CREATING LOGICAL ORGANIZATION (continued)

Now work on organizing your writing.

Use a flow chart to organize your writing. Here is an example of a flow chart one student made to organize a letter about how to take a phone message.

How to take a phone message

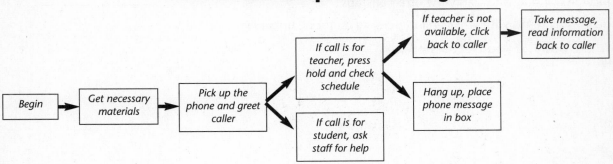

Look at the example. Then, use the steps you outlined on page 134 to make your own flow chart. Show all the steps you want the pet sitter to do.

Draw your flow chart here.

DRAFTING YOUR WRITING

For the body of the letter, you will want to present the rest of the steps in order from first to last. Be sure to explain any confusing points. Include examples and provide transitions between steps.

- list all materials needed
- write each step listed in your flow chart
- add any details needed to explain the step
- include transitions to clarify the order of steps
- define any terms with which your audience might be unfamiliar

Draft the body of your letter here.

Guided Writing Practice, continued

DRAFTING YOUR WRITING, CONTINUED

Write an introductory paragraph to identify the purpose of the letter and the process you will describe.

Include any background information, such as when or why someone might use this process.

Add a conclusion. If appropriate, summarize the process and describe the outcome or final product.

DRAFTING YOUR WRITING, CONTINUED

Business letters are more formal than friendly letters, and they usually require a precise form. For instance, you should use a colon after the salutation. See the example below.

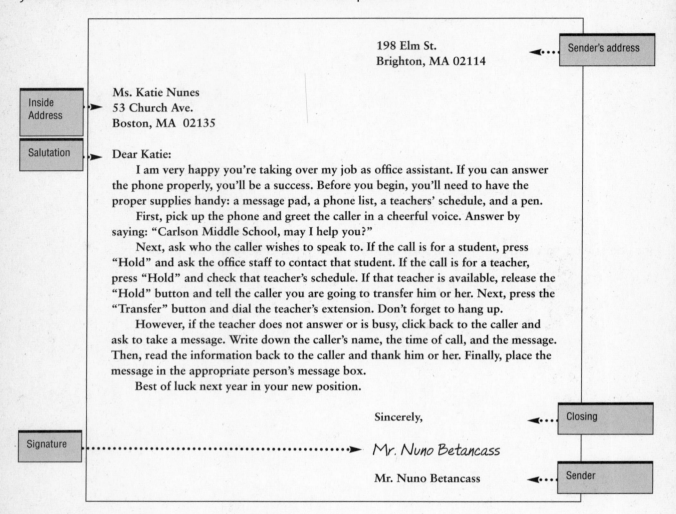

198 Elm St.
Brighton, MA 02114

Sender's address

Inside Address

Ms. Katie Nunes
53 Church Ave.
Boston, MA 02135

Salutation

Dear Katie:

I am very happy you're taking over my job as office assistant. If you can answer the phone properly, you'll be a success. Before you begin, you'll need to have the proper supplies handy: a message pad, a phone list, a teachers' schedule, and a pen.

First, pick up the phone and greet the caller in a cheerful voice. Answer by saying: "Carlson Middle School, may I help you?"

Next, ask who the caller wishes to speak to. If the call is for a student, press "Hold" and ask the office staff to contact that student. If the call is for a teacher, press "Hold" and check that teacher's schedule. If that teacher is available, release the "Hold" button and tell the caller you are going to transfer him or her. Next, press the "Transfer" button and dial the teacher's extension. Don't forget to hang up.

However, if the teacher does not answer or is busy, click back to the caller and ask to take a message. Write down the caller's name, the time of call, and the message. Then, read the information back to the caller and thank him or her. Finally, place the message in the appropriate person's message box.

Best of luck next year in your new position.

Sincerely,

Closing

Signature

Mr. Nuno Betancass

Mr. Nuno Betancass

Sender

Write your letter in proper business form. Use the paragraphs and ideas you developed on pages 136 and 137. Use a separate sheet of paper if you need more space.

USING APPROPRIATE AND GRAMMATICALLY CORRECT LANGUAGE

Review the draft of your composition and pay close attention to the language you used. Correct any errors in usage, grammar, and mechanics. Check for mistakes in paragraph structure. Make sure you used language appropriate to your subject, audience, and purpose. Then, write the final version of your composition below and on the back of this page. Use a separate sheet of paper if necessary.

COMPOSITION PRACTICE: BUSINESS WRITING (LETTER)
Additional Prompts: Levels 6–8

Use the following prompts to complete the writing exercises in this book and to practice your composition skills.

> You are in charge of sending out directions to your school's spring musical. Write a business letter to a local photographer explaining how to get to your school auditorium and where to park.

> You are in charge of organizing a group camping trip. Write a business letter to parents explaining how to help their children pack for the trip. Explain the process in your letter.

> You are applying for financial aid to attend a sports camp. You need to prove you are a good candidate. In your business letter, show that you deserve the scholarship by explaining how you go about training for your favorite sport every day.

> A cooking magazine is looking for recipes and baking instructions. You want your idea to be published. Write a business letter in which you explain how to make your favorite food.

> You have been appointed Master Mentor at your school's computer lab. Part of your job is to write instructions for other students, explaining how to use the computers, printers, and software. Choose one task, and write a letter to other students explaining how to complete the task.

COMPOSITION PRACTICE: BUSINESS WRITING (LETTER)

Scoring Guide: How TAAS Compositions are Scored

TAAS compositions are scored *holistically*. In holistic scoring, graders take into account the overall effect of the content and delivery rather than focusing primarily on grammar, punctuation, and spelling. They expect grammar, punctuation, and spelling to be correct, but they are mainly concerned with how effectively the overall message comes across. To do this, they focus on how well each composition meets several specific objectives.

Scores range from 1 (low) to 4 (high), although an essay may receive a "0" if it is off topic, indecipherable, or presents insufficient information.

BASIC CRITERIA FOR EVALUATION

Topic All TAAS essays must address the topic presented in the prompt. An essay that is off-topic will receive a score of 0, no matter how well it is written.

Purpose If a TAAS essay addresses the topic in the prompt but fails to meet the purpose, it will receive a score of 1, even if the writing is effective. The ability to meet the purpose of the prompt is one of the basic skills the TAAS assesses. The following questions will help determine whether the student has addressed purpose effectively:

- Does the writer follow the correct form of a business letter?
- Does the writer focus on and describe one process?
- Does the writer include all the steps and list them in an organized and logical way?
- Does the writer provide necessary details and transitions between ideas?

ADDITIONAL CRITERIA FOR EVALUATION

The chart below demonstrates the characteristics of each score.

Score 0	Score 1	Score 2	Score 3	Score 4
Off topic Blank paper	Incorrect purpose, audience, or type of writing	Correct purpose, audience, and type of writing	Correct purpose, audience, and type of writing	Correct purpose, audience, and type of writing
Foreign language	Brief or vague	Some elaboration	Moderately well elaborated	Effective elaboration
Illegible, Incoherent	Rambling	Some details	Clear, effective language	Consistent organization
Not enough content to score	Lack of language control Poor organization	Gaps in organization Limited language control	Organized (perhaps with brief digressions)	Sense of completeness, fluency

STANDARDS FOR A SCORE 4 COMPOSITION

Purpose	Names a process and clearly explains it.
Audience	Uses language, tone, and reasons that appeal to the specified audience.
Support	Provides several logical steps. Supports steps with adequate elaboration (details, examples, etc.).
Structure	Arranges main ideas and support according to logical patterns. Includes an introduction, conclusion, and appropriate transitions.
Fluency	Includes good word choice and sentence variety. Exhibits control of language.

Student Self-Evaluation: A Business Letter

The questions on this page will help you see how well your composition meets the objective the evaluators are likely to look for. Become familiar with them so you can use them to evaluate your essay during the TAAS.

The Prompt

1. Does your response meet all the requirements stated in the prompt? Have you stated your topic clearly?

2. Have you addressed the audience appropriately?

3. Does your letter use the proper form for a business letter?

Elaboration

4. Will your audience find your process description easy to follow?

5. Have you listed all needed materials?

6. Have you stated the steps clearly?

7. Have you explained and elaborated unfamiliar terms or confusing points?

Order and Arrangement

8. Have you included a strong opening statement that identifies the process you describe?

9. Have you included a closing statement?

10. Are the points well-organized and arranged in a logical order?

Word Choice

11. Is the language of your letter appropriate for your audience?

12. Have you used precise, vivid words?

Fluency

13. Have you used sentences of varying length and structures?

14. Have you connected ideas with transitions and other devices?

COMPOSITION PRACTICE: INTERPRETIVE WRITING (POETRY)
Guided Writing Practice

Writing Prompt

Interpreting literature means reading between the lines to discover what message the writer wishes to communicate. Before you can write about a piece of literature, you need to first analyze how the poem's sound and images create impressions in the readers' mind. In this section, you will analyze a writing prompt about a poem and develop your ideas and details into an essay.

> ## THE HURRICANE
>
> When the hurricane unfolds
> Its fierce accordion of winds,
> On the tip of its toes,
> Agile dancer, it sweeps whirling
> Over the carpeted surface of the sea
> With the scattered branches of the palm.
>
> —Pales Matos, Translated by Alida Malkus

Write an interpretive essay in which you analyze this poem.

IDENTIFYING YOUR SUBJECT, AUDIENCE, AND PURPOSE

List the subject, audience, and purpose of your writing in response to the prompt shown here. Use a separate sheet of paper if necessary.

Subject: _____

Audience: _____

Purpose: _____

IDENTIFYING POETIC ELEMENTS

Imagery, or words that appeal to the five senses, and figurative language both contribute to the message. Figurative language includes comparisons such as metaphor, simile, and personification. Sound devices such as rhyme, rhythm, and repetition can create a certain "music" or feeling. The form and the speaker, or "voice" from whom the words come, also affect the message.

To help you interpret a poem, first make a chart that shows the imagery, figurative language, sound devices, form, and speaker and the words or phrases that convey the meaning. Use your own paper if you need more space. (For information on poetic elements, refer to *The Language of Literature*.)

	Words/Phrases	Represents	Message
Imagery			
Figurative language			
Sound devices			
Form			
Speaker			

Guided Writing Practice, continued

DEVELOPING IDEAS AND PROVIDING ELABORATION

Review the chart you completed on p. 143. List your key ideas and plans for elaboration below. Use a separate sheet of paper if necessary.

Key Idea (poetic device):

_____

Elaboration (how it contributes to the message/theme):

_____

_____

Key Idea (poetic device):

_____

Elaboration (how it contributes to the message/theme):

_____

_____

Key Idea (poetic device):

_____

Elaboration (how it contributes to the message/theme):

_____

_____

Key Idea (poetic device):

_____

Elaboration (how it contributes to the message/theme):

_____

_____

Now review each key idea and the elaboration you have chosen. Make sure your elaboration actually supports your statement about the poem's message.

FOCUSING YOUR COMPOSITION

Look back at the key points you listed on p. 144. Then reread the poem. What do you think is the poet's main message? On the following lines, list the main message of the poem. Then, rewrite it in the form of a thesis statement. A thesis statement is not simply the main idea, topic, or title of your essay. Instead, it is a sentence or two that summarizes how the poet creates the message.

Main Message: _____

_____

_____

Thesis Statement: _____

_____

_____

CREATING LOGICAL ORGANIZATION

Now review your key ideas and decide how you want to arrange them. Use the space below to outline your compostion.

Use your introductory paragraph to identify the poem and the author and to briefly state your thesis statement.

For the body of the essay, decide which idea you want to present first, and arrange the others in a logical order. Be sure to include examples that best support your main points.

Conclude with a summary of the meaning of the poem.

Guided Writing Practice, continued

DRAFTING YOUR WRITING—INTRODUCTION

Now you should begin writing a draft of your composition. Begin with an **introductory paragraph** that states the subject of your composition—in this case, the poem "The Hurricane." It's important to catch your audience's attention early, so try to include an interesting anecdote or fact that will make the reader want to keep reading. Your introductory paragraph also needs to include a thesis statement—a sentence or two that summarize the main idea and purpose of your essay.

Write a first draft of your introduction below. You might try drafting two or more introductions and then deciding which you think is more effective. Use a separate sheet of paper if necessary.

Introduction 1

Introduction 2

DRAFTING YOUR WRITING—DEVELOPING KEY IDEAS

Continue working on your draft by **developing each of your key ideas** in order below. Use a separate sheet of paper if necessary. As you write, remember to do the following:

- Use language that is appropriate for your audience and purpose.

- Follow the rules of standard written English.

- Be sure your elaboration actually supports the key idea.

- Use appropriate transitions, such as *as a result, then, in contrast, for example, similarly,* and *furthermore* to connect ideas.

Guided Writing Practice, continued

DRAFTING YOUR WRITING—CONCLUSION

Now, write a **concluding** paragraph for your composition. In the conclusion:

- restate the thesis of your essay in different words
- summarize the points you have made

Write a first draft of your conclusion on the lines below. Use a separate sheet of paper if necessary. You might need to draft several versions of your conclusion before you write one that satisfies you. Review the drafts of your conclusions and choose the one you like best.

Conclusion 1

Conclusion 2

Conclusion 3

Name _____ Date _____

USING APPROPRIATE AND GRAMMATICALLY CORRECT LANGUAGE

Review the draft of your composition and pay close attention to the language you used. Correct any errors in usage, grammar, and mechanics. Check for mistakes in paragraph structure. Make sure you used language appropriate to your subject, audience, and purpose. Then, write the final version of your composition below and on the back of this page. Use a separate sheet of paper if necessary.

COMPOSITION PRACTICE: INTERPRETIVE WRITING (POETRY)
Additional Prompts: Level 6

Choose one of the two poems below. Write an interpretive essay in which you analyze this poem.

ANOTHER MOUNTAIN

Sometimes there's a mountain
that I must climb
even after I've climbed one already
But my legs are tired now
and my arms need a rest
my mind is too weary right now
But I must climb before the storm comes
before the earth rocks
and an avalanche of clouds buries me
and smothers my soul
And so I prepare myself for another climb
Another Mountain
and I tell myself it is nothing
it is just some more dirt and stone
and every now and then I should reach
another plateau and enjoy the view
of the trees and the flowers below
And I am young enough to climb
and strong enough to make it to any top
You see the wind has warned me
about settling too long
about peace without struggle
The wind has warned me
and taught me how to fly
But my wings only work
After I've climbed a mountain

—Abiodun Oyewole

WOMAN WITH FLOWER

I wouldn't coax the plant if I were you.
Such watchful nurturing may do it
    harm.
Let the soil rest from so much digging
And wait until it's dry before you water
    it.
The leaf's inclined to find its own
    direction;
Give it a chance to seek the sunlight for
    itself.

Much growth is stunted by too careful
    prodding,
Too eager tenderness.
The things we love we have to learn to leave alone.

—Naomi Long Madgett

COMPOSITION PRACTICE: INTERPRETIVE WRITING (POETRY)
Additional Prompts: Level 7

Choose one of the two poems below. Write an interpretive essay in which you analyze this poem.

NEW WORLD

1.
First Man,
behold:
the earth
glitters
with leaves;
the sky
glistens
with rain.
Pollen
is borne
on winds
that low and lean
upon
mountains.
Cedars
blacken
the slopes—
and pines.

2.
At dawn
eagles
hie and
hover
above
the plain
where light
gathers
in pools.
Grasses
shimmer
and shine.
Shadows
withdraw
and lie away
like smoke.

—N. Scott Momaday

THUMBPRINT

In the heel of my thumb
are whorls, whirls, wheels
in a unique design:
mine alone.
What a treasure to own!
My own flesh, my own feelings.
No other, however grand or base,
can ever contain the same.
My signature,
thumbing the pages of my time.
My universe key,
my singularity.
Impress, implant,
I am myself,
of all my atom parts I am the sum.
And out of my blood and my brain
I make my own interior weather,
my own sun and rain.
Imprint my mark upon the world,
whatever I shall become.

—Eve Merriam

COMPOSITION PRACTICE: INTERPRETIVE WRITING (POETRY)
Additional Prompts: Level 8

Choose one of the two poems below. Write an interpretive essay in which you analyze this poem.

WHAT IS SUPPOSED TO HAPPEN

When you were small,
we watched you sleeping,
waves of breath
filling your chest.
Sometimes we hid behind
the wall of baby, soft cradle
of baby needs.
I loved carrying you between
my own body and the world.

Now you are sharpening pencils,
entering the forest of
lunch boxes, little desks.
People I never saw before
call out your name
and you wave.

This loss I feel,
this shrinking,
as your field of roses
grows and grows ....

Now I understand history.
Now I understand my mother's
ancient eyes.

—Naomi Shihab Nye

WISHES

I'm tired of pacing the petty round of the ring of the thing I know—
I want to stand on the daylight's edge and see where the sunsets go.

I want to sail on a swallow's tail and peep through the sky's blue glass.
I want to see if the dreams in me shall perish or come to pass.

I want to look through the moon's pale crook and gaze on the moon-man's face.
I want to keep all the tears I weep and sail to some unknown place.

—Georgia Douglas Johnson

COMPOSITION PRACTICE: INTERPRETIVE WRITING (POETRY)
Scored Writing Samples: How TAAS Compositions are Scored

TAAS compositions are scored *holistically*. Graders take into account the overall effect of the content and delivery rather than focusing primarily on grammar, punctuation, and spelling. They expect grammar, punctuation, and spelling to be correct, but they are mainly concerned with how effectively the message comes across. They focus on how well each composition meets several specific objectives.

Scores range from 1 (low) to 4 (high), although an essay may receive a "0" if it is off topic, indecipherable, or presents insufficient information.

BASIC CRITERIA FOR EVALUATION

Topic All TAAS essays must address the topic presented in the prompt. An essay that is off-topic will receive a score of 0, no matter how well it is written.

Purpose If a TAAS essay addresses the topic in the prompt but fails to meet the purpose, it will receive a score of 1, even if the writing is effective. Meeting the purpose of the prompt is a basic skill of the TAAS. The following questions will help determine whether the student has addressed purpose effectively:

- Does the writer look beyond the words and interpret the poem's message?
- Does the writer analyze how poetic devices contribute to the message or meaning of the poem?
- Does the writer support that interpretation with examples from the poem?

ADDITIONAL CRITERIA FOR EVALUATION

The chart below demonstrates the characteristics of each score.

Score 0	Score 1	Score 2	Score 3	Score 4
Off topic Blank paper	Incorrect purpose, audience, or type of writing	Correct purpose, audience, and type of writing	Correct purpose, audience, and type of writing	Correct purpose, audience, and type of writing
Foreign language	Brief or vague	Some elaboration	Moderately well elaborated	Effective elaboration
Illegible Incoherent	Insufficient support Rambling	Some details	Clear, effective language	Consistent organization
Not enough content to score	Lack of language control Poor organization	Gaps in organization Limited language control	Organized (perhaps with brief digressions)	Sense of completeness, fluency

STANDARDS FOR A SCORE 4 COMPOSITION

Purpose	Analyzes a poem and describes how poetic elements contribute to the message.
Audience	Uses language, tone, and reasons that appeal to the specified audience.
Support	Provides several thoughtful points. Supports points with adequate elaboration (details, examples, etc.).
Structure	Arranges main ideas and support according to logical patterns. Includes an introduction, conclusion, and appropriate transitions.
Fluency	Includes good word choice and sentence variety. Exhibits control of language.

COMPOSITION PRACTICE: INTERPRETIVE WRITING (POETRY)
Student Self-Evaluation: An Interpretive Composition

The questions on this page will help you see how well your composition meets the objective the evaluators are likely to look for. Become familiar with them so you can use them to evaluate your essay during the TAAS.

The Prompt

1. Does your response meet all the requirements stated in the prompt? Have you stated your purpose clearly and supported it with details?

2. Have you addressed your audience appropriately?

3. Does your essay fit the type of writing suggested in the prompt (letter to the editor, article to the paper, etc.)?

Support

4. Do you use examples from the text and from your own experiences to support your main points?

5. Will your audience find this evidence convincing?

6. Have you stated this evidence clearly?

7. Have you elaborated on your main points?

8. Is your reasoning sound? Have you avoided faulty logic?

Order and Arrangement

9. Have you included a strong introduction?

10. Have you included a strong conclusion?

11. Are the points arranged in a logical order?

Word Choice

12. Is the language of your essay appropriate for your audience?

13. Have you used precise, vivid words and persuasive language?

Fluency

14. Have you used sentences of varying lengths and structures?

15. Have you connected ideas with transitions and other devices?

Scripts for Speaking and Listening Skills Lessons

Interpreting a Speaker's Message

p. 125—Interpreting a Speaker's Message: Understanding the Skill

Use nonverbal and verbal cues as you read the following script aloud to students:

Students of Taber Middle School:

As one of your fellow students and a lifetime dog owner, I am asking that you sign my petition to host a *special* "Dog Adoption Day" at our school. Right now, our school has a no-pet policy, but I believe students would benefit from having the Jones Animal Shelter bring in a selection of dogs. This could happen every other month so that students could learn about dog care. I am a volunteer at the shelter and I have seen the price these *poor* dogs pay.

First, as I'm *sure* you'll agree, dogs are the *innocent* victims of human neglect. People purchase dogs because they think the animals will be cute and cuddly and that they won't have to spend time and money caring for them. Then, when people realize the work involved, they no longer want the dog. Children are usually the culprits.

Second, the Jones Animal Shelter needs our help. The fact is that there isn't enough room or money to support all the dogs. Through our program, students can adopt the dogs advertised.

Finally, the program is educational. Students would learn about science and biology. Above all, they'd learn that dogs are not products you can bring back to a store. Like human beings, they are living creatures with feelings. I think a Dog Adoption Day would be the first step toward creating a more *humane* world. I *urge* you to sign my petition when it crosses your desk.

p. 126—Interpreting a Speaker's Message: Level 6

Use nonverbal and verbal cues as you read the following script aloud to students:

Students of Brighton Middle School:

As a fellow student of Brighton Middle School, I, Arun Singh, am asking for your vote for 6th-grade class Student Council Representative. I have many ideas but only enough time to tell you about a few of the reasons why I am the *best* candidate. First of all, I have *always* been involved in school activities, taking on *numerous responsibilities* including *Yearbook Assistant Editor* and *President* of the Math Team. Last year, *my idea* to have a schoolwide bake was a *huge success*, bringing in over *three hundred dollars*, which paid for *new library furniture*. As I'm sure you'll agree, the new furniture is a *big improvement* over the old and ratty furniture we used to have.

Second, I have *more experience* than my opponent, Mary Roderick. Mary only arrived at our school a few months ago. She also has never participated in school activities. In my opinion, this makes her *unqualified* for the job. Do you really want a representative who *doesn't know* our school?

Finally, I want to improve our cafeteria food. If elected, *I will make sure* that each and every student has *healthy and tasty lunch choices*. Fellow students, I *care* about our school and what happens to our students! I have the *ability, the drive, and the ideas to make our class great.* Vote for me, *Arun Singh*, for Student Council Representative. I *won't disappoint* you!

p. 126—Interpreting a Speaker's Message: Level 7

Use nonverbal and verbal cues as you read the following script aloud to students:

Fellow Students:

As *president* of the 7th grade class, I, Haan Lu, am asking for your support in my *nomination for Student Council President*. Currently, my opponent Susan Cogley is handing out balloons and prizes to win your vote. *Please don't let this convince you!* I think this is *childish* and has *nothing* to do with the issues.

First, our school *doesn't need more balloons and prizes*. What *we need* is a *confident leader* who doesn't have to resort to *bribery* to win votes. I have *two years of solid Student Council experience*. My opponent has no experience. My experience working on the School Talent Show and the Finance Committee makes me qualified to lead our school toward *huge success*. Further, I have proven myself as a *leader* who *listens* when you speak. For example, from talking to fellow students I know that many students want an extra playground. If elected, *I will see to it* that we get our playground as soon as possible.

Fellow students, you must not be *blinded by bribery!* Please vote for *me.* I have solid experience. Do you want a president who takes action on the issues you care about or a president who sits around blowing up balloons? Remember, *vote for me, Haan Lu,* for Student Council President. I will be a president of *action*!

p. 126—Interpreting a Speaker's Message: Level 8

Use nonverbal and verbal cues as you read the following script aloud to students:

Fellow Residents of Maplewood:

As *president* of the Town Parks Committee, I, Ronnika Barnes, stand before you at this town meeting to beg for your support. Currently, big business is *trampling* all over the *little* people of our town. Plans are underway for the building of a *supermarket* which would *squash* our *small* but *beloved* park. I think this is *totally unfair and unnecessary.*

First, our town *doesn't need another supermarket.* We *already* have *three,* including one just *a half mile away* from the town square. And in my opinion a supermarket would be *ugly, an absolute eyesore.* The park that is there now is *beautiful.* People *love* walking through it. Could you tell a happy young mother that the park where her children play is going to be *ripped apart* and *replaced* with *concrete* and air polluting cars?

Sally Bilow, our Town Planner, agrees the idea is a bad one. Based on her studies, the traffic in our town is getting *worse.* A supermarket would just *add* to the problem.

Fellow residents, we must act *now* to save our park! A supermarket is unnecessary, it would be ugly, and it would clog our town with cars. Do you want to *wait* in traffic for *one more half hour* than you *already* do? I don't *think* so! I ask that you support *my* effort to stop the supermarket monsters at once!

Distinguishing Between a Speaker's Opinion and Fact

p. 128—Distinguishing Between a Speaker's Opinion and Fact: Level 6

Read the following script aloud as students take notes.

The Writer, Paula Fox

Anyone who has ever read *The Slave Dancer* agrees that Paula Fox is a most talented author. Her straightforward writing style and her keen insight into the minds of characters have brought her much acclaim through the years. In 1974 she won the Newbery Medal for the book, which was later made into a movie.

The Slave Dancer chronicles the experiences of a white boy and a black slave aboard an American ship returning from Africa. However, this book stands out for more than its heartbreaking subject matter. Fox uses vivid description and creative dialogue to make her characters come to life as they struggle in a suspenseful test of survival. By the end of the book, readers feel that they, too, have fought for dignity and freedom.

Born in New York City in 1923, Paula Fox has written several children's books including *How Many Miles To Babylon?, Blowfish Live in the Sea*, and *Lily and the Lost Boy*. She has also written books for adults.

p. 128—Distinguishing Between a Speaker's Opinion and Fact: Level 7

Read the following script aloud as students take notes.

The Life and Contributions of E. B. White

Anyone who's ever read *Charlotte's Web* has fallen in love with the narrative of E. B. White. The author, named Elwyn Brooks White, was born in Mount Vernon in 1899. In 1925, he started writing for *The New Yorker* magazine. Known chiefly as an essay writer, White wrote in an informal, personal manner. Many of his works tell of his life in Maine. But among children and parents, White's poetry and children's books are the most memorable.

White's children's books are still some of the best around. Featuring animals that talk and act like people, his books highlight the issues of friendship and love. *Stuart Little*, which was published in 1945, tells the story of a mouse with human parents. *Charlotte's Web* explores the friendship between a girl, a pig and a spider. But *The Trumpet of the Swan* is by far his best work. In this story a young cygnet swan overcomes the handicap of having no voice.

In 1963, White received the Presidential Medal of Freedom and in 1978, a Pulitzer Prize special citation for his writings.

White died in 1985. He remains one of the most beloved children's authors of our time.

p. 128—Distinguishing Between a Speaker's Opinion and Fact: Level 8

Read the following script aloud as students take notes.

The Life and Contributions of Judy Blume

Born in Elizabeth, New Jersey in 1938, author Judy Blume has become a favorite of both children and adults. Blume's books are celebrated for their frankness and willingness to tackle today's real life issues. *Are You There God, It's Me, Margaret?*, which chronicles eleven-year old Margaret's search for identity, is by far her most beloved book. Some of Judy Blume's other books for children include *Then Again, Maybe I won't, Tales of a Fourth Grade Nothing, Deenie, Blubber, Superfudge, Tiger Eyes*, and *As Long As We're Together*. Blume has written books for adults, *Wifey*, published in 1978, and *Smart Women*.

Although Judy Blume has had many personal losses, this hasn't changed her views on writing. Blume still incorporates parts of her life into her works. Her grandmother's death, her first period, and her experiences living in different parts of the country all become part of the subject matter. She knows how to make children, teenagers, and adults feel comfortable with the changes in themselves.

In 1986, Judy Blume published a collection of letter from young readers and her responses to them in *Letters to Judy*. This bold move shows her willingness to relate to the issues of the day.

Answer Key

Preparing for TAAS

p. 12 Objective 1—Using Context Clues: Level 6

Word	Context Clues	Best Guess at Meaning
composure	antonym: panic	state of being calm and in control of your actions and feelings
haughty	followed by a definition	an attitude in which one person looks down upon another; arrogant pride
pensively	followed by a definition	as if deep in thought
stupendous	synonym: amazing	something wonderful

Word	Context Clues	Best Guess at Meaning
tedious	antonym: exciting	boring; humdrum; monotonous
gnarled	synonym: twisted	bent or twisted
crevices	synonym: cracks	something like a crack or fissure
plummet	followed by a definition	to fall suddenly and steeply

Word	Context Clues	Best Guess at Meaning
primitive	Described in previous sentence	crude
imminent	Imminent modifies change	soon
initiative	Previous sentence describes how John Kay was the first to develop the flying shuttle.	to take the lead
dwindle	Contrasts with description of the emergence of the factory system.	becomes less; grows smaller

p. 16 Objective 1—Using Word Parts: Level 6

Word	Word Parts	Word Meaning
misfortune	Prefix: *mis-* (bad) Base word: *fortune*	bad luck or bad fortune
disciplinarian	Base word: *discipline* Suffix: *-arian* (believer in)	someone who believes in and enforces discipline
legitimate	Root: *lex* (law) *Suffix: -ate (having, characterized by)*	characterized by or being acceptable to a law; valid
compassionate	Base word: *compassion* Suffix: *-ate* (having, characterized by)	to have compassion or mercy

p. 17 Objective 1—Using Word Parts: Level 7

Word	Word Parts	Word Meaning
inadequate	Prefix: *in-* (not) Base word: *adequate* (sufficient for a need or purpose)	not sufficient to meet a need
unappeasable	Prefix: *un-* (not) Base word: *appease* (to make calm or satisfy) Suffix: *-able* (capable of)	not capable of being satisfied
impunity	Prefix: *im-* (not) Root word: *poena* (punishment) Suffix: *-ity* (state or quality)	being free from punishment
resistance	Base word: *resist* (to keep from giving in) Suffix: *-ance* (act or condition)	the act of not giving in

p. 18 Objective 1—Using Word Parts: Level 8

Word	Word Parts	Word Meaning
privilege	Root word: *privus* (single, alone)	something for one person
inconsequential	Prefix: *in-* (not, without) Base word: *consequential* (important)	not important
infatuated	Prefix: *in-* (in, within) Base word: *fatuous:* (foolish, unreal) Suffix: *-ed* (having, characterized by)	having a foolish or unreasonable attraction to someone
authenticity	Base word: *authentic* (genuine) Suffix: *-ity* (state or quality)	quality of being genuine

p. 20 Objective 2—Recognizing Supporting Details: Level 6

A. Answers will vary. Possible answers:

1. The advantages animals bring to senior citizens living in elderly housing facilities and nursing homes outweigh any disadvantages.

2. Pets replace loneliness with companionship and boredom with interest. Pet visits help residents "come alive", build their self-esteem, and help seniors feel less isolated.

3. Scientific studies prove pets help people relax, lower stress levels, and help prolong life.

4. It shows that seniors would benefit from the pets' visits.

B. Answers will vary. Possible answers:

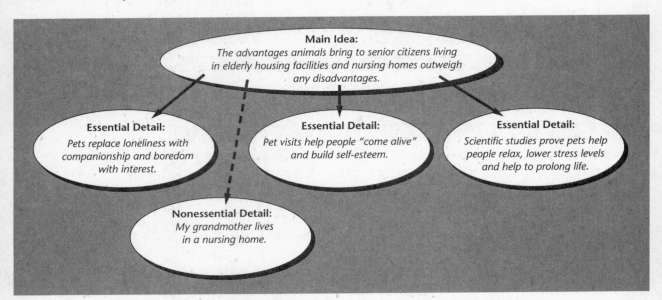

Main Idea:
The advantages animals bring to senior citizens living in elderly housing facilities and nursing homes outweigh any disadvantages.

Essential Detail:
Pets replace loneliness with companionship and boredom with interest.

Essential Detail:
Pet visits help people "come alive" and build self-esteem.

Essential Detail:
Scientific studies prove pets help people relax, lower stress levels and help to prolong life.

Nonessential Detail:
My grandmother lives in a nursing home.

p. 21 Objective 2—Recognizing Supporting Details: Level 7

A. Answers will vary. Possible answers:

1. Every place on Earth has its own climate.

2. Climate is affected by distance from the equator, ocean temperatures and currents, winds, altitude, and many other factors.

3. Scientists recognize that there are 12 major kinds of climate and most of them fall within three climate zones. The tropical zone is closest to the equator; the temperate zone lies between the poles and the tropics; and the polar zone includes areas below the Antarctic Circle and above the Arctic Circle.

4. No, it is a nonessential detail.

B. Answers will vary. Possible answers:

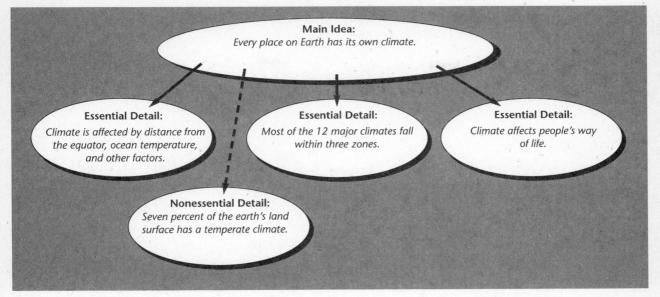

p. 22 Objective 2—Recognizing Supporting Details: Level 8

A. Answers will vary. Possible answer:

1. Rainbows can be seen only under certain conditions.

2. The sun's ray is bent as it enters the water droplet and is separated into different colors. As it passes through the droplet's inner surface, it is reflected. Many droplets make a rainbow.

3. Other key factors are the sun's position in the sky and the time of day.

4. Double rainbows are rare because even single rainbows can be seen only under certain conditions.

B. Answers will vary. Possible answer:

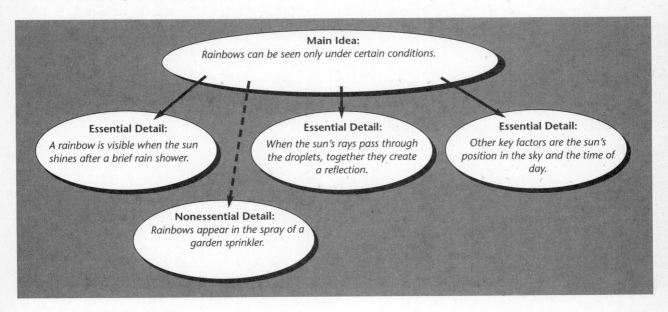

p. 24 Objective 2—Understanding Sequential Order: Level 6

A.

1. 1818; 1835; 1847; 1848; 1865-1888; 1889
2. 1836
3. 1847
4. 1848

B.

1818: Maria is born

1818-1834: Maria is home-schooled by her father

1835: Maria becomes an assistant at a teacher's college

1836: Maria opens her own school

1847: Maria discovers a comet which is later named "Miss Mitchell's Comet"

1848: Maria is voted the first woman astronomer to become a member of American Academy of Arts and Sciences161

1865-1888: Maria is a professor of astronomy at Vassar College

1889: Maria dies at age 70

p. 25 Objective 2—Understanding Sequential Order: Level 7

A.

1. 1917; 1938; 1940s; 1996
2. 1932
3. in the 1940s
4. 79

B.

1917: Ella is born

1932: Ella is orphaned

1938: Ella records the hit song, "A Tisket-A Tasket"

1940s: Ella perfects the art of "scat singing"

1996: Ella dies at age 79

p. 26 Objective 2—Understanding Sequential Order: Level 8

A.

1. 1880; 1904; 1964; 1968
2. 1887
3. 1904
4. 1965

B.

1880: Helen is born

1881: Illness leaves Helen blind and deaf

1887-1904: Annie Sullivan tutors Helen

1904: Helen graduates from Radcliffe College

1964: Helen is awarded the Presidential Medal of Freedom

1965: Helen is elected to the Women's Hall of Fame

1968: Helen dies at age 87

p. 28 Objective 3—Identifying the Main Idea: Level 6

Paragraph with Stated Main Idea

Stated Main Idea: *It's hard to imagine life without chocolate, but there was a time when chocolate candy was unheard of.*

Supporting Statements:
1. *Around 1500 chocolate was introduced to Europe.*
2. *At first only the wealthy could afford chocolate. Later the price dropped, and more people could enjoy it.*
3. *Chocolate was first produced in Dorchester, Massachusetts, in 1765.*

Paragraph with Implied Main Idea

Text Clues:
1. *Chocolate is a popular gift, especially on special occasions.*
2. *Chocolate is given as a sign of love and affection.*
3. *Children often receive chocolate as a reward or treat.*

Implied Main Idea: *Chocolate is not just for eating, but is symbolic as well.*

p. 29 Objective 3—Identifying the Main Idea: Level 7

Paragraph with Stated Main Idea

Stated Main Idea: *Taking a rafting trip down the Colorado River is a great way to experience the Grand Canyon.*

Supporting Statements:
1. *Rafting guides point out rock formations and explain the canyon's history.*
2. *Inside the canyon, you can see how it was formed.*
3. *There are many stops along the way where you can hike, swim, explore waterfalls or relax along the river.*

Paragraph with Implied Main Idea

Text Clues:
1. *Most people choose a guided trip with equipment and meals provided.*
2. *You can take either small rafts with oars or paddles or large, motorized rafts.*
3. *Trips last 6–8 days and rafters experience both calm waters and raging rapids.*

Implied Main Idea: *There's much more to a rafting trip down the Colorado River than just riding the rapids.*

p. 30 Objective 3—Identifying the Main Idea: Level 8

Paragraph with Stated Main Idea	Paragraph with Implied Main Idea
Stated Main Idea: *The garden art of training, pruning, and cutting live shrubs and trees into ornamental designs is known as topiary.*	**Text Clues:** 1. *Topiary hasn't always been elaborate. The Romans practiced topiary, by making geometric shapes.* 2. *Topiary became extremely popular in the 17th and 18th centuries with detailed animal shapes and mazes.* 3. *Topiary is not as common today and is usually found in specialized private gardens, botanical displays, and formal parks.*
Supporting Statements: 1. *The best plants to use for topiary are thickly leaved evergreen shrubs, such as cypress and yew.* 2. *The plants can be shaped into decorations for landscaping, or can be made to resemble "live" statues.*	**Implied Main Idea:** *Topiary has evolved over time, and can be seen in different levels of complexity throughout history.*

p. 32 Objective 3—Summarizing: Level 6

B. *Answers will vary. Possible answers:*

1. Some animals must go into hibernation in order to survive the cold winter months.

2. • Some animals hibernate in order to survive cold climates.

   • Bats, bears, skunks, and squirrels go into a sleep-like state.

   • They hibernate because the plants and berries they eat are not available in the winter.

   • Some animals hibernate from September through March; others may hibernate and come out on warm days.

   • Hibernating animals prepare for hibernation by building up fat. Fat allows them to survive.

   • Bears can gain up to 40 pounds of fat per week before going into hibernation.

   • In hibernation, the body temperature drops and the heart rate decreases.

   • The best hibernating environments are those that are dark, quiet, and well-protected, like burrows and caves.

3. • Some animals hibernate in order to survive cold climates.

   • They hibernate because the plants and berries they eat are not available in the winter.

   • Hibernating animals prepare for hibernation by building up fat. Fat allows them to survive.

   • In hibernation, the body temperature drops and the heart rate decreases.

   • The best hibernating environments are those that are dark, quiet, and well-protected, like burrows and caves.

4. Some animals in northern climates go into hibernation during the winter because the food they rely on disappears. They prepare by building up a fat reserve which allows them to survive, and finding a dark, well-protected shelter. Once they enter the hibernating state, their body temperature and heart rate drop, putting them in a sleep-like state.

p. 33 Objective 3—Summarizing: Level 7

B. *Answers will vary. Possible answers:*

1. Both the male and female Emperor penguin must work hard to care for their young in the harsh Antarctic conditions.

2. • Parenthood is a shared event for the Emperor penguin.

- The male incubates the single egg for two months while the female looks for food.
- The male cradles the egg to protect it from temperatures as low as -112F.
- The males stand close together in groups called "huddles" to keep warm. They take turns standing on the outside edges.
- The male loses over half of his body weight and survives on fat reserves as he endures the 65-mph winds and freezing temperatures.
- When it's time for the egg to hatch, the female returns to provide heat for the chick.
- Both parents take turns finding food for the chick and protecting it from predators.
- Only 10% of chicks survive to adulthood.

3. • <u>Parenthood is a shared event for the Emperor penguin.</u>
- <u>The male incubates the single egg for two months while the female looks for food.</u>
- <u>The female returns when it's time for the egg to hatch, and provides heat for the chick.</u>
- <u>Both parents take turns finding food for the chick and protecting it from predators.</u>
- <u>Only 10% of chicks survive to adulthood.</u>

4. The harsh conditions in the Antarctic make it necessary for the male and female Emperor penguin to care for their young. The male incubates the egg for two months while the female looks for food. She returns around the same time that the egg hatches to help protect the chick. Both parents take turns looking for food. Despite the shared parenting duties, only 10% of the chicks survive.

p. 34 Objective 3—Summarizing: Level 8

B. *Answers will vary. Possible answers:*

1. Many families question whether or not teenagers should be allowed to work during the school year.
2. • Teenagers who work part-time can gain pride and learn responsibility.
- Research indicates that working 20 hours or more a week is not beneficial for teens.
- Teens who work too much have less time for sleep, schoolwork, and extracurricular activities.
- A recent study found that teens who worked 15 hours had lower grades, higher dropout rates, and were less likely to attend college.
- Many states limit the amount of time 16– and 17–year olds can work.
- Some day, the Department of Labor may limit the hours anyone under 18 may work during the school year.
- Families must decide how much a teen can work.
3. • <u>Teenagers who work part-time can gain pride and learn responsibility.</u>
- <u>Research indicates that working 20 hours or more a week is not beneficial for teens.</u>
- <u>Families must decide how much a teen can work.</u>
4. Many families question whether or not teenagers should be allowed to work during the school year. Teens may gain pride and learn responsibility, but working too much might have negative effects. Each family must decide if and how much a teen should work.

p. 36 Objective 4—Perceiving Cause–and–Effect Relationships: Level 6

A. *Answers will vary. Possible answers:*

1. Everything in the tornado's path can be destroyed.
2. Entire towns have been washed away and huge waves destroy piers, boats, and structures close to shore.
3. Hurricanes, tornadoes, and lightning remain in firn control.

B. *Answers will vary. Possible answers:*

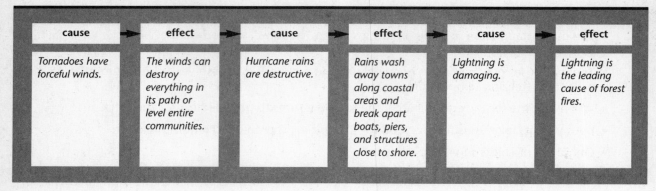

cause	effect	cause	effect	cause	effect
Tornadoes have forceful winds.	The winds can destroy everything in its path or level entire communities.	Hurricane rains are destructive.	Rains wash away towns along coastal areas and break apart boats, piers, and structures close to shore.	Lightning is damaging.	Lightning is the leading cause of forest fires.

p. 37 Objective 4—Perceiving Cause-and-Effect Relationships: Level 7

A. *Answers will vary. Possible answers:*

1. milk, peanuts, walnuts, shellfish, wheat

2. If you eat something you are allergic to, your body reacts to it, releasing histamines and other chemicals to fight off the invader.

3. The best treatment is to stay away from trigger foods.

B. *Answers will vary. Possible answers:*

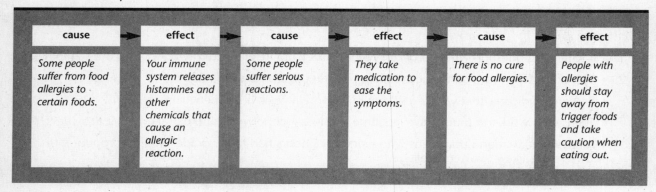

cause	effect	cause	effect	cause	effect
Some people suffer from food allergies to certain foods.	Your immune system releases histamines and other chemicals that cause an allergic reaction.	Some people suffer serious reactions.	They take medication to ease the symptoms.	There is no cure for food allergies.	People with allergies should stay away from trigger foods and take caution when eating out.

p. 38 Objective 4—Perceiving Cause-and-Effect Relationships: Level 8

A. *Answers will vary. Possible answers:*

1. Because of people's dedication and fundraising efforts , enough money was raised to build a new sports center.

2. The pool will allow the school to compete in swimming and diving events.

3. The school will have a new basketball arena and a new pool which town residents can use.

B. *Answers will vary. Possible answers:*

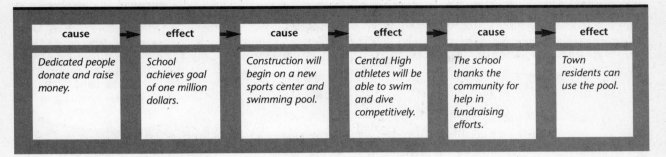

cause	effect	cause	effect	cause	effect
Dedicated people donate and raise money.	School achieves goal of one million dollars.	Construction will begin on a new sports center and swimming pool.	Central High athletes will be able to swim and dive competitively.	The school thanks the community for help in fundraising efforts.	Town residents can use the pool.

p. 40 Objective 4—Predicting Probable Future Actions and Outcomes: Level 6

A. *Answers will vary. Possible answers:*

1. Donata and her fawn were chased by hunters.

2. Her uncle had panicked and ran into an open field.

3. Donata remains calm instead of panicking.

4. Because Donata remains calm and the fact that the hunters will be confused by the windy forest trails, you might infer that she and her fawn have a good chance of escaping.

B. *Answers will vary. Possible answers:*

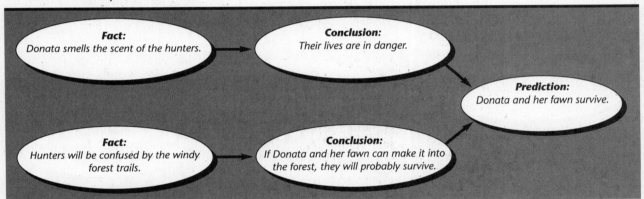

Fact: Donata smells the scent of the hunters.

Conclusion: Their lives are in danger.

Prediction: Donata and her fawn survive.

Fact: Hunters will be confused by the windy forest trails.

Conclusion: If Donata and her fawn can make it into the forest, they will probably survive.

p. 41 Objective 4—Predicting Probable Future Actions and Outcomes: Level 7

A. *Answers will vary. Possible answers:*

1. They are blocking their shots.

2. Because they have an emergency plan for games like the one they are in.

3. When he got "crowded" by the opposing team, Hal would make them think that he was going to shoot; instead, he would get the ball to Kenny who is good at distance shots.

4. He crouches and dribbles and then he whirls around as if he is going to make a shot. Instead, he turns around and throws the ball to Kenny.

5. Because Hal and Kenny have been able to put their plan into action, you may infer that Kenny will be able to make the shot and win the game.

B. *Answers will vary. Possible answers:*

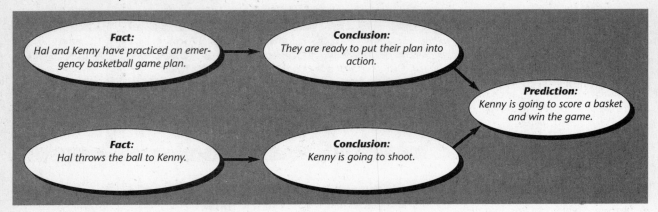

Fact: Hal and Kenny have practiced an emergency basketball game plan. → Conclusion: They are ready to put their plan into action. → Prediction: Kenny is going to score a basket and win the game.

Fact: Hal throws the ball to Kenny. → Conclusion: Kenny is going to shoot.

p. 42 Objective 4—Predicting Probable Future Actions and Outcomes: Level 8

A. *Answers will vary. Possible answers:*

1. Because she is studying for a science test.

2. Because it is Terri's turn to empty it.

3. He discovers that Terri really is studying.

4. Because Bud is obviously impressed that Terri is studying, you may infer that he will take her turn and empty the trash so that she can study and get a good grade.

B. *Answers will vary. Possible answers:*

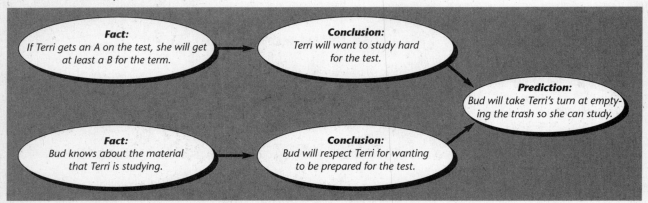

Fact: If Terri gets an A on the test, she will get at least a B for the term. → Conclusion: Terri will want to study hard for the test. → Prediction: Bud will take Terri's turn at emptying the trash so she can study.

Fact: Bud knows about the material that Terri is studying. → Conclusion: Bud will respect Terri for wanting to be prepared for the test.

p. 45 Objective 5—Interpreting Charts and Graphs: Level 6

A.

1. The topic of the line graph is average car sales over a six week period.

2. The horizontal axis represents the week.

3. The vertical axis represents the number of cars sold.

4. The topic of the bar graph is the sixth grade students' favorite bagels.

5. Each individual bar represents those who prefer a particular bagel.

B.

Answers will vary. Possible answers: Car sales rose every other week for six weeks. The most cars were sold during the fifth week of sales.

Sixth grade students liked poppy seed bagels the most, but all the kinds of bagels combined are more popular than any kind listed.

p. 46 Objective 5—Interpreting Charts and Graphs: Level 7

A.

1. The topic of the pie graph is the various investments that make up a financial profile.

2. Each individual slice represents a different type of investment.

3. The topic of the line graph is the number of animals at Midland's animal shelter from January to December.

4. The horizontal axis represents the month of the year.

5. The vertical axis represents the number of animals.

B.

Answers will vary. Possible answers: The largest investment type of the investment profile is government bonds which is almost double the percentage of fine art or stocks.

The number of animals at Midland's shelter rose steadily from January to May, then declined for a couple of months, but peaked in August and declined again through the end of the year.

p. 47 Objective 5—Interpreting Charts and Graphs: Level 8

A.

1. The topic of the pie graph is the kinds of transportation employed by teachers at the James Middle School by percentage.

2. Each individual slice represents the percentage of those who use a particular kind of transportation.

3. The topic of the line graph is the amount of rainfall in Lyle during 1999.

4. The horizontal axis represents the month of the year.

5. The vertical axis represents the inches of rain.

B.

Answers will vary. Possible answer: The majority of teachers at James Middle School take the train or drive to work. Three times as many teachers ride a bicycle than walk to work.

The amount of rainfall in Lyle during 1999 rose from January to April when it peaked at six inches and then decreased each month from May to December.

p. 50 Objective 5—Making Inferences: Level 6

A. *Answers will vary. Possible answers:*

1. The driver is speeding on a highway.

2. It is a police car.

3. She will receive a speeding ticket from the police.

B. *Answers will vary. Possible answers:*

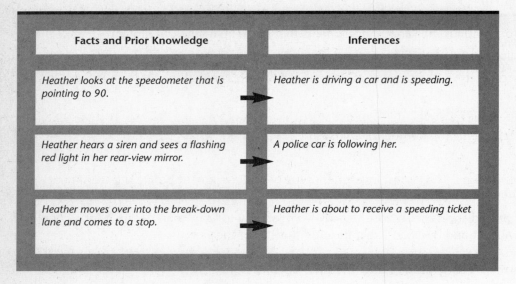

Facts and Prior Knowledge	Inferences
Heather looks at the speedometer that is pointing to 90.	Heather is driving a car and is speeding.
Heather hears a siren and sees a flashing red light in her rear-view mirror.	A police car is following her.
Heather moves over into the break-down lane and comes to a stop.	Heather is about to receive a speeding ticket

p. 51 Objective 5—Making Inferences: Level 7

A. *Answers will vary. Possible answers:*

1. Sarah Winchester was an eccentric and superstitious woman.

2. Since building went on uninterrupted, there was no master plan. The goal was just to continue building.

3. She was afraid something would happen to her.

B. *Answers will vary. Possible answers:*

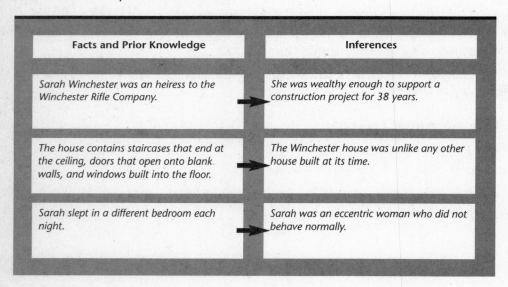

Facts and Prior Knowledge	Inferences
Sarah Winchester was an heiress to the Winchester Rifle Company.	She was wealthy enough to support a construction project for 38 years.
The house contains staircases that end at the ceiling, doors that open onto blank walls, and windows built into the floor.	The Winchester house was unlike any other house built at its time.
Sarah slept in a different bedroom each night.	Sarah was an eccentric woman who did not behave normally.

p. 52 Objective 5—Making Inferences: Level 6

A. *Answers will vary. Possible answers:*

1. The ride takes you from one extreme to the next.

2. People scream helplessly on the ride.

3. The ride is on a roller coaster and although it is frightening, it is exciting and fun.

B. *Answers will vary. Possible answers:*

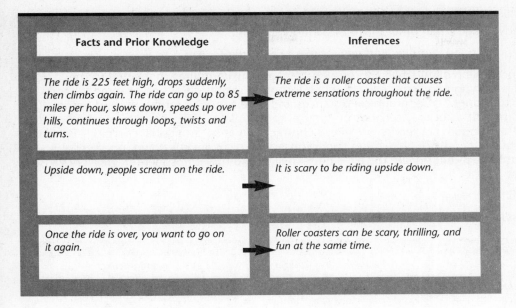

Facts and Prior Knowledge	Inferences
The ride is 225 feet high, drops suddenly, then climbs again. The ride can go up to 85 miles per hour, slows down, speeds up over hills, continues through loops, twists and turns.	The ride is a roller coaster that causes extreme sensations throughout the ride.
Upside down, people scream on the ride.	It is scary to be riding upside down.
Once the ride is over, you want to go on it again.	Roller coasters can be scary, thrilling, and fun at the same time.

p. 54 Objective 5—Evaluating and Making Judgments: Level 6

A. *Answers will vary. Possible answers:*

1. The writer suggests that young people join a program like Roots & Shoots to aid in wildlife protection.

2. Roots & Shoots should be international. It should involve young people of all ages. There should be a variety of activities for young people to perform that are community-based.

3. "Roots & Shoots is an environmental education and humanitarian program," "It is in 50 countries and is open to young people from pre-school through college age."

4. Each individual effort makes a difference.

B. *Answers will vary. Possible answers:*

Criteria	Facts Meeting Criteria	Judgment
To make a difference you should be involved in a cause.	Some people only ask the question—How can I help? Some people help animals that are threatened with extinction and others are trying to improve the quality of life for all living creatures.	
To make a difference people protecting wildlife should perform a variety of activities.	Roots & Shoots members participate in activities that range in in kind and scope.	Each individual effort on behalf of wildlife protection is worthwhile.
Protecting wildlife should involve people from around the world.	Roots & Shoots is in 50 countries and is open to young people from pre-school through college age.	

p. 55 Objective 5—Evaluating and Making Judgments: Level 7

A. *Answers will vary. Possible answers:*

1. Email has more advantages than other forms of communication.

2. Is email convenient, fast, inexpensive, and environmentally sound?

3. "Once you're in possession of an email address, you can use any computer connected to the Internet," "Email is helping people renew and repair forgotten relationships and in some cases it's helping to create new ones," "Geographical distances and time zones no longer present barriers," "Email is immediate," "It takes only seconds or minutes to complete," "Email is inexpensive," "Most of the time email is included in a service provider's contract and at no additional charge," "Email is truly "environmentally friendly," "No writing paper is used, no trees are cut down, nor forests destroyed," "Harmful fuel that pollute the air is not expelled into the atmosphere by delivery vans, trains, or airplanes."

4. Yes, as it meets all the criteria.

B. *Answers will vary. Possible answer:*

Criteria	Facts Meeting Criteria	Judgment
Email should have more benefits than other forms of communication.	*Email is immediate, convenient, and less expensive than other forms of communication.*	
Email should benefit oneself personally.	*Email helps me to stay in contact with more friends. I don't have to stay up late to call another time zone.*	*Email has many advantages over other forms of communication.*
Email should help to protect the environment.	*Email can be sent without using paper products. Vehicles that pollute the atmosphere are not needed to deliver email.*	

p. 56 Objective 5—Evaluating and Making Judgments: Level 8

A. *Answers will vary. Possible answers:*

1. Mahatma Gandhi was a respected and effective leader, so much so, that he won independence for his country, India.

2. An effective leader should be able to unite his or her people and lead them towards a common good. To earn respect, a leader should be both sensitive and strong.

3. Using only non-violent means, Gandhi challenged unfair laws by organizing labor strikes and extended fasts to aid his cause. By using these methods, Gandhi won independence for India from British rule. Gandhi was one of the gentlest of men but he also had an unbending iron will. Millions of followers called him Mahatma or "great soul."

4. Gandhi was a respected and effective leader because, through non-violent means, he was able to unite his people and win independence for India.

B. *Answers will vary. Possible answers:*

Criteria	Facts Meeting Criteria	Judgment
Good leaders are effective if they can unite people in working towards a common good.	Gandhi organized non-violent strikes and fasts and finally won independence for India from British rule.	Gandhi was an effective and respected leader and is held in high regard more than fifty years after his death.
Good leaders earn respect if they are both sensitive and strong.	Gandhi was gentle but he also had an iron will. His followers called him Mahatma or "great soul."	
Good leaders are remembered long after their death.	The world is forever indebted to Gandhi. Martin Luther King adopted Gandhi's principles on non-violent civil disobedience.	

p. 58 Objective 6—Recognizing Propaganda: Level 6

A. *Answers will vary. Possible answers:*

1. Frank Norman is a typical politician: he's against change that will help people. Joe Maxon is a new kind of politician who wants only the kind of change that will help you and your children.

2. "A small police force will turn our streets into safe havens for crime," "Frank Norman will give our students an inferior education that won't prepare them for the future," "Joe Maxon will change our city into a place that is safe and secure for ourselves and our children."

3. "a city that is safe and secure for ourselves and our children," "people are scared and children won't get a good education," "safe havens for crime," "change that will help you and your children"

4. The author wants you to vote for Joe Maxon.

B. *Answers will vary. Possible answers:*

Stereotype	Exaggerated Claims and Emotional Language	Author's Intention
A. Frank Norman is a typical politician: he's against change that will help people.	A. Frank Norman will give our students an inferior education that won't prepare them for the future.	The author wants you to vote for Joe Maxon.
B. Joe Maxon is a new kind of politician who wants only the kind of change that will help you and your children.	A small police force will turn our streets into safe havens for crime.	
	B. Joe Maxon will change our city into a place that is safe and secure for ourselves and our children.	

p. 59 Objective 6—Recognizing Propaganda: Level 7

A. *Answers will vary. Possible answers:*

1. Seemingly innocent messages that appear on your screen, which when opened release a virus.

2. "WATCHDOG is a foolproof virus detection program that surpasses all others on the market," "WATCHDOG can protect companies and businesses and save millions of dollars," "WATCHDOG can protect hospitals and doctors' offices and save lives."

3. "crawl," "eat up," "invade," "infect," "destroy"

4. The author wants you to buy the WATCHDOG computer virus detection program.

B. *Answers will vary. Possible answers:*

Stereotype	Exaggerated Claims and Emotional Language	Author's Intention
Seemingly innocent messages that appear on your screen, which when opened release a virius.	*WATCHDOG is a foolproof virus detection program that surpasses all others on the market. WATCHDOG can protect companies and businesses and save millions of dollars. WATCHDOG can protect hospitals and doctors' offices and save lives.*	*The author wants you to buy the WATCHDOG computer virus detection program by creating feelings of fear about computer viruses and exaggerating the abilities of WATCHDOG as being foolproof.*

p. 60 Objective 6—Recognizing Propaganda: Level 8

A. *Answers will vary. Possible answers:*

1. Big business and lying politicians don't tell the truth.

2. "Every time you bite into your tuna sandwich, you've helped kill amother dolphin," "The meager few which survive are so badly battered that nothing can ensure their survival in the open ocean," "Only your compassion and action can save the few remaining dolphins."

3. "you've helped kill," "entire families of innocent dolphins are the sad vivtims," "meager few which survive are so badly battered," "lovable dolphins," "cruel practices of these fishing fleets," "your compassion and action can save"

4. The author wants the public to boycott tuna fish.

B. *Answers will vary. Possible answers:*

Stereotype	Exaggerated Claims and Emotional Language	Author's Intention
Big business and lying politicians want you to believe that dolphins no longer die in the nets of the tuna fishermen.	*"Every time you bite into your tuna sandwich, you've helped kill another dolphin," "Even one dolphin in those nets is too many," "The meager few which survive are so badly battered that nothing can ensure their survival in the open ocean," "cruel practices," "your compassion," "few remaining dolphins."*	*To make the public aware: that it must save the dwindling dolphin population by not eating tuna fish and that fisherman who catch dolphins lie when they claim that no dolphins are killed in the production of canned tuna.*

p. 62 Objective 6—Recognizing Author's Perspective and Purpose: Level 6

A. *Answers will vary. Possible answers:*

1. The author feels that the new dollar coin is much better and more practical than the old one.

2. "only a few Americans ever saw those," "never caught on," "too much like quarters," "new dollar has changed completely"

3. The author thinks it is an honor for the new dollar to feature Sacajawea, the first Native American woman on a US minted coin.

4. The author's opinion seems sensible and reasonable.

B. *Answers will vary. Possible answers:*

Key Words, Phrases, and Details	Author's Perspective	Author's Purpose
• only a few Americans ever saw one • never caught on for everyday use • too much like quarters • hard to tell them apart • new dollar has changed completely and is identified by a quick touch • golden in color • popular heroine; Sacajawea deserves this honor	The new dollar coin is much better than the old one.	The author's purpose is to express an opinion about why the old dollar coin was not a success, and what makes the new one better.

p. 63 Objective 6—Recognizing Author's Perspective and Purpose: Level 7

A. *Answers will vary. Possible answers:*

1. A number of factors contribute to the increased life expectancy of Americans.

2. social interaction

3. "because people are living longer does not mean they are living better," "according to recent research," "social interaction not only insures that the elderly live longer," "actually improves the quality of their lives," "contact with older adults can also be beneficial," "may have some fun and improve their own lives."

4. It is mutually beneficial for both generations.

5. The author's opinion on healthy aging is strong and convincing.

B. *Answers will vary. Possible answers:*

Key Words, Phrases, and Details	Author's Perspective	Author's Purpose
• genes we inherit also play a role, but probably not as big a role as people used to think • because people are living longer doesn't mean they are living better • according to recent research, social interaction insures elderly live longer and live better • for young people, contact with older adults can also be beneficial • may have some fun	Social interaction is an important part of healthy aging.	The author's purpose is to express the opinion that social interaction deserves more attention when considering the factors for healthy aging, as it improves the lives of both young and old.

p. 64 Objective 6—Recognizing Author's Perspective and Purpose: Level 8

A. *Answers will vary. Possible answers:*

1. The author thinks solar energy is the best form of energy.

2. "safest and cleanest form of energy," "other energy sources commonly in use do not have these advantages," "it is crucial that private energy companies, as well as state and local governments, invest in solar technology."

3. Non-solar energy sources should not be used.

4. The author feels that solar energy should become the main source of energy.

B. *Answers will vary. Possible answers:*

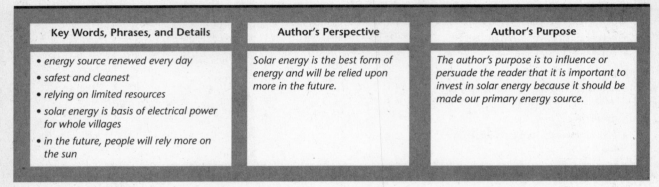

Key Words, Phrases, and Details	Author's Perspective	Author's Purpose
• energy source renewed every day • safest and cleanest • relying on limited resources • solar energy is basis of electrical power for whole villages • in the future, people will rely more on the sun	Solar energy is the best form of energy and will be relied upon more in the future.	The author's purpose is to influence or persuade the reader that it is important to invest in solar energy because it should be made our primary energy source.

p. 66 Objective 6—Distinguishing Between Fact and Opinion: Level 6

A. *Answers will vary. Possible answers:*

1. Rodeos are sporting contests where cowboys and cowgirls display their skills and form in roping and riding events. In 1888, the first rodeo was held before an audience. Young people take part in them as well as adults.

2. This was not fair to the cowgirls.

3. "eventually," "achieved a balance," "enjoyable recreation"

B. *Answers will vary. Possible answers:*

Facts	Opinions
• Rodeos are sporting contests where cowboys and cowgirls display their skills and form in roping and riding events. • In 1888, the first rodeo was held before an audience. • Events fall into two categories: stock events and timed events. • Today there are all-girl rodeos.	• It was not fair to cowgirls that women and girls were excluded from many rodeo events. • Today, rodeos have achieved a balance in competition, now that men and women have their own shows.

p. 67 Objective 6—Distinguishing Between Fact and Opinion: Level 7

A. *Answers will vary. Possible answers:*

1. On March 20, 1999, the *Breitling Orbiter 3* flew non-stop around the world. Numerous other attempts to circle the globe by balloon had ended in failure. The *Orbiter 3* was in the air longer than any balloon on record.

2. Like the first people to land on the moon, Jones and Picard are true modern day heroes.

3. "adventurous and courageous," "true modern day heroes," "helped by sheer luck"

B. *Answers will vary. Possible answers:*

Facts	Nonfacts
• On March 20, 1999, the Breitling Orbiter 3 *flew around the world non-stop in just over 20 days.*	• *Jones and Picard were adventurous and courageous.*
• *Brian Jones and Bertrand Picard piloted the balloon.*	• *They achieved one of the biggest goals in aviation history.*
• *Meteorologists and satellite experts mapped the route for the pilots in the air.*	• *Jones and Picard are true modern day heroes.*
• *The* Orbiter 3 *was in the air longer than any balloon on record.*	• *The pilots were helped by sheer luck.*

p. 68 Objective 6—Distinguishing Between Fact and Opinion: Level 8

A. *Answers will vary. Possible answers:*

1. A statue of Friedrich Schiller can be found in the following cities: Cleveland, Omaha, St. Louis, New Orleans, San Francisco, and New York.

   Schiller's plays were produced in the US almost a decade before his death.

   Schiller died in 1805.

2. Schiller was inspired by the American Revolution and by the belief that all men are created equal.

3. "an idea prized by Americans," "Schiller was inspired," "Schiller is certainly worth remembering"

B. *Answers will vary. Possible answer:*

Facts	Opinions
• *A statue of Schiller can be found in each of these cities: Cleveland, Omaha, St. Louis, New Orleans, San Francisco, and New York.*	• *The people living in the cities that erected monuments respected Schiller.*
• *Schiller's plays began to be produced in the US almost a decade before his death.*	• *Schiller is important to people because of his idea of freedom.*
• *Two important advocates were Abraham Lincoln and Frederick Douglass.*	• *Schiller was inspired by the American Revolution and by the belief that all men are created equal.*
• *Schiller died in 1805 at the age of 45.*	• *At the time Schiller wrote, the belief in human freedom was not widely accepted.*
	• *Schiller was admired more 50 years after his death.*
	• *Schiller is to be remembered for making the idea of freedom more acceptable and popular.*

p. 76 Objective 1—Analyzing the Prompt: Subject, Purpose, and Audience

Subject: asking permission for a new pet

Purpose: persuade

Audience: family members

Subject: relating a weather experience

Purpose: to describe or to inform

Audience: science class

Subject: explaining the best thing about school

Purpose: to state an opinion or to inform

Audience: classmates, students in other grades, faculty

p. 78 Objectives 2—Exploring Ideas and Planning a Composition

Answers will vary.

p. 83 Objectives 2 and 4—Organizing and Elaborating Ideas

Answers will vary.

p. 86 Objectives 3, 5, 6, and 7—Following Language Conventions

Movie Ratings should not <u>preevent</u> teenagers under the age of seventeen from seeing whatever movie they want. <u>Too see</u>. <u>Its</u> not <u>fare</u>. If a teenager <u>wan'ts</u> to see a movie that's rated "R<u>.</u>" <u>they</u> should be <u>alowed</u> <u>too</u>. Teenagers under the age of seventeen have <u>responsibly</u> <u>jobbs</u>. They have to make <u>judgements</u> about <u>alot</u> of things<u>,</u> <u>everyday</u> in order for them to keep those jobs. They should be able to <u>pic</u> <u>there</u> own movies. Otherwise, they <u>wont</u> <u>never</u> be <u>alowed</u> to <u>grough</u> up.

Corrected: Movie ratings should not prevent teenagers under the age of seventeen from seeing whatever movie they want to see. It's not fair. If a teenager wants to see a movie that's rated "R," he or she should be allowed to. Teenagers under the age of seventeen have responsible jobs. They have to make judgments about a lot of things every day in order for them to keep those jobs. They should be able to pick their own movies. Otherwise, they won't ever be allowed to grow up.

p. 125—Interpreting a Speaker's Message: Understanding a Skill

Answers will vary.

NOTES	
Before Listening	
• purpose	• *Answers will vary.*
• barriers	• *Students may state judgments about the speaker or topic.*
During Listening	
• main idea	• *Sign the petition.*
• nonverbal cues	• *Students may note changes in body language.*
• verbal cues	• *Students may note intonation, voice modulation, pacing.*
• comparisons	• *Answers will vary. Dogs are not products.*
After Listening	
• questions	• *Answers will vary.*
• conclusions	• *Answers will vary.*
• causes	• *Answers will vary.*

p. 126—Interpreting a Speaker's Message: Level 6

Answers will vary.

NOTES	
Before Listening	
• purpose	• *Answers will vary.*
• barriers	• *Students may state judgments about the speaker.*
During Listening	
• main idea	• Vote for Arun Singh.
• nonverbal cues	• *Students may note changes in body language.*
• verbal cues	• *Students may note intonation, voice modulation, pacing.*
• comparisons	• new furniture is an improvement
	• more experience than opponent
	• participation in school activities
After Listening	
• questions	• *Answers will vary.*
• conclusions	• *Answers will vary.*
• causes	• *Answers will vary.*

p. 126—Interpreting a Speaker's Message: Level 7

Answers will vary.

NOTES	
Before Listening • purpose • barriers	• *Answers will vary.* • *Students may state judgments about the speaker.*
During Listening • main idea • nonverbal cues • verbal cues • comparisons	• Nominate Haan Lu for Student Council President • *Students may note changes in body language.* • *Students may note intonation, voice modulation, pacing.* • opponent handing out balloons and prizes; speaker doesn't resort to briberty • more experience than opponent
After Listening • questions • conclusions • causes	• *Answers will vary.* • *Answers will vary.* • *Answers will vary.*

p. 126—Interpreting a Speaker's Message: Level 8

Answers will vary.

NOTES	
Before Listening • purpose • barriers	• *Answers will vary.* • *Students may state judgments about the speaker.*
During Listening • main idea • nonverbal cues • verbal cues • comparisons	• Support Ronnika Barnes-save the park • *Students may note changes in body language.* • *Students may note intonation, voice modulation, pacing.* • people love the park, parking lot would be an eyesore • happy mother in beautiful park vs. concrete and pollution
After Listening • questions • conclusions • causes	• *Answers will vary.* • *Answers will vary.* • *Answers will vary.*

p. 128—Distinguish Between a Speaker's Opinion and Fact: Level 6

Answers will vary. Possible answers are shown below

Facts	Opinions
• In 1994 she won the Newbery Medal • the book was later made into a movie • chronicles the experiences of a white boy and a black slave... • Born in New York City in 1923...has written several children's books.... She has also written books for adults.	• Anyone...agrees that Paula Fox is a most talented author. • ...the book stands out for more than its heartbreaking subject matter... • By the end of the book, readers feel they have fought...

B.

1. Answers will vary. See above chart.

2. Answers will vary. See above chart.

3. anyone...agrees, most talented, straightforward writing style, keen insight, book stands out, heart-breaking subject matter, readers feel

p. 128—Distinguish Between a Speaker's Opinion and Fact: Level 7

Answers will vary. Possible answers are shown below.

Facts	Opinions
• The author, named Elwyn...was born in Mount Vernon in 1899. • In 1925, he started writing for *The New Yorker* magazine. • Many of his works tell of his life in Maine. • Born in New York City in 1923...has written several children's books.... She has also written books for adults. • *Stuart Little*, which was published in 1945... • In 1963, White received the Presidential Medal of Freedom and in 1985, a Pulitzer... • White died in 1985.	• Anyone...has fallen in love with the narrative of E. B. White. • Known chiefly as an essay writer, White wrote in an informal.... • But among children and parents, White's poetry and children's books are the most memorable. • White's children's books...best around. • *The Trumpet of the Swan* is by far his best work. • He remains one of the most beloved children's authors of our time.

B.

1. Answers will vary. See above chart.

2. Answers will vary. See above chart.

3. has fallen in love, most memorable, best around, his best work, most beloved

p. 128—Distinguish Between a Speaker's Opinion and Fact: Level 8

Answers will vary. Possible answers are shown below.

Facts	Opinions
• Born in Elizabeth, New Jersey in 1938 • Some of Judy Blume's other books for children.... • Blume has written two books for adults.... • In 1986, Judy Blume published....	• become a favorite of both children... • Blume's books are celebrated for their ... • *Are You There God*....is by far her most beloved book. • Blume won over adult audiences.... • ...this hasn't changed her views on writing. • She knows how to make children... • This bold move shows her willingness...

B.

1. Answers will vary. See above chart.

2. Answers will vary. See above chart.

3. become a favorite, books are celebrated, is by far her most beloved, she knows how, this bold move, shows her willingness

p. 130—Interpreting and Analyzing Advertisements: Level 6

A. Advertisement: R. J. Sneakers

1. R. J. Sneakers; to sell this brand of sneakers

2. Preteens and teenage boys

3. "The fastest feet in town!" "These sneakers are cool!"

4. Sale; uses a celebrity endorsement

5. You'll be cool and good at sports like this celebrity.

B. Answers will vary.

Images and Words	Target Audience	Associations
Picture of R. J. Thomas Celebrity	boys	power
		Message: You'll be famous. You'll be admired, maybe even make millions of dollars. People will want to be like you.
images of boys playing basketball, sinking a basket	boys	competition, winning Message: You'll be good at sports, jump higher. You'll be a winner.
slogan: the fastest feet in town	boys	Message: You'll be a winner.
20% off sale	boys, parents	savings, great deal Message: Buy now!

p. 131—Interpreting and Analyzing Advertisements: Level 7

A. Advertisement: Daisy Dee Cereal

1. Daisy Dee Cereal; to sell this brand of cereal

2. preteen and teenage girls

3. "Famous movie star Daisy Dee says it's the best!"

4. Special Offer- a plastic ring, uses celebrity appeal

5. popularity, romance, beauty

B.

Answers will vary.

Images and Words	Target Audience	Associations
Celebrity Daisy Dee	preteen and teenage girls	beauty, fame, charisma Message: You'll be popular and beautiful if you buy this product.
Special Offering	preteen and teenage girls	free gift ring means love
"Famous movie star Daisy Dee says it's the best!"	preteen and teenage girls	having the best Message: If she says it's the best, then it must be true. If I buy it then I have the best.

p. 132—Interpreting and Analyzing Advertisements: Level 8

A. Advertisement: A. D. O. Radio

1. A.D.O. Radio, purpose-to sell radios

2. teenagers, parents

3. On Sale Now

4. portrays a "cool" image, you will be popular if you buy this product

5. popularity, independence

B.

Images and Words	Target Audience	Associations
teenage girls	preteen and teenage girls	being part of a crowd following the "cool guy" friendship popularity romance Message: You'll be part of the cool crowd.
girls following	teenage boys	popularity independence Message: Girls will like you.
On Sale Now	parents teens	savings Message: Buy this product before it's too late.

TAAS Practice Test Copymasters, Grade 6
TEST I—WRITING: PART 1

Note: For Writing practice test items, the correct answer is given, followed by

- the targeted TAAS Objective;
- the specific skill or rule tested; and
- references to pages in *The Language of Literature* (*LoL*) and *Language Network* (*LN*) on which the targeted skill is taught.

SA-1. **B** Writing Obj. 5. Run-on sentence. *LoL*, pp. T171, 635; *LN*, pp. 25–27.

SA-2. **F** Writing Obj. 5. Correctly written sentences that should be combined. *LoL*, pp. T685, 713; *LN*, pp. 282–285.

SA-3. **D** Writing Obj. 5.

SB-1. **F** Writing Obj. 6. Use the present tense to show that an action occurs in the present. *LoL*, p. R85; *LN*, pp. 107–110.

SB-2. **D** Writing Obj. 6. Use the superlative degree of comparison to compare three or more people, things, or actions. *LoL*, pp. 380, T380; *LN*, pp. 133–135.

SC-1. **H** Writing Obj. 7. Use commas to set off a nonessential clause. *LoL*, p. R56.

SC-2. **D** Writing Obj. 7.

1. **D** Writing Obj. 6. Use the present perfect tense to show that an action was completed at some indefinite time in the past. *LoL*, p. R85; *LN*, pp. 107–110.

2. **J** Writing Obj. 6. Use an adverb to modify a verb, an adjective, or another adverb. Word modified: *changed. LoL*, pp. T339, 434; *LN*, pp. 130–132.

3. **A** Writing Obj. 6. An intensive pronoun emphasizes the noun or pronoun in the same sentence. Intensive pronouns are not necessary to the sense of the sentence. *LoL*, pp. R54, R83; *LN*, pp. 64–65.

4. **H** Writing Obj. 6. Use the past tense to show that an action occurred in the past. *LoL*, p. R85; *LN*, pp. 107–110.

5. **B** Writing Obj. 6. A pronoun must agree with its referent in number, gender, and person. Referents: *movies* and *basketball. LoL*, pp. R66, R80; *LN*, pp. 69–71.

6. **H** Writing Obj. 6. Use the comparative degree of comparison to compare two persons, places, or things. *LoL*, pp. T380, 434, 862; *LN*, pp. 133–135.

7. **A** Writing Obj. 6. Use the present tense to show that an action occurs in the present. *LoL*, p. R85; *LN*, pp. 107–110.

8. **G** Writing Obj. 6. A pronoun must agree with its referent in number, gender, and person. Referent: *actors. LoL*, pp. R66, R80; *LN*, pp. 69–71.

9. **D** Writing Obj. 6. Use the present tense to show that an action occurs in the present. *LoL*, p. R85; *LN*, pp. 107–110.

10. **H** Writing Obj. 6. Use the superlative degree of comparison to compare three or more people, things, or actions. *LoL*, pp. 380, T380; *LN*, pp. 133–135.

11. **B** Writing Obj. 6. Use the possessive case of a personal pronoun to show ownership or possession. Do not confuse a contraction with a possessive pronoun. *LoL*, pp. T288, 302; *LN*, pp. 61–63.

12. **F** Writing Obj. 6. Use the present tense to show that an action occurs in the present. *LoL*, p. R85; *LN*, pp. 107–110.

13. **D** Writing Obj. 5.

14. **F** Writing Obj. 5. Incomplete sentence. *LoL*, pp. T33, T635, 694; *LN*, pp. 25–27.

15. **C** Writing Obj. 5. Correctly written sentences that should be combined. *LoL*, pp. T685, 713; *LN*, pp. 282–285.

16. **G** Writing Obj. 5. Run-on sentence. *LoL*, T171, 635; *LN*, pp. 25–27.

17. **B** Writing Obj. 5. Incomplete sentence. *LoL*, pp. T33, T635, 694; *LN*, pp. 25–27.

18. **H** Writing Obj. 5. Incomplete sentence. *LoL*, pp. T33, T635, 694; *LN*, pp. 25–27.

19. **B** Writing Obj. 5. Correctly written sentences that should be combined. *LoL*, pp. T685, 713; *LN*, pp. 282–285.

20. **F** Writing Obj. 5. Incomplete sentence. *LoL*, pp. T33, T635, 694; *LN*, pp. 25–27.

21. **A** Writing Obj. 5. Incomplete sentence. *LoL*, pp. T33, T635, 694; *LN*, pp. 25–27.

22. **J** Writing Obj. 5. Correctly written sentences that should be combined. *LoL*, pp. T685, 713; *LN*, pp. 282–285.

23. **D** Writing Obj. 5.

24. **J** Writing Obj. 5.

25. **A** Writing Obj. 5. Correctly written sentences that should be combined. *LoL*, pp. T685, 713; *LN*, pp. 282–285.

26. **F** Writing Obj. 5. Run-on sentence. *LoL*, p.

T171, 635; *LN*, pp. 25–27.

27. A Writing Obj. 7. *it's* should be *its*.

28. G Writing Obj. 7. *roman catholic church* should be *Roman Catholic Church*; Capitalize religious denominations. *LoL*, p 229; *LN*, p. 187.

29. C Writing Obj. 7. Use commas to set off a nonessential clause. *LoL*, p. R56

30. F Writing Obj. 7. *bread* should be *bred*.

31. B Writing Obj. 7. *alps* should be *Alps*; Capitalize proper nouns. *LoL*, p 229; *LN*, p. 36.

32. J Writing Obj. 7.

33. A Writing Obj. 7. *Bernard's* should be *Bernards*.

34. H Writing Obj. 7. Use a period to punctuate a declarative sentence. *LoL*, p. T47; *LN*, pp. 16–17.

35. A Writing Obj. 7. *for* should be *four*.

36. J Writing Obj. 7.

37. A Writing Obj. 7. *runing* should be *running*.

38. J Writing Obj. 7.

39. C Writing Obj. 7. In a series of three or more items, use a comma after every item except the last one. *LoL*, pp. R56, R77; *LN*, p. 209.

40. G Writing Obj. 7. *athens* should be *Athens*; Capitalize proper nouns. *LoL*, p. 229; *LN*, p. 36.

TEST I—WRITING: PART 2

Writing Obj. 1–4. To score students' compositions, use the rubric on p. 113.

TEST I—READING

Note: For Reading practice test items, the correct answer is given, followed by a paragraph identifying

- the targeted TAAS Objective and skill name,
- references to pages in *Preparing for TAAS* and *The Language of Literature* (*LoL*) on which the targeted skill is taught, and
- explanations to assist you with error analysis and remediation.

SD-1. B Reading Obj. 1: Context Clues, pp. 11–14; *LoL*, p. 79.

SD-2. J Reading Obj. 5: Inferences, pp. 49–52; *LoL*, p. 613.
No evidence in the passage supports G or H. F is a possible explanation, but J is the answer best supported by the text. The play has already occurred.

1. C Reading Obj. 5: Inferences, pp. 49–52; *LoL*, p. 613.
No evidence in the passage supports A or D. B is a possible explanation, but C is the answer best supported by the text. The passage states that "biology became more fun than gym class."

2. J Reading Obj. 1: Context Clues, pp. 11–14; *LoL*, p. 79.

3. D Reading Obj. 2, 3: Main Idea, pp. 27–30; *LoL*, pp. 101, 636.
A is an inference. B and C are supporting details.

4. F Reading Obj. 5: Inferences, pp. 49–52; *LoL*, p. 613.
No evidence in the passage supports G, H, or J. F is the answer best supported by the text. The brochure indicates that Monique and Francoise have rescued animals whose owners no longer wanted them.

5. B Reading Obj. 5: Fact-Opinion, pp. 65–68; *LoL*, p. 699.
A, C, and D are not stated in the passage. B is stated in the last para. of the brochure.

6. J Reading Obj. 2: Supporting Details, pp. 19–22; *LoL*, p. 201.
F, G, and H are not stated in the passage. J is stated in the brochure.

7. A Reading Obj. 5: Inferences, pp. 49–52; *LoL*, p. 613.
No evidence in the passage supports B or C. D is a possible explanation, but A is the answer best supported by the text. The rules ask visitors not to make too much noise. It is clear from the rules that not all the zoo's animals like to be petted, so D can be eliminated.

8. F Reading Obj. 5: Inferences, pp. 49–52; *LoL*, p. 613.
No evidence in the passage supports G, H, or J. F is the answer best supported by the text. Because Terri's sister is old enough to drive, she is most likely a high-school student.

9. B Reading Obj. 3: Summarizing, pp. 31–34; *LoL*, p. 340.
A is not addressed in the passage. C omits essential details. D is false.

10. G Reading Obj. 5: Inferences, pp. 49–52; *LoL*, p. 613.
No evidence in the passage supports F or J. H is a possible explanation, but G is the answer best supported by the text. Mr. Siddall says they did a terrific job, not that he is upset with them.

11. C Reading Obj. 1: Context Clues, pp. 11–14;

LoL, p. 79.

12. F Reading Obj. 5: Inferences, pp. 49–52; *LoL*, p. 613.
No evidence in the passage supports G, H, or J. F is the answer best supported by the text. Terri received a letter in her mailbox, indicating that she is most likely at her parents' house.

13. D Reading Obj. 1: Context Clues, pp. 11–14; *LoL*, p. 79.

14. H Reading Obj. 5: Inferences, pp. 49–52; LoL, p. 613.
No evidence in the passage supports F or J. G is a possible explanation, but H is the answer best supported by the text. Amanda Debs's letter mentions libraries and says that the float "looks just right"; Terri sits on the float to read her letter as though "it really were quiet like a library."

15. D Reading Obj. 6: Author's Perspective & Purpose, pp. 61–64; *LoL*, pp. 135, 418.
A and C are not addressed in the passage. B is not supported: Two paragraphs address the studio system, but the author also discusses other parts of the history of film. D is the best answer: Each paragraph in the passage describes a way that the film industry has changed.

16. G Reading Obj. 5: Inferences, pp. 49–52; *LoL*, p. 613.
No evidence in the passage supports F, H, or J. G is the answer best supported by the text. The passage states that Hollywood became the movie capital between 1908 and 1912. Producers had moved to California from New York City, so it is most likely that New York City is where movies were shot before 1908.

17. C Reading Obj. 5: Inferences, pp. 49–52; *LoL*, p. 613.
A and D are false. No evidence in the passage supports B. C is the answer best supported by the text. *The Jazz Singer* was the first film in which the audience could hear the actors.

18. F Reading Obj. 3: Summarizing, pp. 31–34; *LoL*, p. 340.
G omits essential points. H is false. J is not addressed in the passage.

19. B Reading Obj. 5: Inferences, pp. 49–52; *LoL*, p. 613.
No evidence in the passage supports A or C. D is a possible explanation, but B is the answer best supported by the text. The passage states that during the period in which studios ran the industry, American writers and directors became restless because they saw that writers and directors in Europe had

greater freedom.

20. J Reading Obj. 5: Inferences, pp. 49–52; *LoL*, p. 613.
No evidence in the passage supports F or G. H is a possible explanation, but J is the answer best supported by the text. The passage states that in the future movies may use computer-generated actors instead of real people.

21. A Reading Obj 5: Inferences, pp. 49–52; *LoL*, p. 613.
No evidence in the passage supports B. D is false. C is a possible explanation, but A is the answer best supported by the text. The passage states that the XP patient must be completely covered when he or she goes outside, even if it is cloudy, because no light can be allowed to touch him or her.

22. G Reading Obj. 2, 3: Main Idea, pp. 27–30; *LoL*, pp. 101, 636.
F and H are false. J is a supporting detail. G is stated in para. 6.

23. C Reading Obj. 2: Supporting Details, pp. 19–22; *LoL*, p. 201.
A and B are not stated in the passage. D is contradicted in para. 5. C is stated in para. 2.

24. J Reading Obj. 2: Supporting Details, pp. 19–22; *LoL*, p. 201.
F, G, and H are not stated in the passage. J is stated in para. 2.

25. C Reading Obj. 5: Inferences, pp. 49–52; *LoL*, p. 613.
No evidence in the passage supports A. B and D are false. C is the answer best supported by the text. According to the passage, carcinoma cancers do not spread to internal organs, which makes them less dangerous than melanoma skin cancer.

26. J Reading Obj. 5: Inferences, pp. 49–52; *LoL*, p. 613.
No evidence in the passage supports F, G, or H. J is the answer best supported by the text. According to the passage, XP patients should wear sunscreen inside the house to protect them from the longer wavelength ultraviolet light in sun coming through windows.

27. A Reading Obj. 6: Author's Perspective & Purpose, pp. 61–64; *LoL*, pp. 154, 363.
B and C are not addressed in the passage. D is not supported: The passage demonstrates that the author has a good understanding of XP. A is the best answer: The author states that life is difficult for those with XP.

28. G Reading Obj. 1: Context Clues, pp. 11–14; *LoL*, p. 79.

29. D Reading Obj. 5: Fact-Opinion, pp. 65–68; *LoL*,

p. 699.
A is not stated in the passage. B is contradicted in para. 4. C is contradicted in para. 2. D is stated in para. 1.

30. **G** Reading Obj. 5: Fact-Opinion, pp. 65–68; *LoL,* p. 699.
F and H are not stated in the passage. J is a fact. G is stated in para. 3.

31. **B** Reading Obj. 5: Inferences, pp. 49–52; *LoL,* p. 613.
No evidence in the passage supports A, C, or D. B is the answer best supported by the text. While teaching at Ferry Hall School, Perkins came in contact with Chicago's settlement houses.

32. **F** Reading Obj. 2: Supporting Details, pp. 19–22; *LoL,* p. 201.
G, H, and J are not stated in the passage. F is stated in para. 6.

33. **B** Reading Obj. 5: Inferences, pp. 49–52; *LoL,* p. 613.
No evidence in the passage supports A, C, or D. B is the answer best supported by the text. The passage states that Perkins was labor secretary for all four of FDR's terms and that she left her post in 1945.

34. **H** Reading Obj. 3: Summarizing, pp. 31–34; *LoL,* p. 340.
F and J include nonessential details. G is false.

35. **C** Reading Obj. 2: Sequential Order, pp. 53–56; *LoL,* p. 364.
B and D are not stated in the passage. C occurs before A.

36. **F** Reading Obj. 5: Inferences, pp. 49–52; *LoL,* p. 613.
No evidence in the passage supports G, H, or J. F is the answer best supported by the text. The passage states that Rhonda is excited to come to art class, and then states that the subject of the class is self portraits.

37. **A** Reading Obj. 5: Fact-Opinion, pp. 65–68; *LoL,* p. 699.
B and C are not stated in the passage. D is contradicted in the flier. A is stated in para. 1 of the flier.

38. **H** Reading Obj. 5: Inferences, pp. 49–52; *LoL,* p. 613.
No evidence in the passage supports F, G, or J. H is the answer best supported by the text. The flier says that entrants should not paint copies of their photographs.

39. **D** Reading Obj. 2, 3: Main Idea, pp. 27–30; *LoL,* pp. 101, 636.
A and C are false. B is a generalization. D is stated in the "WIN" section.

40. **J** Reading Obj. 2: Supporting Details, pp. 19–22; *LoL,* p. 201.
F, G, and H are not stated in the passage. J is stated in the "PRIZES" section of the flier.

TEST II—WRITING: PART 1

Note: For Writing practice test items, the correct answer is given, followed by

- the targeted TAAS Objective;
- the specific skill or rule tested; and
- references to pages in *The Language of Literature* (*LoL*) and *Language Network* (*LN*) on which the targeted skill is taught.

SA-1. **B** Writing Obj. 5. Incomplete sentence. *LoL,* pp. T33, T635, 694; *LN,* pp. 25–27.

SA-2. **F** Writing Obj. 5. Correctly written sentences that should be combined. *LoL,* pp. T685, 713; *LN,* pp. 282–285.

SA-3. **D** Writing Obj. 5.

SB-1. **H** Writing Obj. 6. Use the present tense to show that an action occurs in the present. *LoL,* p. R85; *LN,* pp. 107–110.

SB-2. **B** Writing Obj. 6. A pronoun must agree with its referent in number, gender, and person. Referent: *calendar. LoL,* pp. R66, R80; *LN,* pp. 69–71.

SC-1. **H** Writing Obj. 7. Use a comma to separate an introductory adverb clause from the rest of the sentence. *LoL,* p. R56.

SC-2. **D** Writing Obj. 7.

1. **D** Writing Obj. 6. Use the present tense to show that an action occurs in the present. *LoL,* p. R85; *LN,* pp. 107–110.

2. **F** Writing Obj. 6. A pronoun must agree with its referent in number, gender, and person. Referent: *ozone. LoL,* pp. R66, R80; *LN,* pp. 69–71.

3. **D** Writing Obj. 6. Use the comparative degree of comparison to compare two persons, places, or things. *LoL,* pp. 380, T380; *LN,* pp. 133–135.

4. **G** Writing Obj. 6. Use the future tense to show that an action will occur in the future. *LoL,* p. T274: *LN,* pp. 107–110.

5. **A** Writing Obj. 6. Use the superlative degree of comparison to compare three or more people, things, or actions. *LoL,* pp. 380, T380; *LN,* pp. 133–135.

6. **H** Writing Obj. 6. Use the possessive case of a personal pronoun to show ownership or pos-

session. Do not confuse a contraction with a possessive pronoun. *LoL*, pp. T288, 302; *LN*, pp. 61–63.

7. C Writing Obj. 6. A pronoun must agree with its referent in number, gender, and person. Referent: *common flea*. *LoL*, pp. R66, R80; *LN*, pp. 69–71.

8. F Writing Obj. 6. Use the possessive case of a personal pronoun to show ownership or possession. Do not confuse a contraction with a possessive pronoun. *LoL*, pp. T288, 302; *LN*, pp. 61–63.

9. B Writing Obj. 6. Use a demonstrative pronoun to point out a specific person, place, thing, or idea. The demonstrative pronouns are *this, these, that,* and *those*. *LoL*, pp. R54, R83; *LN*, pp. 67–68.

10. H Writing Obj. 6. Use the past tense to show that an action occurred in the past. *LoL*, p. R85; *LN*, pp. 107–110.

11. D Writing Obj. 6. Use an adverb to modify a verb, an adjective, or another adverb. Words modified: *had worn*. *LoL*, pp. T339, 434; *LN*, pp. 130–132.

12. H Writing Obj. 6. Use the objective form of a personal pronoun when the pronoun functions as the object of a preposition. *LoL*, pp. 218, T218; *LN*, pp. 59–60.

13. C Writing Obj. 5. Incomplete sentence. *LoL*, pp. T33, T635, 694; *LN*, pp. 25–27.

14. F Writing Obj. 5. Incomplete sentence. *LoL*, pp. T33, T635, 694; *LN*, pp. 25–27.

15. C Writing Obj. 7. Correctly written sentences that should be combined. *LoL*, pp. T685, 713; *LN*, pp. 282–285.

16. J Writing Obj. 5.

17. C Writing Obj. 5. Correctly written sentences that should be combined. *LoL*, pp. T685, 713; *LN*, pp. 282–285.

18. J Writing Obj. 5.

19. C Writing Obj. 5. Run-on sentence. *LoL*, pp. T171, 635; *LN*, pp. 25–27.

20. F Writing Obj. 5. Incomplete sentence. *LoL*, pp. T33, T635, 694; *LN*, pp. 25–27.

21. A Writing Obj. 5. Incomplete sentence. *LoL*, pp. T33, T635, 694; *LN*, pp. 25–27.

22. H Writing Obj. 5. Incomplete sentence. *LoL*, pp. T33, T635, 694; *LN*, pp. 25–27.

23. D Writing Obj. 5.

24. J Writing Obj. 5. Correctly written sentences that should be combined. *LoL*, pp. T685, 713; *LN*, pp. 282–285.

25. D Writing Obj. 5.

26. H Writing Obj. 5. Incomplete sentence. *LoL*, pp. T33, T635, 694; *LN*, pp. 25–27.

27. C Writing Obj. 7. *persons* should be *person's*; To form the possessive of a singular noun, add an apostrophe and an *s*. *LoL*, pp. T253, 302, T303; *LN*, pp. 222–223.

28. F Writing Obj. 7. *concentrateons* should be *concentrations*.

29. C Writing Obj. 7. Use commas to set off a nonessential clause. *LoL*, p. R56.

30. F Writing Obj. 7. *proceses* should be *processes*.

31. B Writing Obj. 7. *new Mexico* should be *New Mexico*; Capitalize proper nouns. *LoL*, p. 229; *LN*, p. 36.

32. G Writing Obj. 7. *bottles aware, inc.* should be *Bottles Aware, Inc.*; Capitalize proper nouns. *LoL*, p. 229; *LN*, p. 36.

33. D Writing Obj. 7.

34. G Writing Obj. 7. *texas* should be *Texas*; Capitalize proper nouns. *LoL*, p. 229; *LN*, p. 36.

35. A Writing Obj. 7. *busness* should be *business*.

36. H Writing Obj. 7. In a series of three or more items, use a comma after every item except the last one. *LoL*, pp. R56, R77; *LN*, p. 209.

37. D Writing Obj. 7.

38. F Writing Obj. 7. *distric* should be *district*.

39. B Writing Obj. 7. *Art* should be *art*; *Music* should be *music*; Do not capitalize common nouns. *LoL*, p. 229; *LN*, p. 36.

40. H Writing Obj. 7. Use a comma before the coordinating conjunction that joins the two independent clauses of a compound sentence. *LoL*, pp. R56, R76: *LN*, p. 155.

TEST II—WRITING: PART 2

Writing Obj. 1–4. To score students' compositions, use the rubric on p. 95.

TEST II—READING

Note: For Reading practice test items, the correct answer is given, followed by a paragraph identifying

- the targeted TAAS Objective and skill name,
- references to pages in *Preparing for TAAS* and *The Language of Literature* (*LoL*) on which the targeted skill is taught, and
- explanations to assist you with error analysis and remediation.

SD-1. B Reading Obj. 1: Context Clues, pp. 11–14; *LoL*, p. 79.

SD-2. J Reading Obj. 5: Inferences, pp. 49–52; *LoL*, p. 613.
No evidence in the passage supports G or H. F is a possible explanation, but J is the answer best supported by the text. After diving for the ball, Edward dusts himself off and notices that his joystick has disappeared and that there are other people around him.

1. B Reading Obj. 3: Summarizing, pp. 31–34; *LoL*, p. 340.
A and C are false. D is a generalization.

2. H Reading Obj. 5: Inferences, pp. 49–52; *LoL*, p. 613.
No evidence in the passage supports F, G, or J. H is the answer best supported by the text. Tina thinks that Ursula's talents would be good for the yearbook staff.

3. A Reading Obj. 2: Supporting Details, pp. 19–22; *LoL*, p. 201.
B, C, and D are not stated in the passage. A is stated in para. 2.

4. F Reading Obj. 5: Inferences, pp. 49–52; *LoL*, p. 613.
No evidence in the passage supports J. G and H are possible explanations, but F is the answer best supported by the text. Ursula's sister had been editor-in-chief, and Ursula thinks that she could follow in her sister's footsteps.

5. C Reading Obj. 5: Evaluating & Making Judgments, pp. 53–56; *LoL*, p. 462.
Omitting A or D on the application would not affect its usefulness. B is a possible explanation, but C is the best answer. As long as an application contained the student's name, the student could be contacted to fill in any missing information.

6. J Reading Obj. 5: Fact-Opinion, pp. 65–68; *LoL*, p. 699.
F, G, and H are not stated in the passage. J is stated in the application under "Copy Editor."

7. D Reading Obj. 1: Context Clues, pp. 11–14; *LoL*, p. 79.

8. J Reading Obj. 3: Summarizing, pp. 31–34; *LoL*, p. 340.
F is false. G is a generalization. H omits essential details.

9. B Reading Obj. 5: Evaluating & Making Judgments, pp. 53–56; *LoL*, p. 462.
A is false. No evidence in the passage supports D. C is a possible explanation, but B is the answer best supported by the text. According to the passage, Gabriela already

knows how to make friends, so C can be eliminated. The passage states that Gabriela's nervousness is mixed with excitement, which supports answer B.

10. H Reading Obj. 5: Inferences, pp. 49–52; *LoL*, p. 613.
No evidence in the passage supports F, G, or J. H is the answer best supported by the text. In the passage, Gabriela is not yet a student at Finley, but she will be one the following day.

11. C Reading Obj. 5: Inferences, pp. 49–52; *LoL*, p. 613.
No evidence in the passage supports A, B, or D. C is the answer best supported by the text. The idea of starting over at Finley makes Gabriela nervous.

12. G Reading Obj. 1: Context Clues, pp. 11–14; *LoL*, p. 79.

13. D Reading Obj. 5: Inferences, pp. 49–52; *LoL*, p. 613.
No evidence in the passage supports B or C. A is a possible explanation, but D is the answer best supported by the text. Gabriela thinks that croutons "didn't taste like stale bread."

14. G Reading Obj. 4: Cause-Effect, pp. 35–38; *LoL*, p. 446.
There is no basis in the passage for F and H. J is stated but is not a cause. G is stated in para. 5.

15. A Reading Obj. 4: Cause-Effect, pp. 35–38; *LoL*, p. 446.
There is no basis in the passage for B, C, or D. A is stated in para. 1.

16. G Reading Obj. 2: Supporting Details, pp. 19–22; *LoL*, p. 201.
F, H, and J are not stated in the passage. G is stated in para. 2.

17. A Reading Obj. 5: Fact-Opinion, pp. 65–68; *LoL*, p. 699.
B and C are not stated in the passage. D is a fact. A is stated in para. 3.

18. J Reading Obj. 2, 3: Main Idea, pp. 27–30; *LoL*, pp. 101, 636.
F is a supporting detail. G is an inference. H is a generalization. J is stated in para. 1.

19. C Reading Obj. 6: Author's Perspective & Purpose, pp. 61–64; *LoL*, pp. 135, 418.
A is not supported: The passage mentions waterfalls, but does not try to persuade the reader to visit them. B and D are not addressed in the passage. C is the best answer: The author states that the reason many people visit Highlands is to go to the Condiment Shop, and devotes three of the five paragraphs to discussing the jellies and

jams.

20. G Reading Obj. 1: Context Clues, pp. 11–14; *LoL*, p. 79.

21. A Reading Obj 5: Evaluating & Making Judgments, pp. 53–56; *LoL*, p. 462.
No evidence in the passage supports C or D. B is a possible explanation, but A is the answer best supported by the text. Mrs. Edwards used to pick the fruit for the jellies herself, and although she is elderly, she still visits the store.

22. G Reading Obj. 5: Inferences, pp. 49–52; *LoL*, p. 613.
No evidence in the passage supports F or H. J is false. G is the answer best supported by the text. According to the passage, origami can be "used in other ways," and is a practical art.

23. A Reading Obj. 2, 3: Main Idea, pp. 27–30; *LoL*, pp. 101, 636.
B and D are supporting details. C is false.

24. H Reading Obj. 1: Context Clues, pp. 11–14; *LoL*, p. 79.

25. D Reading Obj. 5: Inferences, pp. 49–52; *LoL*, p. 613.
No evidence in the passage supports A or B. C is a possible explanation, but D is the answer best supported by the text. The illustrations portray animal shapes, and the passage mentions folding paper into a dragonfly or a swan. Geometric figures are only mentioned once.

26. H Reading Obj. 6: Author's Perspective & Purpose, pp. 61–64; *LoL*, pp. 154, 363.
F, G, and J are not addressed in the passage. H is the best answer: The author calls origami beautiful, powerful, and practical.

27. A Reading Obj. 2: Supporting Details, pp. 19–22; *LoL*, p. 201.
B and C are not stated in the passage. D is contradicted in para. 3. A is stated in para. 3.

28. J Reading Obj. 5: Fact-Opinion, pp. 65–68; *LoL*, p. 699.
F and H are not stated in the passage. G is contradicted in para. 2. J is stated in para. 2.

29. B Reading Obj. 2: Supporting Details, pp. 19–22; *LoL*, p. 201.
A, C, and D are not stated in the passage. B is stated in para. 2.

30. J Reading Obj. 5: Inferences, pp. 49–52; *LoL*, p. 613.
No evidence in the passage supports F or G. H is a possible explanation, but J is the answer best supported by the text. The passage says that birds come to Texas because the state's climate is comfortable even when it is cold elsewhere.

31. A Reading Obj. 5: Inferences, pp. 49–52; *LoL*, p. 613.
No evidence in the passage supports B, C, or D. A is the answer best supported by the text. The passage refers to "all the golden eagles that are left," which suggests that their numbers are small, and says that they have found safety in Texas.

32. H Reading Obj. 2, 3: Main Idea, pp. 27–30; *LoL*, pp. 101, 636.
F is an inference. G is a generalization. J is not stated in the passage. H is stated in the section.

33. B Reading Obj. 5: Inferences, pp. 49–52; *LoL*, p. 613.
No evidence in the passage supports A, C, or D. B is the answer best supported by the text. As woodpeckers like to live in forests, it is likely that the reason for this has to do with trees.

34. H Reading Obj. 5: Fact-Opinion, pp. 65–68; *LoL*, p. 699.
F and G are facts. J not stated in the passage. H is stated in para. 2.

35. A Reading Obj. 5: Inferences, pp. 49–52; *LoL*, p. 613.
No evidence in the passage supports B, C, or D. A is the answer best supported by the text. The fact that Jimmy's mother is reading the newspaper and that Jimmy is asking permission to go out supports A.

36. G Reading Obj. 2: Supporting Details, pp. 19–22; *LoL*, p. 201.
F, H, and J are not stated in the passage. G is stated in Letter 1.

37. C Reading Obj. 3: Summarizing, pp. 31–34; *LoL*, p. 340.
A and D are false. B omits essential details.

38. J Reading Obj. 2: Supporting Details, pp. 19–22; *LoL*, p. 201.
F, G, and H are not stated in the passage. J is stated in Letter 2.

39. A Reading Obj. 5: Inferences, pp. 49–52; *LoL*, p. 613.
B and D are false. No evidence in the passage supports C. A is the answer best supported by the text. The text states that "Even in parks that have natural history museums. . .", which suggests that not all parks have museums.

40. J Reading Obj. 5: Inferences, pp. 49–52; *LoL*, p. 613.
No evidence in the passage supports F or G. H is false. J is the answer best supported by the text. Both letters discuss crime in the park.

TAAS Practice Test Copymasters, Grade 7

TEST I—WRITING: PART 1

Note: For Writing practice test items, the correct answer is given, followed by

- the targeted TAAS Objective;

- the specific skill or rule tested; and

- references to pages in *The Language of Literature* (*LoL*) and *Language Network* (*LN*) on which the targeted skill is taught.

SA-1. **C** Writing Obj. 5. Run-on sentence. *LoL*, pp. T50, 79, T183; *LN*, pp. 26–27.

SA-2. **F** Writing Obj. 5. Correctly written sentences that should be combined. *LoL*, pp. 45, T126; *LN*, pp. 330–331.

SA-3. **D** Writing Obj. 5.

SB-1 **H** Writing Obj. 6. Use the present tense to show that an action occurs in the present. *LoL*, p. T683; *LN*, pp. 111–114.

SB-2. **B** Writing Obj. 6. Use the possessive case of a personal pronoun to show ownership or possession. Do not confuse a contraction with a possessive pronoun. *LoL*, p. T329; *LN*, pp. 65–67.

SC-1. **H** Writing Obj. 7. In a series of three or more items, use a comma after every item except the last one. *LoL*, p. T744; *LN*, p. 253.

SC-2. **D** Writing Obj. 7.

1. **B** Writing Obj. 6. Use an adverb to modify a verb, an adjective, or another adverb. Word modified: *chosen. LoL*, p. T457; *LN*, pp. 134–136.

2. **H** Writing Obj. 6. Use the pronoun *who* in questions and in subordinate clauses. To figure out the correct form, decide if the pronoun is the subject or object in the clause. Use *who* as the subject and *whom* as the object. *LoL*, p. R67; *LN*, p. 70.

3. **B** Writing Obj. 6. Use the present tense to show that an action occurs in the present. *LoL*, p. T683; *LN*, pp. 111–114.

4. **F** Writing Obj. 6. To form the plural of most nouns add *s. LoL*, p. R64; *LN*, p. 39.

5. **D** Writing Obj. 6. Use the possessive case of a personal pronoun to show ownership or possession. Do not confuse a contraction with a possessive pronoun. *LoL*, p. T329; *LN*, pp. 65–67.

6. **J** Writing Obj. 6. A pronoun must agree with its referent in number, gender, and person.

Referent: *tail. LoL*, p. 328; *LN*, pp. 73–78.

7. **C** Writing Obj. 6. Use the future tense to show that an action will occur in the future. *LoL*, p. T683; *LN*, pp. 111–114.

8. **F** Writing Obj. 6. Use the past tense to show that an action occurred in the past. *LoL*, p. T683; *LN*, pp. 111–114.

9. **C** Writing Obj. 6. Use the past perfect tense to show that an action or condition in the past preceded another past action or condition. *LoL*, p. T889; *LN*, pp. 111–114.

10. **G** Writing Obj. 6. To form the possessive of a singular noun, add an apostrophe and an *s. LoL*, p. T662; *LN*, pp. 42–43.

11. **C** A pronoun must agree with its referent in number, gender, and person. Referents: *Marsha* and *father. LoL*, p. 328; *LN*, pp. 73–78.

12. **J** Writing Obj. 6. Two negatives should not be used to express one negative meaning. *LoL*, p. T450; *LN*, pp. 142–143.

13. **D** Writing Obj. 5.

14. **F** Writing Obj. 5. Run-on sentence. *LoL*, pp. T50, 79, T183; *LN*, pp. 26–27.

15. **B** Writing Obj. 5. Incomplete sentence. *LoL*, pp. 64, 786; *LN*, pp. 25–27.

16. **J** Writing Obj. 5. Correctly written sentences that should be combined. *LoL*, pp. 45, T126; *LN*, pp. 330–331.

17. **A** Writing Obj. 5. Incomplete sentence. *LoL*, pp. 64, 786; *LN*, pp. 25–27.

18. **G** Writing Obj. 5. Correctly written sentences that should be combined. *LoL*, pp. 45, T126; *LN*, pp. 330–331.

19. **D** Writing Obj. 5.

20. **G** Writing Obj. 5. Run-on sentence. *LoL*, pp. T50, 79, T183; *LN*, pp. 26–27.

21. **B** Writing Obj. 5. Incomplete sentence. *LoL*, pp. 64, 786; *LN*, pp. 25–27.

22. **H** Writing Obj. 5. Correctly written sentences that should be combined. *LoL*, pp. 45, T126; *LN*, pp. 330–331.

23. **D** Writing Obj. 5.

24. **J** Writing Obj. 5. Correctly written sentences that should be combined. *LoL*, pp. 45, T126; *LN*, pp. 330–331.

25. **A** Writing Obj. 5. Run-on sentence. *LoL*, pp. T50, 79, T183; *LN*, pp. 26–27.

26. **G** Writing Obj. 5. Run-on sentence. *LoL*, pp. T50, 79, T183; *LN*, pp. 26–27.

27. **B** Writing Obj. 7. *lincoln* should be *Lincoln*; *kennedy* should be *Kennedy*; Capitalize proper nouns and adjectives. *LoL*, p. T80; *LN*, p. 36.

28. **J** Writing Obj. 7.

29. **C** Writing Obj. 7. Use a period to punctuate a declarative sentence. *LoL*, p. T172; *LN*, pp. 16–17.

30. **H** Writing Obj. 7. In a contraction an apostrophe is used to take the place of one or more missing letters. *LoL*, pp. R57, R81; *LN*, p. 266.

31. **A** Writing Obj. 7. *dissagreed* should be *disagreed*.

32. **H** Writing Obj. 7. Use a comma to set off a participial phrase. *LoL*, p. T616; *LN*, p. 176.

33. **C** Writing Obj. 7. Use a question mark to punctuate an interrogative sentence. *LoL*, p. 172; *LN*, pp. 16–17.

34. **F** Writing Obj. 7. *beleived* should be *believed*.

35. **A** Writing Obj. 7. *no* should be *know*.

36. **G** Writing Obj. 7. *Planets* should be *planets*; Do not capitalize common nouns. *LoL*, p. T80; *LN*, p. 36.

37. **D** Writing Obj. 7.

38. **J** Writing Obj. 7.

39. **B** Writing Obj. 7. *saturn* should be *Saturn*; *uranus* should be *Uranus*; Capitalize proper nouns and adjectives. *LoL*, p. T80; *LN*, p. 36.

40. **H** Writing Obj. 7. To form the possessive of a singular noun, add an apostrophe and an *s*. *LoL*, p. T662; *LN*, pp. 42–43.

TEST I—WRITING: PART 2

Writing Obj. 1–4. To score students' compositions, use the rubric on p. 95.

TEST I—READING

Note: For Reading practice test items, the correct answer is given, followed by a paragraph identifying

- the targeted TAAS Objective and skill name,
- references to pages in *Preparing for TAAS* and *The Language of Literature* (*LoL*) on which the targeted skill is taught, and
- explanations to assist you with error analysis and remediation.

SD-1. **B** Reading Obj. 1: Context Clues, pp. 11–14; *LoL*, p. 67.

SD-2. **J** Reading Obj. 5: Inferences, pp. 49–52; *LoL*, p. 347.

No evidence in the passage supports F or G. H is false. J is the answer best supported by the text. In the passage, the coach does not include Lucy in the play and tells her to "get ready for overtime."

1. **C** Reading Obj. 5: Inferences, pp. 49–52; *LoL*, p. 347.
No evidence in the passage supports A, B, or D. C is the answer best supported by the text. Jesse's birthday is two days after Saturday.

2. **F** Reading Obj. 3: Summarizing, pp. 31–34; *LoL*, p. 396.
G, H, and J are false.

3. **B** Reading Obj. 6: Fact-Opinion, pp. 65–68; *LoL*, p. 657.
A is a fact. C and D are not stated in the passage. B is stated in para. 1.

4. **G** Reading Obj. 5: Inferences, pp. 49–52; *LoL*, p. 347.
No evidence in the passage supports F or H. J is a possible explanation, but G is the answer best supported by the text. Jesse does not stop to talk to his neighbors, indicating that he is eager to reach the post office.

5. **D** Reading Obj. 5: Inferences, pp. 49–52; *LoL*, p. 347.
A is false. No evidence in the passage supports C. B is a possible explanation, but D is the answer best supported by the text. Jesse recalls happy memories of activities at his grandfather's, and says it "was a great old house."

6. **H** Reading Obj. 2, 3: Main Idea, pp. 27–30; *LoL*, p. 223.
F is not stated in the passage. G and J are supporting details.

7. **A** Reading Obj. 5: Evaluating & Making Judgments, pp. 53–56; *LoL*, p. 138.
No evidence in the passage supports C or D. B is a possible explanation, but A is the answer best supported by the text. Although Jesse does not understand the gift at first, by the end of the passage he recalls happy memories of the house and smiles when he shows the number on the brick to his father.

8. **H** Reading Obj. 6: Author's Perspective & Purpose, pp. 61–64; *LoL*, p. 414.
F is not addressed in the passage. G is not supported: Jesse's grandpa mentions the sale of the house, but most of the card is about the brick. J is not supported: Jesse's grandpa wants to explain the unusual gift, not entertain Jesse. H is the best answer: The passage shows how Jesse's opinion about the gift changes as a result of the card.

9. **B** Reading Obj. 3: Summarizing, pp. 31–34; *LoL*,

p. 396.
A omits essential points. C is a generalization. D is a judgment.

10. **F** Reading Obj. 6: Fact-Opinion, pp. 65–68; *LoL*, p. 657.
F is an opinion. G is contradicted in para. 1. H is not stated in the passage. J is stated in para. 1.

11. **D** Reading Obj. 5: Evaluating & Making Judgments, pp. 53–56; *LoL*, p. 138.
The picture does not support A, B, or C. D is the answer best supported by the picture. The pictures of the coffee and cookies look like refreshments that one might serve a house-guest.

12. **F** Reading Obj. 1: Context Clues, pp. 11–14; *LoL*, p. 67.

13. **C** Reading Obj. 2, 3: Main Idea, pp. 27–30; *LoL*, p. 223.
A and D are not addressed in the passage. B is a supporting detail.

14. **J** Reading Obj. 4: Cause-Effect, pp. 35–38; *LoL*, p. 708.
There is no basis in the passage for F. G and H are stated but are not causes.

15. **B** Reading Obj. 5: Charts & Graphs, pp. 43–47; *LoL*, p. R95–R96.
Students should find Suburbia's Passbook Savings account on the chart and read across to find its interest rate. They then divide that interest rate in half, find the resulting interest rate on the chart, and read across to find the name of the corresponding account.

16. **J** Reading Obj. 5: Inferences, pp. 49–52; *LoL*, p. 347.
No evidence in the passage supports F or G. H is false. J is the answer best supported by the text. The passage states that inflation occurs in the United States and in "many smaller countries."

17. **C** Reading Obj. 4: Cause-Effect, pp. 35–38; *LoL*, p. 708.
There is no basis in the passage for A or B. D is an effect. C is stated in para. 3.

18. **G** Reading Obj. 5: Inferences, pp. 49–52; *LoL*, p. 347.
No evidence in the passage supports F, H, or J. G is the answer best supported by the text. The passage states that many smaller countries have higher inflation rates than larger countries, and that smaller countries often rely on one source of money.

19. **B** Reading Obj. 2: Supporting Details, pp. 19–22; *LoL*, p. 732.
A, C, and D are not stated in the passage. B is

stated in para. 4.

20. **H** Reading Obj. 1: Context Clues, pp. 11–14; *LoL*, p. 67.
A is not stated in the passage. B and C are opinions. D is stated in para. 2.

21. **A** Reading Obj 5: Fact-Opinion, pp. 65–68; *LoL*, p. 657.
B and D are not stated in the passage. C is an opinion. A is stated in para. 4.

22. **F** Reading Obj. 2, 3: Main Idea, pp. 27–30; *LoL*, p. 223.
G is not stated in the passage. H is a generalization. J is a supporting detail.

23. **B** Reading Obj. 1: Context Clues, pp. 11–14; *LoL*, p. 67.

24. **G** Reading Obj. 2: Supporting Details, pp. 19–22; *LoL*, p. 732.
F is contradicted in para. 2. H is contradicted in para. 4. J is contradicted in para. 1. G is stated in para. 3.

25. **D** Reading Obj. 5: Evaluating & Making Judgments, pp. 53–56; *LoL*, p. 138.
No evidence in the passage supports A, B, or C. D is the answer best supported by the text. The passage states that asteroids and mete-oroids are found in space.

26. **J** Reading Obj. 1: Context Clues, pp. 11–14; *LoL*, p. 67.

27. **A** Reading Obj. 2, 3: Main Idea, pp. 27–30; *LoL*, p. 223.
B and D are false. C is a supporting detail.

28. **H** Reading Obj. 4: Cause-Effect, pp. 35–38; *LoL*, p. 708.
There is no basis in the passage for F, G, or J.

29. **D** Reading Obj. 5: Charts & Graphs, pp. 43–47; *LoL*, p. R95–R96.
Students should choose two consecutive dates of appearances of Halley's comet on the time line. By subtracting the earlier date from the later one, they will find the number of years between each appearance of Halley's comet (76 years). They should then add that number to the date of the comet's last appearance.

30. **F** Reading Obj. 6: Author's Perspective & Purpose, pp. 61–64; *LoL*, p. 414.
G and J are not addressed in the passage. H is not supported: The passage states that people often confuse asteroids, meteors, and comets. F is the best answer: The passage discusses the features that distinguish one astronomical phenomenon from the other.

31. **D** Reading Obj. 2: Supporting Details, pp. 19–22; *LoL*, p. 732.

A, B, and C are contradicted in para. 1. D is stated in para. 1.

32. H Reading Obj. 4: Cause-Effect, pp. 35–38; *LoL*, p. 708.
There is no basis in the passage for F or G. J is contradicted in para. 1.

33. C Reading Obj. 5: Inferences, pp. 49–52; *LoL*, p. 347.
Each of the following titles contains a word or words that relate to Reese's topic: The Ongoing Struggle to Free Caledonia; Where Do We Go When We Die? A Study of Ritual Among the Strictest Belief Systems; The Freedom to Believe and the Patience to Remain a Monk; What Do I Wear and Do I Have to Believe? Funeral Fashion and Etiquette.

34. G Reading Obj. 5: Inferences, pp. 49–52; *LoL*, p. 347.
F, H, and J each contain a word or words that refer to Reese's topic. Only G contains no reference to the topic.

35. C Reading Obj. 6: Author's Perspective & Purpose, pp. 61–64; *LoL*, p. 414.
A and B are not addressed in the passage. D is not supported: as she looks at the works cited, Reese is not optimistic about finding books with information on her topic. C is the best answer: Several books on the Works Cited page may possibly contain information on Reese's topic.

36. G Reading Obj. 3: Summarizing, pp. 31–34; *LoL*, p. 396.
F is false. H omits essential points. J is a generalization.

37. A Reading Obj. 5: Inferences, pp. 49–52; *LoL*, p. 347.
No evidence in the passage supports B or C. D is a possible explanation, but A is the answer best supported by the text. The book's title is specifically about funeral practices.

38. G Reading Obj. 3: Summarizing, pp. 31–34; *LoL*, p. 396.
F and H are false. J is a generalization.

39. A Reading Obj. 5: Evaluating & Making Judgments, pp. 53–56; *LoL*, p. 138.
No evidence in the passage supports B or D. C is a possible explanation, but A is the answer best supported by the text. The other students admire Kendra's courage, not her friendliness.

40. J Reading Obj. 2: Sequential Order, p. 23–26; *LoL*, p. 87.
F occurs after Felicia enters Kendra's room. H is not stated in the passage. J occurs after G.

41. A Reading Obj. 2: Supporting Details, pp. 19–22; *LoL*, p. 732.
C and D are not stated in the passage. B is an inference. A is stated in para. 1.

42. H Reading Obj. 5: Inferences, pp. 49–52; *LoL*, p. 347.
No evidence in the passage supports F or G. J is a possible explanation, but H is the answer best supported by the text. Felicia criticizes Kendra's outfit, not her speech.

43. C Reading Obj. 5: Fact-Opinion, pp. 65–68; *LoL*, p. 657.
A and B are not stated in the passage. D is a fact. C is stated in para. 4.

44. F Reading Obj. 5: Inferences, pp. 49–52; *LoL*, p. 347.
No evidence in the passage supports G or H. J is false. A is the answer best supported by the text. Kendra has already written her whole speech when Felicia arrives.

45. B Reading Obj. 5: Inferences, pp. 49–52; *LoL*, p. 347.
No evidence in the passage supports C or D. A is a possible explanation, but B is the answer best supported by the text. The passage states that by the end of Kendra's speech, the other students "weren't making fun of her outfit anymore."

TEST II—WRITING: PART 1

Note: For Writing practice test items, the correct answer is given, followed by

- the targeted TAAS Objective;
- the specific skill or rule tested; and
- references to pages in *The Language of Literature* (*LoL*) and *Language Network* (*LN*) on which the targeted skill is taught.

SA-1. A Writing Obj. 5. Correctly written sentences that should be combined. *LoL*, pp. 45, T126; *LN*, pp. 330–331.

SA-2. H Writing Obj. 5. Incomplete sentence. *LoL*, pp. 64, 786; *LN*, pp. 25–27.

SA-3. D Writing Obj. 5.

SB-1. G Writing Obj. 6. Use the present tense to show that an action occurs in the present. *LoL*, p. T683; *LN*, pp. 111–114.

SB-2. A Writing Obj. 6. To form the plural of most nouns add *s*. *LoL*, p. R64; *LN*, p. 39.

SC-1. F Writing Obj. 7. *too* should be *two*.

SC-2. C Writing Obj. 7. Use a comma to separate an introductory adverb clause from the rest of the sentence. *LoL*, p. T41; *LN*, p. 204.

1. **A** Writing Obj. 6. Use the passive voice when the action of the verb is being performed upon the subject. *LoL*, pp. 295, 298, T298.

2. **G** Writing Obj. 6. Use the comparative degree of comparison to compare two persons, places, or things. *LoL*, p. T544; *LN*, pp. 137–139.

3. **A** Writing Obj. 6. Use a demonstrative pronoun to point out a specific person, place, thing, or idea. The demonstrative pronouns are *this*, *these, that,* and *those*. *LoL*, pp. R53, R83; *LN*, p. 71.

4. **H** Writing Obj. 6. Use the present tense to show that an action occurs in the present. *LoL*, p. T683; *LN*, pp. 111–114.

5. **B** Writing Obj. 6. Use an adverb to modify a verb, an adjective, or another adverb. Word modified: *faded*. *LoL*, p. T457; *LN*, pp. 134–136.

6. **J** Writing Obj. 6. Use the possessive case of a personal pronoun to show ownership or possession. *LoL*, p. 328; *LN*, pp. 73–78.

7. **C** Writing Obj. 6. Use the past tense to show that an action occurred in the past. *LoL*, p. T683; *LN*, pp. 111–114.

8. **F** Writing Obj. 6. Use the future tense to show that an action will occur in the future. *LoL*, p. T683; *LN*, pp. 111–114.

9. **C** Writing Obj. 6. Use the present tense to show that an action occurs in the present. *LoL*, p. T683; *LN*, pp. 111–114.

10. **G** Writing Obj. 6. Use the possessive case of a personal pronoun to show ownership or possession. Do not confuse a contraction with a possessive pronoun. *LoL*, p. T329; *LN*, pp. 65–67.

11. **D** Writing Obj. 7. To form the possessive of a singular noun, add an apostrophe and an *s*. *LoL*, p. 662; *LN*, pp. 42–43.

12. **J** Writing Obj. 6. Use the present perfect tense to show that an action was completed at some indefinite time in the past. *LoL*, p. T889; *LN*, pp. 111–114.

13. **B** Writing Obj. 5. Incomplete sentence. *LoL*, pp. 64, 786; *LN*, pp. 25–27.

14. **J** Writing Obj. 5.

15. **B** Writing Obj. 5. Incomplete sentence. *LoL*, pp. 64, 786; *LN*, pp. 25–27.

16. **J** Writing Obj. 5.

17. **D** Writing Obj. 5.

18. **H** Writing Obj. 5. Correctly written sentences that should be combined. *LoL*, pp. 45, T126; *LN*, pp. 330–331.

19. **D** Writing Obj. 5.

20. **F** Writing Obj. 5. Incomplete sentence. *LoL*, pp. 64, 786; *LN*, pp. 25–27.

21. **A** Writing Obj. 5. Run-on sentence. *LoL*, pp. T50, 79, T183; *LN*, pp. 26–27.

22. **H** Writing Obj. 5. Correctly written sentences that should be combined. *LoL*, pp. 45, T126; *LN*, pp. 330–331.

23. **D** Writing Obj. 5.

24. **G** Writing Obj. 5. Incomplete sentence. *LoL*, pp. 64, 786; *LN*, pp. 25–27.

25. **C** Writing Obj. 5. Run-on sentence. *LoL*, pp. T50, 79, T183; *LN*, pp. 26–27.

26. **H** Writing Obj. 5. Correctly written sentences that should be combined. *LoL*, pp. 45, T126; *LN*, pp. 330–331.

27. **D** Writing Obj. 7.

28. **G** Writing Obj. 7. *department of commerce* should be *Department of Commerce*; Capitalize the names of legislative bodies. *LoL*, p. R58; *LN*, p. 241.

29. **A** Writing Obj. 7. *questionair* should be *questionnaire*.

30. **H** Writing Obj. 7. In a series of three or more items, use a comma after every item except the last one. *LoL*, p. T744; *LN*, p. 253.

31. **D** Writing Obj. 7

32. **H** Writing Obj. 7. *states* should be *state's*; To form the possessive of a singular noun, add an apostrophe and an *s*. *LoL*, p. 662; *LN*, pp. 42–43.

33. **A** Writing Obj. 7. *recieved* should be *received*.

34. **H** Writing Obj. 7. In a series of three or more items, use a comma after every item except the last one. *LoL*, p. T744; *LN*, p. 253.

35. **B** Writing Obj. 7. *Concrete* should be *concrete*; Do not capitalize common nouns. *LoL*, p. T80; *LN*, p. 36.

36. **J** Writing Obj. 7.

37. **B** Writing Obj. 7. *harrisbug* should be *Harrisburg*; Capitalize proper nouns and adjectives. *LoL*, p. T80; *LN*, p. 36.

38. **F** Writing Obj. 7. *too* should be *two*.

39. **D** Writing Obj. 7.

40. **G** Writing Obj. 7. *golden gate bridge* should be *Golden Gate Bridge*; Capitalize proper nouns. *LoL*, p. T80; *LN*, p. 36.

TEST II—WRITING: PART 2

Writing Obj. 1–4. To score students' compositions, use the rubric on p. 95.

TEST II—READING

Note: For Reading practice test items, the correct answer is given, followed by a paragraph identifying

- the targeted TAAS Objective and skill name,
- references to pages in *Preparing for TAAS* and *The Language of Literature* (*LoL*) on which the targeted skill is taught, and
- explanations to assist you with error analysis and remediation.

SD-1. A Reading Obj. 1: Context Clues, pp. 11–14; *LoL*, p. 67.

SD-2. H Reading Obj. 5: Inferences, pp. 49–52; *LoL*, p. 347.
No evidence in the passage supports F or G. J is a possible explanation, but H is the answer best supported by the text. The fact that Tasha could call from the tent to her mother in the kitchen indicates that they are camping at Tasha's house.

1. C Reading Obj. 5: Inferences, pp. 49–52; *LoL*, p. 347.
No evidence in the passage supports A, B, or D. C is the answer best supported by the text. The passage states that Sheri and Terry had a "short walk to the shelter" after their parents spoke to them about the responsibilities of owning a dog.

2. J Reading Obj. 5: Inferences, pp. 49–52; *LoL*, p. 347.
No evidence in the passage supports F or G. H is a possible explanation, but J is the answer best supported by the text. In the passage, Sheri thinks about the extra activities and schoolwork she will have in junior high, and then thinks, "Maybe a puppy wasn't the best idea."

3. A Reading Obj. 2: Supporting Details, pp. 19–22; *LoL*, p. 732.
B, C, and D are not stated in the passage. A is stated in para. 4.

4. H Reading Obj. 5: Evaluating & Making Judgments, pp. 53–56; *LoL*, p. 138.
No evidence in the passage supports F or G. J is a possible explanation, but H is the answer best supported by the text. Sheri's behavior toward the dogs is more caring than playful.

5. B Reading Obj. 5: Inferences, pp. 49–52; *LoL*, p. 347.

No evidence in the passage supports A or C. D is a possible explanation, but B is the answer best supported by the text. The passage states that the dog had to sit down quickly after standing, but not why.

6. G Reading Obj. 3: Summarizing, pp. 31–34; *LoL*, p. 396.
F is a judgment. H is false. J omits essential points.

7. A Reading Obj. 4: Cause-Effect, pp. 35–38; *LoL*, p. 708.
There is no basis in the passage for B, C, or D.

8. G Reading Obj. 5: Inferences, pp. 49–52; *LoL*, p. 347.
No evidence in the passage supports H or J. F is a possible explanation, but G is the answer best supported by the text. The cousins are exploring the creek bed in an area where there are bushes, rocks, and hills, which suggests they are in the park rather than the housing development.

9. D Reading Obj. 3: Summarizing, pp. 31–34; *LoL*, p. 396.
A is false. B and C omit essential details.

10. F Reading Obj. 1: Context Clues, pp. 11–14; *LoL*, p. 67.

11. C Reading Obj. 5: Inferences, pp. 49–52; *LoL*, p. 347.
The puppy is described in the passage as brown with white spots, which matches the description given in the flier for the dog lost from 5121 Calico Road.

12. G Reading Obj. 5: Evaluating & Making Judgments, pp. 53–56; *LoL*, p. 138.
No evidence in the passage supports F, H, or J. G is the answer best supported by the text. The flier states that the reward is offered to the person who returns Belvedere to her owners.

13. D Reading Obj. 2, 3: Main Idea, pp. 27–30; *LoL*, p. 223.
A and C are judgments. B is false.

14. G Reading Obj. 5: Inferences, pp. 49–52; *LoL*, p. 347.
No evidence in the flier and map supports F or J. H is a possible explanation, but G is the answer best supported by the flier and the map. The flier states that Goliath was last seen in the back yard of 4810 Persian Lane. House number 3 is the closest to 4810 Persian Lane.

15. B Reading Obj. 5: Inferences, pp. 49–52; *LoL*, p. 347.
No evidence in the passage supports A, C, or D. B is the answer best supported by the text. The passage states that the flags of France,

Spain, and Mexico have flown over Texas.

16. G Reading Obj. 2, 3: Main Idea, pp. 27–30; *LoL*, p. 223.
F and H are supporting details. J is a judgment.

17. D Reading Obj. 5: Fact-Opinion, pp. 65–68; *LoL*, p. 657.
A and C are not stated in the passage. B is a fact. D is stated in para. 1.

18. J Reading Obj. 2: Supporting Details, pp. 19–22; *LoL*, p. 732.
F, G, and H are not stated in the passage. J is stated in para. 3.

19. A Reading Obj. 2: Sequential Order, p. 23–26; *LoL*, p. 87.
B and D are not stated in the passage. A occurred before C.

20. G Reading Obj. 1: Context Clues, pp. 11–14; *LoL*, p. 67.

21. C Reading Obj 4: Cause-Effect, pp. 35–38; *LoL*, p. 708.
A states nonessential details. There is no basis in the passage for B or D.

22. J Reading Obj. 6: Author's Perspective & Purpose, pp. 61–64; *LoL*, p. 414.
F is not supported: The author describes the ten-year existence of the Republic as a bumpy ride. G is not supported: The author states that Texas was eventually forced to reapply to join the United States. H is not addressed in the passage. J is the best answer: The author states that "Texas is the only state in the Union to have been its own country."

23. D Reading Obj. 2, 3: Main Idea, pp. 27–30; *LoL*, p. 223.
A, B, and C are false. D is stated in para. 1.

24. H Reading Obj. 5: Fact-Opinion, pp. 65–68; *LoL*, p. 657.
F and J are not stated in the passage. G is contradicted in para. 1. H is stated in para. 1.

25. C Reading Obj. 2, 3: Main Idea, pp. 27–30; *LoL*, p. 223.
A and D are supporting details. B is a judgment.

26. J Reading Obj. 1: Context Clues, pp. 11–14; *LoL*, p. 67.

27. C Reading Obj. 2: Supporting Details, pp. 19–22; *LoL*, p. 732.
A and D are contradicted in para. 4. B is not stated in the passage. C is stated in para. 4.

28. F Reading Obj. 5: Inferences, pp. 49–52; *LoL*, p. 347.
G, H, and J are false. F is the answer best sup-ported by the text. The passage states that "not all imitations are so valueless," and that the Black Prince's Ruby and the Timur Ruby are two of the most famous gems in the world, although they are not actually rubies.

29. B Reading Obj. 4: Cause-Effect, pp. 35–38; *LoL*, p. 708.
There is no basis in the passage for A, C, or D.

30. F Reading Obj. 5: Charts & Graphs, pp. 43–47; *LoL*, p. R95–R96.
Students should reread the descriptions of the various gemstone cuts in para. 4 and match the shape and appearance of the diamond to the correct cut. The diamond is round and has kite-shaped cuts on it, so the correct answer is F.

31. A Reading Obj. 5: Inferences, pp. 49–52; *LoL*, p. 347.
No evidence in the passage supports B or C. D is a possible answer, but A is the answer best supported by the text. The passage states that Ms. Ravel and her students discuss the issue "after attending a school meeting" and during a class period.

32. G Reading Obj. 4: Predicting, pp. 39–42; *LoL*, p. 521.
No evidence in the passage supports F or J. H is a possible answer, but G is the answer best supported by the text. The passage states that the "do's and don'ts" may be posted at every school, not that students and parents may be required to read them.

33. C Reading Obj. 6: Author's Perspective & Purpose, pp. 61–64; *LoL*, p. 414.
B and D are not addressed in the passage. A is not supported: The "do's and don'ts" do not define sportsmanship, and it was not just students who were involved in the incident of bad sportsmanship. C is the best answer: The class's goal is to improve sportsmanship among everyone attending games.

34. J Reading Obj. 5: Fact-Opinion, pp. 65–68; *LoL*, p. 657.
F is contradicted in para. 2. G is not stated in the passage. H is an opinion. J is stated under "Do's" on the poster.

35. D Reading Obj. 5: Evaluating & Making Judgments, pp. 53–56; *LoL*, p. 138.
No evidence in the passage supports C. A and B are possible explanations, but D is the answer best supported by the text. Two of the "Do's" use forms of the word *encourage*, while none mention courtesy or expression.

36. H Reading Obj. 3: Summarizing, pp. 31–34; *LoL*, p. 396.
F and G omit essential points. J is false.

37. B Reading Obj. 5: Evaluating & Making Judgments, pp. 53–56; *LoL*, p. 138.
No evidence in the passage supports C or D. A is a possible explanation, but B is the answer best supported by the text. The bad sportsmanship is described as embarrassing, and it disgusted the other people at the game. Although the people involved in the incident are described as loud, there is nothing in the passage to suggest that they are dedicated.

38. G Reading Obj. 6: Author's Perspective & Purpose, pp. 61–64; *LoL*, p. 414.
No evidence in the passage supports H or J. F is a possible explanation, but G is the answer best supported by the text. F can be eliminated; while the poster encourages spectators to be respectful, it also urges them to cheer loudly. G is the best answer because the poster states that spectators should not put the goal of winning before good sportsmanship.

39. B Reading Obj. 5: Inferences, pp. 49–52; *LoL*, p. 347.
No evidence in the passage supports A or C. D is a possible explanation, but B is the answer best supported by the text. According to the passage, Malory knows that the carnival is not an important event; knowing that Nyssa Jones will be at the carnival is what convinces Malory that her band should play there.

40. G Reading Obj. 5: Inferences, pp. 49–52; *LoL*, p. 347.
No evidence in the passage supports F or J. H is a possible explanation, but G is the answer best supported by the text. The passage makes clear that Malory and her bandmates write their own songs, so H can be eliminated. The passage states that Malory has practically worn out her *Agony and Irony* CDs, indicating that she has listened to them many times.

41. C Reading Obj. 2: Supporting Details, pp. 19–22; *LoL*, p. 732.
A, B, and D are not stated in the passage. C is stated in para. 4.

42. H Reading Obj. 3: Summarizing, pp. 31–34; *LoL*, p. 396.
F omits essential points. G and J are false.

43. B Reading Obj. 5: Inferences, pp. 49–52; *LoL*, p. 347.
No evidence in the passage supports A or D. C is false. B is the answer best supported by the text. When Malory sees Nyssa Jones walking toward her, Malory's throat gets clogged up and she loses her voice.

44. F Reading Obj. 5: Fact-Opinion, pp. 65–68; *LoL*, p. 657.
G is not stated in the passage. H is contradicted in para. 6. J is a fact. F is stated in para. 6.

45. C Reading Obj. 5: Evaluating & Making Judgments, pp. 53–56; *LoL*, p. 138.
No evidence in the passage supports A, B, or D. C is the answer best supported by the text. After Malory's conversation with Nyssa Jones, Malory thinks her teachers are more important than anyone in the music business.

TAAS Practice Test Copymasters, Grade 8
TEST I—WRITING: PART 1

Note: For Writing practice test items, the correct answer is given, followed by

- the targeted TAAS Objective;
- the specific skill or rule tested; and
- references to pages in *The Language of Literature* (*LoL*) and *Language Network* (*LN*) on which the targeted skill is taught.

SA-1. B Writing Obj. 5. Correctly written sentences that should be combined. *LoL*, pp. 732, T732; *LN*, pp. 332–337.

SA-2. F Writing Obj. 5. Run-on sentence. *LoL*, p. 98; *LN*, pp 26–27, 291.

SA-3. D Writing Obj. 5.

SB-1. J Writing Obj. 6. Use the past tense to show that an action occurred in the past and is completed. *LoL*, p. T67; *LN*, pp. 105–114.

SB-2. B Writing Obj. 6. Use the past perfect tense to show that an action or condition in the past preceded another past action or condition. *LoL*, p. T67; *LN*, pp. 105–114.

SC-1. H Writing Obj. 7. Use a comma to separate an introductory adverb clause from the rest of the sentence. *LoL*, p. R58; *LN*, p. 195.

SC-2. D Writing Obj. 7.

1. B Writing Obj. 6. Two negatives should not be used to express one negative meaning. *LoL*, p. 179; *LN*, p. 142.

2. G Writing Obj. 6. Use an adverb to modify a verb, an adjective, or another adverb. Word modified: *lit*. *LoL*, pp. 533, T533; *LN*, pp. 134–135.

3. C Writing Obj. 6. Use the superlative degree of comparison to compare three or more people, things, or actions. *LoL*, p. 500; *LN*, pp.

137–139.

4. **F** Writing Obj. 6. Use the future tense to show that an action will occur in the future. *LoL*, p. T67; *LN*, pp. 105–114.

5. **A** Writing Obj. 6. Use the objective form of a personal pronoun when the pronoun functions as a direct object. *LoL*, p. T270; *LN*, pp. 63–64.

6. **J** Writing Obj. 6. Use the future tense to show that an action will occur in the future. *LoL*, p. T67; *LN*, pp. 105–114.

7. **B** Writing Obj. 6. Use the objective form of a personal pronoun when the pronoun functions as the object of a preposition. *LoL*, pp. T270, T282; *LN*, pp. 63–64.

8. **F** Writing Obj. 6. Use the present tense to show that an action is occurring in the present. *LoL*, p. T67; *LN*, pp. 105–114.

9. **C** Writing Obj. 6. Use the present tense to show that an action is occurring in the present. *LoL*, p. T67; *LN*, pp. 105–114.

10. **H** Writing Obj. 6. Use the past tense to show that an action occurred in the past. *LoL*, p. T67; *LN*, pp. 105–114.

11. **B** Writing Obj. 6. Use the present tense to show that an action is occurring in the present. *LoL*, p. T67; *LN*, pp. 105–114.

12. **J** Writing Obj. 6. Use the possessive case of a personal pronoun to show ownership or possession. Do not confuse a contraction with a possessive pronoun. *LoL*, p. T270; *LN*, pp. 65–67.

13. **C** Writing Obj. 5. Correctly written sentences that should be combined. *LoL*, pp. 732, T732; *LN*, pp. 332–337.

14. **G** Writing Obj. 5. Correctly written sentences that should be combined. *LoL*, pp. 732, T732; *LN*, pp. 332–337.

15. **C** Writing Obj. 5. Incomplete sentence. *LoL*, p. 31; *LN*, pp. 25, 290.

16. **F** Writing Obj. 5. Incomplete sentence. *LoL*, p. 31; *LN*, pp. 25, 290.

17. **A** Writing Obj. 5. Correctly written sentences that should be combined. *LoL*, pp. 732, T732; *LN*, pp. 332–337.

18. **F** Writing Obj. 5. Incomplete sentence. *LoL*, p. 31; *LN*, pp. 25, 290.

19. **D** Writing Obj. 5.

20. **G** Writing Obj. 5. Incomplete sentence. *LoL*, p. 31; *LN*, pp. 25, 290.

21. **B** Writing Obj. 5. Run on sentence. *LoL*, p. 98; *LN*, pp 26–27, 291.

22. **J** Writing Obj. 5.

23. **C** Writing Obj. 5. Incomplete sentence. *LoL*, p. 31; *LN*, pp. 25, 290.

24. **J** Writing Obj. 5.

25. **B** Writing Obj. 5. Run-on sentence. *LoL*, p. 98; *LN*, pp 26–27, 291.

26. **J** Writing Obj. 5.

27. **C** Writing Obj. 7. Use a question mark to punctuate an interrogative sentence. *LoL*, p. 152; *LN*, p. 250.

28. **F** Writing Obj. 7. *twenteth* should be *twentieth*.

29. **C** Writing Obj. 7. In a series of three or more items, use a comma after every item except the last one. *LoL*, pp. T596, R58; *LN*, p. 253.

30. **G** Writing Obj. 7. *greek* should be *Greek*; Capitalize proper nouns and adjectives. *LoL*, p. 295; *LN*, p. 127.

31. **B** Writing Obj. 7. *italian* should be *Italian*; Capitalize proper nouns and adjectives. *LoL*, p. 295; *LN*, p. 127.

32. **F** Writing Obj. 7. *writen* should be *written*.

33. **D** Writing Obj. 7.

34. **J** Writing Obj. 7.

35. **C** Writing Obj. 7. Use a comma to separate an introductory adverb clause from the rest of the sentence. *LoL*, p. R58; *LN*, p. 195.

36. **F** Writing Obj. 7. *moutain* should be *mountain*.

37. **B** Writing Obj. 7. *gutzon borglum* should be *Gutzon Borglum*; Capitalize proper nouns and proper adjectives. *LoL*, p. 295; *LN*, p. 127.

38. **F** Writing Obj. 7. *themsefs* should be *themselves*.

39. **C** Writing Obj. 7. Use a period to punctuate a declarative sentence. *LoL*, p. 152; *LN*, p. 250.

40. **H** Writing Obj. 7. To form the possessive of a singular noun, add an apostrophe and an *s*. *LoL*, p. R66; *LN*, pp. 42–43.

TEST I—WRITING: PART 2

Writing Obj. 1–4. To score students' compositions, use the rubric on p. 113.

TEST I—READING

Note: For Reading practice test items, the correct answer is given, followed by a paragraph identifying

• the targeted TAAS Objective and skill name,

- references to pages in *Preparing for TAAS* and *The Language of Literature (LoL)* on which the targeted skill is taught, and

- explanations to assist you with error analysis and remediation.

SD-1. B Reading Obj. 1: Context Clues, pp. 11–14; *LoL*, p. 301.

SD-2. J Reading Obj. 5: Inferences, pp. 49–52; *LoL*, p. 553, 875.
F is false. No evidence in the passage supports G. H is false. J is the answer best supported by the text. Only J accomodates the facts that Natasha had been hiking and was able to see a bird flying below where she stood.

1. B Reading Obj. 5: Evaluating & Making Judgments, pp. 53–56; *LoL*, p. 877.
A is false. No evidence in the passage supports D. C is a possible answer, but B is the answer best supported by the text. By the end of the passage, Belinda has come to share her mother's belief that Belinda does not need another pair of shoes.

2. F Reading Obj. 4: Predicting, pp. 39–42; *LoL*, p. 22.
No evidence in the passage supports G or H. J is a possible explanation, but F is the answer best supported by the text. The passage states that volunteering at the soup kitchen made Belinda feel good, so F is the most likely explanation.

3. D Reading Obj. 1: Context Clues, pp. 11–14; *LoL*, p. 301.

4. H Reading Obj. 3: Summarizing, pp. 31–34; *LoL*, p. 283.
F is a generalization. G and J omit essential points.

5. B Reading Obj. 6: Author's Perspective and Purpose, pp. 61–64; *LoL*, p. 118, 426.
A is not supported: Belinda gives her time, not her money. C and D are not addressed in the passage. B is the best answer: The passage shows how the main character's feelings about poverty change.

6. H Reading Obj. 5: Inferences, pp. 49–52; *LoL*, p. 553, 875.
F and J are false. No evidence in the passage supports G. H is the answer best supported by the text. Belinda thinks her mother is driving her home, but without telling her, Belinda's mother drives them to a place where Belinda has never been before—the soup kitchen.

7. A Reading Obj. 2: Sequential Order, pp. 23–26; *LoL*, p. 285.
C and D are not stated in the passage. B occurs before Belinda's mother enters the warehouse. A is the only response that occurs after Belinda's mother goes into the warehouse.

8. H Reading Obj. 5: Evaluating & Making Judgments, pp. 53–56; *LoL*, p. 877.
F is illogical. G is false. J is a possible explanation, but H is the answer best supported by the text. The passage shows Belinda's understanding that although she does not have money to buy things at the mall, she has much more than the people she sees at the soup kitchen.

9. C Reading Obj. 3: Summarizing, pp. 31–34; *LoL*, p. 283.
A omits essential points. B is a generalization. D summarizes only the first review.

10. H Reading Obj. 6: Fact-Opinion, pp. 65–68; *LoL*, p. 829.
F is contradicted in para. 3. G is an opinion. J is not stated in the passage. H is stated in para. 6.

11. A Reading Obj. 2: Sequential Order, pp. 23–26; *LoL*, p. 285.
B is an opinion stated in only one review. C is not stated in the passage. A occurs before D.

12. J Reading Obj. 5: Inferences, pp. 49–52; *LoL*, p. 553, 875.
No evidence in the passage supports F and G. H is a possible explanation, but J is the answer best supported by the text. O'Quinn writes that "a waitperson tries to explain to you how the restaurant works" but her waiter "really flubbed his lines."

13. B Reading Obj. 3: Summarizing, pp. 31–34; *LoL*, p. 283.
A and C omit essential points. D is false.

14. G Reading Obj. 4: Cause-Effect, pp. 35–38; *LoL*, p. 32.
There is no basis in the passage for F. H and J are stated in L. O'Quinn's review, not in A. Sonora's.

15. D Reading Obj. 5: Inferences, pp. 49–52; *LoL*, p. 553, 875.
No evidence in the passage supports A, B, or C. D is the answer best supported by the text. In his review, A. Sonora states that The Surprise Gourmet was "fantastic."

16. H Reading Obj. 2, 3: Main Idea, pp. 27–30; *LoL*, p. 106, 408.
F is not stated in the review. G and J are supporting details.

17. D Reading Obj. 1: Context Clues, pp. 11–14; *LoL*, p. 301.

18. G Reading Obj. 6: Fact-Opinion, pp. 65–68; *LoL*, p. 829.

F, H, and J are facts. G is stated in para. 3.

19. C Reading Obj. 2, 3: Main Idea, pp. 27–30; *LoL*, p. 106, 408.
A is not stated in the passage. B and D are supporting details.

20. J Reading Obj. 5: Inferences, pp. 49–52; *LoL*, p. 553, 875.
No evidence in this passage supports F, G, or H. J is the answer best supported by the text. The passage states, "The basenji's feelings are shown in its eyes."

21. D Reading Obj. 5: Fact-Opinion, pp. 65–68; *LoL*, p. 829.
A is not stated in the passage. B and C are opinions. D is stated in para. 2.

22. H Reading Obj 4: Cause-Effect, pp. 35–38; *LoL*, p. 32.
There is no basis in the passage for F, G, or J.

23. C Reading Obj. 1: Context Clues, pp. 11–14; *LoL*, p. 301.

24. F Reading Obj. 5: Inferences, pp. 49–52; *LoL*, p. 553, 875.
G is an opinion. No evidence in the passage supports H. J is a possible answer, but F is the answer best supported by the text. The passage states that basenji were kept by the pharoahs of ancient Egypt and that the breed has been used as hunting dogs for "thousands of years."

25. C Reading Obj. 5: Evaluating & Making Judgments, pp. 53–56; *LoL*, p. 877.
No evidence in the passage supports A or B. D is false. C is the answer best supported by the text. The passage explains that each time zone is either one hour earlier or later than the zone before it, so by counting the number of zones between the two cities, one can find the number of hours difference in time.

26. G Reading Obj. 6: Author's Perspective & Purpose, pp. 61–64; *LoL*, p. 118, 426.
H is not supported: the author does not express any negative opinions of the system of time zones. J is not supported: the author clearly thinks that the system of time zones is useful. F is a possible answer, but G is the best answer, because the author writes that the system makes "it possible to figure out what time it is anywhere in the world" and that it assists "in the conduct of business and travel."

27. D Reading Obj. 5: Inferences, pp. 49–52; *LoL*, p. 553, 875.
No evidence in the passage supports A, B, or C. D is the answer best supported by the text. The passage states that the countries that do not participate in the time zone system heard "about the plan at a later date," indicating

that they were not represented at the conference.

28. H Reading Obj. 4: Cause-Effect, pp. 35–38; *LoL*, p. 32.
There is no basis in the passage for F, G, or J.

29. C Reading Obj. 5: Charts & Graphs, pp. 43–47; *LoL*, pp. R98–R99.
Students should find South America on the map, find the time zone lines to the east and to the west of the continent, and then read down to find the labels at the bottom of each time zone.

30. F Reading Obj. 5: Charts & Graphs, pp. 43–47; *LoL*, pp. R98–R99.
Students should find each city on the map. The passage states that "time zones east of the Prime Meridian are each an hour later than the previous zone," so the answer will be a city east of Greenwich. Students can also read down from each city on the map to find the time in that time zone relative to the time at the Prime Meridian.

31. B Reading Obj. 2, 3: Main Idea, pp. 27–30; *LoL*, p. 106, 408.
A and D are supporting details. C is a judgment.

32. F Reading Obj. 5: Evaluating & Making Judgments, pp. 53–56; *LoL*, p. 877.
No evidence in the passage supports H or J. G is a possible answer, but F is the answer best supported by the text. When Ivan tells Tracey that he wants to sell his car, but doesn't know how to, Tracey thinks of placing a classified ad and looks over the ads with Ivan.

33. D Reading Obj. 2: Sequential Order, pp. 23–26; *LoL*, p. 285.
A, B, and C are not stated in the passage.

34. F Reading Obj. 5: Inferences, pp. 49–52; *LoL*, p. 553, 875.
No evidence in the passage supports G, H, or J. F is the answer best supported by the text. Tracey and Ivan look at classified ads for ideas on how to sell Ivan's car, and the passage states that the classifieds are organized by type of car. Because Tracey turns to the ads for Jupiters, the reader can infer that Ivan's car is a Jupiter.

35. C Reading Obj. 2: Supporting Details, pp. 19–22; *LoL*, p. 528, R29–R30.
A, B, and D are not mentioned in all the ads, while C is.

36. J Reading Obj. 5: Fact-Opinion, pp. 65–68; *LoL*, p. 829.
F is not stated in the passage. G and H are facts. J is stated in para. 5.

37. C Reading Obj. 5: Inferences, pp. 49–52; *LoL*, p. 553, 875.
No evidence in the passage supports A, B, or D. C is the answer best supported in the text. The reader can infer from the statement "needs front end body work" in the passage that the car could have been damaged in an accident.

38. G Reading Obj. 2, 3: Main Idea, pp. 27–30; *LoL*, p. 106, 408.
F is a supporting detail. H and J are not mentioned in every ad. G is mentioned in every ad and states the key information found in the ads.

39. B Reading Obj. 5: Fact-Opinion, pp. 65–68; *LoL*, p. 829.
A and D are opinions. C is false. B is stated in para. 3.

40. H Reading Obj. 2: Sequential Order, p.23–26; *LoL*, p. 285.
G and J are not stated in the passage. F happens before Tia writes the poem to her sister.

41. B Reading Obj. 5: Evaluating & Making Judgments, pp. 53–56; *LoL*, p. 877.
C is false. No evidence in the passage supports D. A is a possible explanation, but B is the answer best supported in the text. The passage states that after writing the poem to her sister, Tia was much less nervous about being called on to read in class.

42. F Reading Obj. 1: Context Clues, pp. 11–14; *LoL*, p. 301.

43. A Reading Obj. 5: Fact-Opinion, pp. 65–68; *LoL*, p. 829.
B and C are not stated in the passage. D is a fact. A is stated in para. 13.

44. J Reading Obj. 5: Inferences, pp. 49–52; *LoL*, p. 553, 875.
No evidence in the passage supports F or H. G is false. J is the answer best supported by the text. In the passage, Tia writes a poem telling her sister that she is loved.

45. A Reading Obj. 5: Inferences, pp. 49–52; *LoL*, p. 553, 875.
No evidence in the passage supports B, C, or D. A is the answer best supported by the text. Before pointing to Tia, Monica states that "it would be nice to allow any first-time visitors" to read.

46. J Reading Obj. 5: Inferences, pp. 49–52; *LoL*, p. 553, 875.
No evidence in the passage supports F, G, or H. J is the answer best supported by the text. Tia's first response to Deep River's question is a list of social issues, to which Deep River responds, "but what, or who, brings out your strongest feelings?"

47. C Reading Obj. 3: Summarizing, pp. 31–34; *LoL*, p. 283.
A and B are false. D omits essential points.

48. H Reading Obj. 5: Inferences, pp. 49–52; *LoL*, p. 553, 875.
No evidence in the passage supports F or J. G is a possible explanation, but H is the answer best supported by the text. The class applauded because they thought Tia's poem was good, not because she cried. The passage states that, after reading, Tia "wiped a teardrop from her paper," which suggests that reading the poem made her cry.

TEST II—WRITING: PART 1

Note: For Writing practice test items, the correct answer is given, followed by

- the targeted TAAS Objective;
- the specific skill or rule tested; and
- references to pages in *The Language of Literature* (*LoL*) and *Language Network* (*LN*) on which the targeted skill is taught.

SA-1. C Writing Obj. 5. Run-on sentence. *LoL*, p . 98; *LN*, pp 26–27, 291.

SA-2. J Writing Obj. 5.

SA-3. A Writing Obj. 5. Incomplete sentence. *LoL*, p. 31; *LN*, pp. 25, 290.

SB-1. G Writing Obj. 6. Use the future tense to show that an action will occur in the future. *LoL*, p. T67; *LN*, pp. 105–114.

SB-2. A Writing Obj. 6. Maintain consistent verb tense when relating events that occur at the same time. *LoL*, p. 68, p. T68; *LN*, p. 298.

SC-1. H Writing Obj. 7. Use a comma to separate an introductory adverb clause from the rest of the sentence. *LoL*, p. R58; *LN*, p. 195

SC-2. D Writing Obj. 7.

1. D Writing Obj. 6. A pronoun must agree with its referent in number, gender, and person. Referent: *Recycling*. *LoL*, p. T74; *LN*, pp. 73–78.

2. H Writing Obj. 6. Use the past tense to show that an action occurred in the past. *LoL*, p. T67; *LN*, pp. 105–114.

3. A Writing Obj. 6. A pronoun must agree with its referent in number, gender, and person. Referent: *kids*. *LoL*, p. T74; *LN*, pp. 73–78.

4. H Writing Obj. 6. Use the future tense to show that an action will occur in the future. *LoL*, p.

T67; *LN*, pp. 105–114.

5. A Writing Obj. 6. Use a demonstrative pronoun to point out a specific person, place, thing, or idea. The demonstrative pronouns are *this, these, that,* and *those. LoL,* p. R56; *LN*, pp. 71–72.

6. J Writing Obj. 6. Use the past tense to show that an action occurred in the past. *LoL,* p. T67; *LN*, pp. 105–114

7. B Writing Obj. 6. Use an adverb to modify a verb, an adjective, or another adverb. Word modified: *recognizable. LoL,* pp. 533, T533; *LN*, pp. 134–135.

8. H Writing Obj. 6. Use the present tense to show that an action or condition occurs in the present. *LoL,* p. T67; *LN*, pp. 105–114.

9. B Writing Obj. 6. Use the objective form of a personal pronoun when the pronoun functions as a direct object. *LoL,* pp. T270, T282; *LN*, pp. 63–64.

10. J Writing Obj. 6. Use the past perfect tense to show that an action or condition in the past preceded another past action or condition. *LoL,* p. T67; *LN*, pp. 105–114.

11. B Writing Obj. 6. Use the comparative degree of comparison to compare two persons, places, or things. *LoL,* p. 500; *LN*, pp. 137–139.

12. G Writing Obj. 6. Use the present tense to show that an action occurs in the present. *LoL,* p. T67; *LN*, pp. 105–114.

13. A Writing Obj. 5. Incomplete sentence. *LoL,* p. 31; *LN*, pp. 25, 290.

14. G Writing Obj. 5. Incomplete sentence. *LoL,* p. 31; *LN*, pp. 25, 290.

15. C Writing Obj. 5. Correctly written sentences that should be combined. *LoL,* p. 732, p. T732; *LN*, pp. 332–337.

16. D Writing Obj. 5. Correctly written sentences that should be combined. *LoL,* p. 732, p. T732; *LN*, pp. 332–337.

17. F Writing Obj. 5. Run on sentence. *LoL,* p. 98; *LN*, pp 26–27, 291.

18. B Writing Obj. 5. Incomplete sentence. *LoL,* p. 31; *LN*, pp. 25, 290.

19. J Writing Obj. 5.

20. G Writing Obj. 5. Incomplete sentence. *LoL,* p. 31; *LN*, pp. 25, 290.

21. C Writing Obj. 5. Incomplete sentence. *LoL,* p. 31; *LN*, pp. 25, 290.

22. H Writing Obj. 5. Run-on sentence. *LoL,* p. 98; *LN*, pp 26–27, 291.

23. D Writing Obj. 5. Correctly written sentences that should be combined. *LoL,* pp. 732, T732; *LN*, pp. 332–337.

24. F Writing Obj. 5. Correctly written sentences that should be combined. *LoL,* pp. 732, T732; *LN*, pp. 332–337.

25. A Writing Obj. 5. Run-on sentence. *LoL,* p. 98; *LN*, pp 26–27, 291.

26. G Writing Obj. 5. Run-on sentence. *LoL,* p. 98; *LN*, pp 26–27, 291.

27. B Writing Obj. 7. *austin* should be *Austin*; Capitalize proper nouns and adjectives. *LoL,* p. 295; *LN*, p. 36.

28. J Writing Obj. 7.

29. C Writing Obj. 7. Use a period to punctuate a declarative sentence. *LoL,* p. 152; *LN*, p. 250.

30. F Writing Obj. 7. *desparately* should be *desperately.*

31. A Writing Obj. 7. *undar* should be *under.*

32. H Writing Obj. 7. *Austins* should be *Austin's*; To form the possessive of a singular noun, add an apostrophe and an *s. LoL,* R66; *LN*, pp. 42–43.

33. B Writing Obj. 7. *History* should be *history*; Do not capitalize a common noun. *LoL,* p. 295; *LN*, p. 36.

34. J Writing Obj. 7.

35. C Writing Obj. 7. Use quotation marks at the beginning and end of a direct quotation. *LoL,* p. T26; *LN*, pp. 258–260.

36. H Writing Obj. 7. Use a question mark to punctuate an interrogative sentence. *LoL,* p. 152; *LN*, p. 250.

37. C Writing Obj. 7. Use a period to punctuate a declarative sentence. *LoL,* p. 152; *LN*, p. 250.

38. J Writing Obj. 7.

39. A Writing Obj. 7. *peace* should be *piece.*

40. F Writing Obj. 7. *beckun* should be *beckon.*

TEST II—WRITING: PART 2

Writing Obj. 1–4. To score students' compositions, use the rubric on p. 95.

TEST II—READING

Note: For Reading practice test items, the correct answer is given, followed by a paragraph identifying

- the targeted TAAS Objective and skill name,

- references to pages in *Preparing for TAAS* and *The Language of Literature* (*LoL*) on which the targeted skill is taught, and

- explanations to assist you with error analysis and remediation.

SD-1. B Reading Obj. 1: Context Clues, pp. 11–14; *LoL*, p. 301.

SD-2. F Reading Obj. 5: Evaluating & Making Judgments, pp. 53–56; *LoL*, p. 877. No evidence in the passage supports G or H. J is a possible explanation, but F is the answer best supported by the text. After handing the book to her mother, Angie says that her mother is an "excellent writer."

1. B Reading Obj. 1: Context Clues, pp. 11–14; *LoL*, p. 301

2. H Reading Obj. 5: Inferences, pp. 49–52; *LoL*, pp. 553, 875 No evidence in the passage supports F, G, or J. H is the answer best supported by the text. Pietro speaks "sheepishly" and says that he hopes his friends don't recognize him in the play.

3. D Reading Obj. 3: Summarizing, pp. 31–34; *LoL*, p. 283. A and B are false. C omits essential points.

4. G Reading Obj. 5: Inferences, pp. 49–52; *LoL*, pp. 553, 875. No evidence in the passage supports F, H, or J. G is the answer best supported by the text. Pietro is wearing a cape and carrying a stage-prop sword when he comes into the kitchen.

5. A Reading Obj. 5: Inferences, pp. 49–52; *LoL*, pp. 553, 875. No evidence in the passage supports B, C, or D. A is the answer best supported by the text. After the sentence, "Then, his mother remembered," Pietro's mother predicts that the school play will be a success, from which the reader can infer that Pietro must be practicing his lines for the play.

6. J Reading Obj. 2: Sequential Order, pp. 23–26; *LoL*, p. 285. G and H are not stated in the passage. J occurs before F.

7. C Reading Obj. 5: Evaluating & Making Judgments, pp. 53–56; *LoL*, p. 877. No evidence in the passage supports A or D. B is a possible explanation, but C is the answer best supported by the text. When Pietro sees the soccer players at the school play, Rosario tells him "We couldn't let a team member go on without fans."

8. H Reading Obj. 4: Predicting, pp. 39–42; *LoL*, p. 22.

No evidence in the passage supports F, G, or J. H is the answer best supported by the text. Since the players clearly support Pietro's decision to appear in the play, it is likely that, in the future, they will respect Pietro's decision not to play soccer.

9. B Reading Obj. 2: Sequential Order. pp. 23–26; *LoL*, p. 285. C is not stated in the passage. A and D occur the day before the field trip. B occurs just before they reach the museum.

10. J Reading Obj. 6: Fact-Opinion, pp. 65–68; *LoL*, p. 829. F and H are not stated in the passage. G is a fact. J is stated in the brochure.

11. B Reading Obj. 5: Inferences, pp. 49–52; *LoL*, pp. 553, 875. No evidence in the passage supports A or C. Not enough information is given in the passage to make the inference in D. B is the answer best supported by the text. The exhibits appear to move chronologically, from the origins of life in the West Wing to early humans in the South Wing.

12. F Reading Obj. 5: Inferences, pp. 49–52; *LoL*, pp. 553, 875. No evidence in the passage supports G or H. J is a possible explanation, but alligators are small, and do not seem to fit the description "Thunder." F is the answer best supported by the text. The brochure text says that one of the questions that the museum can answer is "What was it like in the days when dinosaurs roamed the earth?" and dinosaurs are not mentioned in any of the other exhibit titles.

13. A Reading Obj. 2: Sequential Order, pp. 23–26; *LoL*, p. 285. B is not on the floor where the exhibits on Platinum County are located. D is not mentioned in the text. C is a possible explanation, but A is the first exhibit on the Fourth Floor.

14. G Reading Obj. 2: Supporting Details, pp. 19–22; *LoL*, pp. 528, R29–R30 F and H are stated, but not in connection with calling the information line. J is not stated in the passage. G is stated in the brochure.

15. C Reading Obj. 6: Fact-Opinion, pp. 65–68; *LoL*, p. 829. A is contradicted in the brochure. B is not stated in the passage. D is an opinion. C is stated in the brochure.

16. J Reading Obj. 2, 3: Main Idea, pp. 2730; *LoL*, pp. 106, 408. F and H are supporting details. G is a judgment.

17. **D** Reading Obj. 6: Fact-Opinion, pp. 65–68; *LoL*, p. 829.
A is contradicted in para. 1. B is not stated in the passage. C is an opinion. D is stated in para. 2.

18. **F** Reading Obj. 2, 3: Main Idea, pp. 27–30; *LoL*, pp. 106, 408.
G is a supporting detail. H is a generalization. J is a supporting detail.

19. **B** Reading Obj. 5: Inferences, pp. 49–52; *LoL*, p. 553, 875.
No evidence in the passage supports A or D. C is a possible explanation, but B is the answer best supported by the text. The passage states that "there are some instances of stuttering recurring in the same family," but not many instances. B is the best answer because the passage states that many people who stutter "desperately want to speak with ease."

20. **H** Reading Obj. 4: Cause-Effect, pp. 35–38; *LoL*, p. 32.
There is no basis in the passage for F. G and J are stated but are not effects.

21. **C** Reading Obj. 5: Inferences, pp. 49–52; *LoL*, pp. 553, 875.
No evidence in the passage supports A, B, or D. C is the answer best supported by the text. The passage discusses how to "avoid 'blocks,'" from which the reader can infer that blocks are something undesirable.

22. **G** Reading Obj. 6: Author's Perspective & Purpose, pp. 61–64; *LoL*, pp. 118, 426.
F is not addressed in the passage. H is not supported: The passage discusses the causes of stuttering, but does not ask the reader to investigate. J is not supported: The passage discusses the National Stuttering Project, but does not encourage or discourage membership. G is the best answer: The passage shows some of the hardships that people who stutter face and mentions the poor way they have been treated in the past.

23. **D** Reading Obj. 1: Context Clues, pp. 11–14; *LoL*, p. 301.

24. **F** Reading Obj. 5: Inferences, pp. 49–52; *LoL*, pp. 553, 875.
No evidence in the passage supports G, H, or J. F is the answer best supported by the text. The passage states that in the Middle Ages, it was thought that torture could "heal" people who stuttered.

25. **A** Reading Obj. 1: Context Clues, pp. 11–14; *LoL*, p. 301.

26. **F** Reading Obj. 6: Fact-Opinion, pp. 6568; *LoL*, p. 829.

G is contradicted in para. 4. H and J are not stated in the passage. F is stated in para. 3.

27. **C** Reading Obj. 5: Inferences, pp. 49–52; *LoL*, pp. 553, 875.
No evidence in the passage supports A or D. B is false. C is the answer best supported by the text. The passage states that the first Interface Message Processor "was the 'shot heard round the world' in the Internet Revolution."

28. **F** Reading Obj. 2: Sequential Order, pp. 23–26; *LoL*, p. 285.
G occured after the TCP/IP address system was worked out. H is not stated in the passage. Not enough information is given in the passage to determine when J occurred.

29. **C** Reading Obj. 2, 3: Main Idea, pp. 27–30; *LoL*, pp. 106, 408.
A is an inference. B and D are not stated in the passage.

30. **G** Reading Obj. 1: Context Clues, pp. 11–14; *LoL*, p. 301.

31. **D** Reading Obj. 5: Inferences, pp. 49–52; *LoL*, pp. 553, 875.
No evidence in the passage supports A, B, or C. D is the answer best supported by the text. The passage states that depending on whether an Internet address ends in .com or .org, the user reaches the "network of a large corporation or a non-profit organization."

32. **J** Reading Obj. 6: Fact-Opinion, pp. 65–68; *LoL*, p. 829.
F and G are not stated in the passage. H is contradicted in para. 6. J is stated in para. 5.

33. **D** Reading Obj. 3: Summarizing, pp. 31–34; *LoL*, p. 283.
A is false. B and C omit essential points.

34. **H** Reading Obj. 5: Inferences, pp. 49–52; *LoL*, pp. 553, 875.
F is false. No evidence in the passage supports G or J. H is the answer best supported by the text. The passage states that Trudy wants to try to answer the extra-credit question "because she needs all the help she can get."

35. **A** Reading Obj. 2: Supporting Details, pp. 19–22; *LoL*, pp. 528, R29–R30.
B and C are contradicted in para. 1. D is not stated in the passage. A is stated in para. 1.

36. **H** Reading Obj. 5: Evaluating & Making Judgments, pp. 53–56; *LoL*, p. 877.
No evidence in the passage supports F, G, or J. H is the answer best supported by the text. The review states that the player is missing a feature that "at its price it should have."

37. **A** Reading Obj. 2: Supporting Details, pp.

19–22; *LoL*, pp. 528, R29–R30.
B, C, and D are contradicted in the reviews.
Only A is found in every review.

38. **J** Reading Obj. 2, 3: Main Idea, pp. 27–30; *LoL*,
pp. 106, 408.
F and G are inferences. H is a generalization.

39. **A** Reading Obj. 5: Evaluating & Making
Judgments, pp. 53–56; *LoL*, p. 877.
No evidence in the passage supports B or D.
C is a possible explanation, but A is the
answer best supported by the text. The
reviews list the features of each player.

40. **J** Reading Obj. 5: Charts & Graphs, pp. 43–47;
LoL, pp. R98–R99.
Students should find on the chart the two
players that received a rating of "excellent"
and then read across to find the prices of the
players. Since the question is about "value,"
the lower-priced player rated "excellent" is
the correct answer.

41. **A** Reading Obj. 5: Inferences, pp. 49–52; *LoL*,
pp. 553, 875.
No evidence in the passage supports B, C, or
D. A is the answer best supported by the text.
In the passage, Monique states that the "only
good thing about going to a farm for summer
vacation is that there should be plenty of
space."

42. **G** Reading Obj. 3: Summarizing, pp. 3134; *LoL*,
p. 283.
F and J omit essential points. H is a generalization.

43. **B** Reading Obj. 2: Supporting Details, pp.
19–22; *LoL*, pp. 528, R29–R30
A is contradicted in para. 2. C and D are contradicted in para. 5. B is stated in para. 3.

44. **F** Reading Obj. 5: Inferences, pp. 49–52; *LoL*,
pp. 553, 875.
No evidence in the passage supports G. H
and J are false. F is the answer best supported
by the text. In the passage, Monique writes
that Nate showed her and Jasmine how to
splash in the pond to "keep the snakes away."

45. **D** Reading Obj. 6: Fact-Opinion, pp. 65–68; *LoL*,
p. 829.
A and B are not stated in the passage. C is a
fact. D is stated in para. 5.

46. **J** Reading Obj. 3: Summarizing, pp. 31–34; *LoL*,
p. 283.
F, G, and H omit essential details.

47. **C** Reading Obj. 5: Inferences, pp. 49–52; *LoL*,
pp. 553, 875.
No evidence in the passage supports A, B, or
D. C is the answer best supported by the text.
The reader can infer that Nate is friendly from
his actions in the passage, such as teaching
Monique and Jasmine, convincing his father
to let Monique work on the farm, and playing
dolls with Jasmine.

48. **G** Reading Obj. 5: Inferences, pp. 49–52; *LoL*,
pp. 553, 875.
No evidence in the passage supports F, H, or
J. G is the answer best supported by the text.
In the passage, Monique at first says that she
hopes she won't have to spend time with
Jasmine's dolls, but later has fun at a tea party
for the dolls.

ACKNOWLEDGMENTS (continued)

Naomi Long Madgett: "Woman With Flower," from *Star by Star* by Naomi Long Madgett. Copyright ©
1965, 1970 by Naomi Long Madgett. Reprinted by permission of the author.

N. Scott Momaday: "New World," from *The Gourd Dancer* by N. Scott Momaday. Copyright © 1976 by
N. Scott Momaday. Reprinted by permission of the author.

Marian Reiner, Literary Agent: "Thumbprint," from *A Sky Full of Poems* by Eve Merriam. Copyright
© 1964, 1970, 1973 by Eve Merriam. Used by permission of Marian Reiner.

Naomi Shihab Nye: "What Is Supposed To Happen," from *Red Suitcase* by Naomi Shihab Nye.
Copyright © 1994 by Naomi Shihab Nye. All rights reserved. Reprinted by permission of the author.

National Association for the Advancement of Colored People/Crisis Magazine: "Wishes" by Georgia
Douglas Johnson, from *Crisis Magazine*, April 1927. McDougal Littell Inc. wishes to thank The Crisis
Publishing Co., Inc., the publisher of the magazine of the National Association for the Advancement of
Colored People, for authorizing the use of this work.